BELORUSSIA UNDER SOVIET RULE, 1917-1957

BELORUSSIA
UNDER SOVIET RULE
1917-1957

Ivan S. Lubachko

The University Press
of Kentucky

ISBN 978-0-8131-5334-6

Library of Congress Catalog Card Number: 79–160047

Copyright © 1972 by The University Press of Kentucky

A statewide cooperative scholarly publishing agency serving Berea College, Centre College of Kentucky, Eastern Kentucky University, Kentucky State College, Morehead State University, Murray State University, University of Kentucky, University of Louisville, and Western Kentucky University.

Editorial and Sales Offices: Lexington, Kentucky 40506

In memory of my parents
  Stsepan and Melaniia Lubachko

CONTENTS

	Preface	xiii
1	Historical Background	1
2	The Formation of the Belorussian Republic	12
3	The Partition of Belorussia	31
4	Belorussia & the Formation of the USSR	47
5	Belorussia under the New Economic Policy	62
6	A Golden Age of Belorussian Culture	80
7	Collectivization & Industrialization	93
8	The Liquidation of Belorussian Nationalism	107
9	West Belorussia under Poland	127
10	The Reunion of West & East Belorussia	139
11	Belorussia under German Occupation	146
12	Belorussia after World War II	165
13	Belorussia & War Diplomacy	177
14	Conclusion	187
	Selected Bibliography	193
	Index	211

TABLES

Ethnic Groups as Percentages of the Total Population of Belorussia, 1897	37
National Composition of the Population of the BSSR According to the Census of 1926	67
Percentages of National Groups Elected to Belorussian Local Soviets in 1926–1927	68
National Composition of Employees of the Central Soviet Administrative Institutions of Belorussia in 1927	69
Party Affiliations of Members Elected to Belorussian Village and Town Soviets in 1926 and 1927	69
Proportions of Party and Non-Party Members among Employees of Belorussian Commissariats of Education, Finance, and Agriculture, 1930	70
Production of Industries in Belorussia, 1924–1927	77
Comparative Volume of State, Cooperative, and Private Trade in the BSSR, 1923–1926	78
Relation between Industrial and Agricultural Production in the Belorussian National Income, 1923–1927	79
Extent of Belorussification in the Belorussian Government by February 1, 1927	85
Development of Schools in the BSSR, 1924–1928	86
Growth of Schools for Adults in the BSSR, 1925–1928	87
Development of Professional Education in the BSSR, 1925–1928	88

*National Composition of Schools in the BSSR
in the 1926–1927 School Year*   90

*Social Origins of Students in Belorussian Higher
and Professional Schools, 1926–1929*   91

*Progress of Collectivization in the BSSR from the
Fifteenth Party Congress to the Beginning of Forced
Collectivization*   97

Ethnographic Composition of West Belorussia, 1931   129

MAPS

Poland between 1921 and 1939	33
The Belorussian National Republic	34
The Partition of Belorussia, 1921	41
Geographical Distribution of Belorussian Dialects	44
The Belorussian S.S.R. between 1921 and 1939	65
The Partition of Poland, September 1939	140
Belorussia under German Occupation during World War II	151
The Belorussian S.S.R. after World War II	178

PREFACE

Little is known about the history of the Belorussian Soviet Socialist Republic, even though it is a charter member of the United Nations. My primary aim in this book has been to collect and present available data on Belorussia since World War I. If my work contributes to a wider knowledge of the history of Belorussia under Soviet rule, as well as to an understanding of Communist rule, especially during the Stalin era, the purpose of this study will have been well served.

The information contained in this book is based mainly upon primary sources published in the Russian and Belorussian languages, supplemented by other pertinent studies. The Library of Congress system of transliteration for Belorussian, Russian, and Ukrainian words, slightly simplified when it seemed practical, is used throughout, except that in referring to Russian authors who have published works in English I have given the names as they appear in the English editions.

Different chapters of the manuscript have been read by Professors Robert F. Byrnes and John M. Thompson of Indiana University, Vladimir I. Seduro of Rensselaer Polytechnic Institute, W. Frank Steely of Northern Kentucky State College, Donald W. Whisenhunt of Thiel College, and Roy O. Hatton of Murray State University. I wish to express my deep gratitude for their comments and valuable suggestions.

Other individuals to whom I am deeply indebted for their advice and the use of their private materials are Nikolai Latushkin, Vladimir Klishevich, Masei Sedneu, George Kolada, and Andrew Turchyn.

I am indebted also to the Graduate School of Indiana University for a grant-in-aid and to Murray State University for a similar grant which made it possible for me to travel to various libraries in connection with this research.

Last but not least, I wish to thank Morgan C. McIlwain, the cartographer, and the staff members of the Indiana University Library, the Library of Congress, and the New York Public Library.

BELORUSSIA UNDER SOVIET RULE, 1917-1957

I.

Historical Background

Belorussians are people of an ancient culture. Together with the Russians and Ukrainians, they are descended from the eastern Slavic tribes. From the time when, according to historical legend, the first Russian state was formed by Rurik in c. 862 until the Mongol invasion and occupation of Kiev in 1240, all three of these Slavic peoples lived in a number of principalities broadly designated as Kievan Rus' (Kievan Russia). By family relationship among the princes, the region had a certain degree of political unity, with primacy centered in Kiev. Geographically, the area now called Belorussia occupied the central western portion of Kievan Russia. Like the Russians and the Ukrainians, the Belorussians inherited their religion from Kievan Russia, whose prince Vladimir I, or St. Vladimir, adopted Christianity from Byzantium in c. 988.

At present the western part of this area is known in English under several, often confusing, names: Belorussia (Bielorussia, Byelorussia), White Russia, and White Ruthenia.[1] The origin of the term Belaia Rus' or Belarus' has not yet been clarified, but in recent years, attempts have been made to determine it. Several linguists support the theory that the area is so called because the people there have light-colored hair and blue eyes.[2] There is, however, another and probably more authentic explanation of the term. In the period of Kievan Russia, the territory which later became known as Belaia Rus' was not occupied by the Mongols. Furthermore, the term Belaia Rus' appeared in documents only after the Mongolian invasion of the Kievan state.[3] Thus, it is possible that the term came into use at that time as a means of differentiating the unoccupied lands from the areas under Mongol domination.

Invasion by the Mongols in the thirteenth century caused the division of Kievan Russia into three separate areas: West Russia, South Russia, and North-East Russia, which later became known respectively as Belorussia, Ukraine, and Russia. This division, which was followed by a long separation of the people of these areas, laid the foundation for the division of the Eastern Slavs into the Belorussians, Ukrainians, and Russians.[4]

There were, to be sure, some linguistic differences already apparent among the Eastern Slavs at the end of the Kievan period. These differences increased during the period of isolation following the division of Kievan Russia. Thereafter the Belorussian and Ukrainian languages developed gradually on the basis of local dialects and popular idioms, "into which Polish words penetrated" later when Belorussia and most of the Ukraine fell under Polish domination.[5]

When Kiev was occupied by the Mongols in 1240, the western principalities sought protection in vassalage to Lithuania. The Lithuanians, still pagan and backward, accepted in turn the superior civilization of the West Russians. Gradually, Old Slavonic in its West Russian version (which later came to be called Belorussian) became the official language of the united Lithuano-Belorussian state, known as the Grand Duchy of Lithuania.[6] The two united peoples, in the common cause of defense against the Mongols and Teutonic Knights, continued to expand their state during the Middle Ages, and by the fifteenth century it extended from the Baltic Sea to the Black Sea.[7]

Perhaps the greatest accomplishment of the Grand Duchy of Lithuania was the promulgation in 1529 of a code of laws. This code was originally written in the Belorussian language, and is considered one of the most complete handwritten codes of the Middle Ages.[8] Thus, because of the position the Belorussians occupied in the Grand Duchy, "they can boast of an illustrious past and can

---

[1] All these terms are synonymous. The term "White Russia" is often confused with anti-Bolshevik political factions and exile groups that emerged after the Revolution of 1917.

[2] *Bol'shaia sovetskaia entsiklopediia*, 2d ed. (Moscow, 1950–1958) 4:479.

[3] Nicholas P. Vakar, *Belorussia: The Making of a Nation* (Cambridge, Mass., 1956), p. 2.

[4] Francis Dvornik, *The Slavs in European History and Civilization* (New Brunswick, N. J., 1962), p. 248.

[5] Ibid., p. 307.   [6] Ibid., p. 216.

[7] Wiktor Ostrowski, *Spotlight on Byelorussia and her Neighbours* (London, 1959), p. 62.

[8] Before the nineteenth century, the Code of Laws of the Grand Duchy of Lithuania circulated in the form of handwritten copies. In the nineteenth century it was published twice, in 1841 and 1854. In Soviet Belorussia, it was published for the first time in 1960 in the Russian language. See *Statut Velikogo Kniazhestva Litovskogo 1529 goda* (Minsk, 1960).

Historical Background

claim for themselves the Lithuanian state of the Middle Ages whose most important documents were couched in the Belorussian language."[9]

Polish influence in Lithuania began in 1386 when the illiterate Grand Duke of Lithuania, Jagiello, married the Polish queen, Jadwiga, in what became known as the Union of Krevo. He thus became king of Poland, as Ladislaus II, as well as Grand Duke of Lithuania. The chief reason for this union was the need for a common front against the Teutonic Knights.[10] The Lithuanian duchy now fell increasingly under the political and cultural supremacy of Poland, a process facilitated by the pressure of Muscovy. Because of the growing conflict with Muscovy, the Grand Duchy gradually lost its ability to resist enemies and had to seek further agreement with Poland to assure cooperation in defense.[11] In this situation, Poland saw a good opportunity for tightening its control over Lithuania, and in 1569 the so-called Union of Lublin was concluded. The Union of Krevo had been only a personal union, directed primarily against the Teutonic Knights. The Union of Lublin established a joint kingdom directed against Muscovy and was forced through by Polish magnates: "Not people but rulers, of the most oligarchical ruling classes, effected it."[12]

The Union of Lublin marked the beginning of the direct Polonization of the former Grand Duchy of Lithuania. Many of its nobles accepted Polish customs and nationality. Those nobles, predominantly Orthodox in faith, who resisted Polonization eventually lost their lands to Polish colonists.[13] Furthermore, under increasing pressure from the Roman Catholic Church and through growing interference of the state in the affairs of the Orthodox Church, a part of the Orthodox nobility was forced into closer relationship with Rome. This led to the religious union with the Catholic Church which was concluded at Brest in 1596 on the pattern of the political Union of Lublin. At that time "it was decided that all official documents in the administration of the grand duchy should be composed in Polish."[14]

The process of Polonization, however, did not extend to the

[9] Walter Kolarz, *Russia and Her Colonies* (New York, 1952), p. 153.
[10] Constantine R. Jurgela, *History of the Lithuanian Nation* (New York, 1948), p. 210.
[11] Ostrowski, *Spotlight on Byelorussia*, p. 65.
[12] William John Rose, *Poland, Old and New* (London, 1948), p. 43.
[13] Harold William Vazeille Temperley, ed., *A History of the Peace Conference of Paris* (London, 1920–1924), 6:223.
[14] Dvornik, *Slavs in European History*, p. 346.

lower classes. The Lithuanian, Belorussian, and Ukrainian peasantry retained their languages and national customs, thus becoming a barrier to the solid establishment of Polish nationality throughout the eastern territories of the artificially created Polish "royal republic." This lack of a homogeneous population remained one of the weaknesses of the Polish state. Furthermore, Poland suffered from the phenomenon that while it was a republic in name, the nominal head of the state was an elected king. Political rights and privileges were restricted almost exclusively to the nobility.[15]

In the three partitions of Poland between 1772 and 1795, Russia took over all the Belorussian lands of the former Grand Duchy of Lithuania. At first, the Russian government tried to convince the population that it was not in favor of the Polish landlords and wanted to improve the position of the Belorussian peasantry.[16] "In reality the sympathies of the Russian tsars were limited by their desire to give to the Belorussian villages a Russian landlord instead of a Polish one."[17] The lands of Polish landlords who refused to take the oath of allegiance to the tsar were confiscated and distributed among Russian citizens. In the last decades of the eighteenth century "persons close to Catherine II were allotted land and peasants in abundance."[18]

The Belorussians and Ukrainians, tied by bonds of religion and memories of common origin with the Russians, but separated by cultural, social, and economic differences, were now subjected by the Russians to treatment almost identical with that which they had received from the Polish government. Belorussia was denied separate nationhood and renamed the North Western Territory. Nicholas I, by a decree of July 18, 1840, even prohibited use of the term Belorussia.[19] National persecution was interwoven with feudal oppression. According to official data, on the eve of the Reform of 1861 nearly 54 percent of the Belorussian peasants were serfs, compared with 38 percent in Russia as a whole.[20] A great achievement was the manifesto of Alexander II, dated February 19, 1861, promulgating liberation of the serfs without compensation to their masters. But the land which the peasants received did not become their private

---

[15] Temperley, *History of the Peace Conference*, p. 224.
[16] Aleksandr Charviakou, *Za Savetskuiu Belarus'* (Minsk, 1927), p. 16.
[17] Ibid., p. 17.
[18] Efim F. Karski, *Kurs Belorussovedeniia* (Moscow, 1920), p. 52.
[19] *Istoriia BSSR*, 2d ed. (Minsk, 1961), 1:312.
[20] I. I. Kostiushko, "K stoletiiu vosstaniia 1863 g. v tsarstve Pol'skom, Litve, Belorussii i na pravoberezhnoi Ukraine," *Voprosy istorii*, no. 1 (1963): 90.

property. It continued to be regarded as the property of the landowner until such time as he could be compensated for it.[21] Thus, despite the agrarian reform in Belorussia the peasants owned only 38.8 percent of the land.[22] A song which became very popular in Belorussia after the Reform of 1861 declares,

> They gave the peasants freedom
> On February nineteenth
> But they gave no land to the people
> That is the "mercy" of nobles and tsars.[23]

The manifesto and conditions of the reform did not satisfy the peasants, nor did "freedom without land" solve their problem. Consequently, the agrarian reform was immediately followed by a wave of peasant unrest in Belorussia.[24] This culminated in an uprising in 1863 which was closely tied to revolutionary events in Poland, Lithuania, and the Ukraine. Both peasants and nobles took part in the 1863 Belorussian revolt. At one time as many as 75,000 peasants were involved in the uprising.[25] The Belorussian leader of the uprising was Kostus' (Constantine) Kalinouski. In his organ *Muzhytskaia prauda* (Peasant Truth), published in the Belorussian language, Kalinouski attacked the predatory nature of the reform and demanded social equality, vast land reforms, and political autonomy for Belorussia and Lithuania.[26]

The uprising was suppressed in Belorussia, as in other parts of the former Grand Duchy of Lithuania and kingdom of Poland. Kalinouski was captured and hanged in Vilna on March 23, 1864. When the sentence was read at the scaffold, he was named "nobleman Constantine Kalinouski"; upon hearing this, he cried, "We do not have nobles, we all are equal."[27] Kalinouski became a symbol of the Belorussian national revival, having led the struggle against both Polish and Russian oppression.

The tsarist regime refused to recognize the striving for autonomy of the national minorities within the Russian Empire. Despite

---

[21] George Vernadsky, *A History of Russia* (New York, 1944), p. 159.
[22] Karski, *Kurs Belorussovedeniia*, p. 65.
[23] *Istoriia BSSR*, 1:427.
[24] Ibid., p. 344.
[25] U.S., Congress, House, Select Committee on Communist Aggression, *Communist Takeover and Occupation of Byelorussia* (Washington, D. C.: G.P.O., 1955), p. 5.
[26] Vakar, *Belorussia*, p. 72.
[27] *Istoriia BSSR*, 1:369.

the abolition of serfdom in 1861, the minority peoples obtained no real improvement of their situation, and the uprising of 1863 led to new restrictions. Any demand for national freedom and equality was suppressed in brutal fashion.[28] The tsarist regime proceeded to a more vigorous policy of Russification and conversion to Orthodoxy of those who had abandoned it under Polish pressure before the partition. "In only one year, 1865–1866, more than 30,000 nobles and gentry abandoned the Catholic for the Orthodox faith."[29]

Shortcomings of the Reform of 1861 and the refusal of the tsarist regime to recognize the demands of the national minorities were the main causes of the spread of the populist movement in the 1870s. In the towns of Belorussia, as in those of Russia, hundreds of young people started giving up their privileges and going to the villages. At that time a club of the "Land and Freedom" movement was organized in Minsk,[30] and during the early 1880s a "social revolutionary" group was organized among the Belorussian populists. Some Belorussians living in St. Petersburg were members of this group and in 1884 started illegally publishing the newspaper *Homan* (Talk), in which they advocated autonomy for Belorussia within a federal Russia.[31]

Generally, the independent national movement in Belorussia did not get well under way until 1902, when with the assistance of the Polish Socialist Party, the Belorussian students in St. Petersburg founded the Belorussian Revolutionary Hramada,[32] in 1903 renamed the Belorussian Socialist Hramada. This was the first exclusively Belorussian revolutionary party with a definite social-democratic program. It sought to gain the same position of importance in Belorussia which the Polish Socialist Party occupied in Poland. Its members wished, first of all, to establish a Belorussian national state, and then to solve the social problems of that state.[33]

Belorussia remained one of the least developed areas of European Russia at the beginning of the twentieth century. It was predominantly an agrarian region. Its industrial production per capita was about half that of Russia as a whole. Seventy-four percent of the population was engaged in agriculture.[34] Many of those living

[28] Charviakou, *Za Savetskuiu Belarus'*, p. 17.
[29] Vakar, *Belorussia*, p. 74.
[30] S. Ahurski, *Ocherki po istorii revoliutsionnogo dvizheniia v Belorussii, 1863–1917* (Minsk, 1928), p. 23.
[31] *Istoriia BSSR*, 1:397.
[32] The Belorussian word *hramada* means party or association.
[33] Charviakou, *Za Savetskuiu Belarus'*, p. 25.
[34] *Bol'shaia sovetskaia entsiklopediia*, 2d ed., 4:483.

in the villages had insufficient land and had to work part-time for the landlords. Generally the peasants' farms were very small, averaging less than twenty acres.[35] Large-scale ownership of land continued to predominate, the small upper class—mostly Polish and Russian—owning most of the land.[36] One large landowner, Princess Gogenloe, for example, owned 1,729,000 acres in the province of Minsk, and the Polish Count Potocki owned 592,800 acres in the same province.[37] Moreover, Belorussia had the highest rate of illiteracy in the European part of the empire. In 1897, 71 percent of the population was illiterate, and in 1905, 63 percent.[38]

Marxist ideas began to spread in Belorussia at the very end of the nineteenth century. At first the Marxist organizations were in the form of "Circles of Self-Development," mostly organized by Jews or Catholics,[39] elements of the population who had suffered intensive oppression based on religious discrimination.[40] Generally, the Marxist Socialist movement in Belorussia had no relation to the Belorussian national movement. "It was a component part of the all-Russian revolutionary movement."[41] The First Congress of the Russian Social Democratic Labor Party, which aimed at organizing all local Social Democratic organizations into a united Marxist party, took place in Minsk, the largest city of Belorussia, March 1–3, 1898. Organization of the party intensified the appearance of Marxist literature, including Lenin's works, "To the Rural Poor," written in 1903, and "The Proletariat and the Peasantry," written in 1905. In the first of these, Lenin, explaining the agrarian program of the Social Democrats, wrote: "The Social Democrats not only demand the complete and immediate abolition of land redemption payments (quit rent) and imposts of all kinds, but they also demand that the money taken from the people in the form of land redemption payments should be restored to the people."[42] In the second article,

[35] *Istoriia BSSR*, 1:442.
[36] *Belorussia*, Subcontractor's Monograph HRAF-19 (New Haven, Conn.: Human Relations Area Files, 1954–1955), p. 58.
[37] *Bol'shaia sovetskaia entsiklopediia*, 2d ed., 4:483.
[38] "Dannye o gramotnosti naseleniia Belorusskikh gubernii v 1905 godu" [The Facts about the Literacy of the Population in the Belorussian Regions in 1905], *Dokumenty i materialy po istorii Belorussii, 1900–1917 gg.* (Minsk, 1953), vol. 3, document no. 302, p. 269.
[39] Ahurski, *Ocherki po istorii*, pp. 34–35.
[40] N. Nedasek, *Bol'shevizm v revoliutsionnom dvizhennii Belorussii: issledovaniia i materialy* (Munich, 1956), p. 143.
[41] *Istoriia BSSR*, 1:409.
[42] Vladimir Lenin, "K derevenskoi bednote" [To the Rural Poor], *Sochineniia*, 3d ed. (Moscow, 1929–1939), 5:301.

Lenin stated: "The peasants want the land and freedom, and the working class aims to achieve just that."[43] Lenin's views on the land were known not only in Russia but in the other regions of the Empire, and had great appeal to land-hungry peasants.

The defeat of Russia in the war with Japan in 1905 was the signal for a revolutionary outbreak against the autocratic regime. This gave an opportunity for the non-Russian nationalities within the Empire to express their dissatisfaction with Russian autocracy. The revolutionary movement in Belorussia in 1905 took the form of a series of demonstrations by workers, demanding better working conditions and higher wages. Many strikes and demonstrations were brutally suppressed. Clashes with the police at a meeting in Minsk on November 1, 1905, for example, left about a hundred dead and several hundred wounded.[44]

In 1905, encouraged by the Northern Committee of the Russian Social Democratic Labor Party, the peasant movement in Belorussia was organized, culminating in a peasant convention in Minsk that same year. The convention formed a peasant union, which proceeded to organize fighting groups against the police.[45] In most cases, however, the peasants did not use physical violence but limited their actions to disobedience of the law. This expressed itself mainly in refusal to adhere to various restrictions: without permission the peasants cut trees from woods belonging to the landlords and used open meadowlands for grazing. In the summer of 1905, the peasants' actions were often directed toward seizure of the landlords' lands.[46] It must be pointed out, however, that the workers' strikes and the peasants' disorders in Belorussia in 1905-1906 were a part of the all-Russian revolutionary movement. The Belorussian national movement was still weak and "exercised no influence on political developments in prerevolutionary Russia."[47]

Frightened by revolutionary disturbances throughout Russia, Tsar Nicholas II on October 30, 1905, promised the people a constitution, an Imperial Duma (parliament) based on universal suffrage, and civil liberties. Although the promised constitution was

[43] Idem, "Proletariat i krest'ianstvo" [The Proletariat and the Peasantry], *ibid.*, 8:382.
[44] "Rasstrel demonstratsii v Minske" [The Shooting Down of the Demonstrators in Minsk], *Dokumenty i materialy po istorii Belorussii*, vol. 3, document no. 495, p. 428.
[45] Vakar, *Belorussia*, p. 85.
[46] *Istoriia BSSR*, 1:489.
[47] Richard Pipes, *The Formation of the Soviet Union* (Cambridge, Mass., 1954), p. 12.

not properly executed and human rights were not extended to all, the work of the Third and Fourth Dumas (1907–1917) did result in certain improvements and raised hopes for the future. After the election of the Third Duma, the conservative nationalist prime minister, Peter Stolypin, succeeded in having his agrarian reform bill passed. Stolypin's reforms, aimed at building up prosperous middle-class farms, were especially welcomed in Belorussia, where such farms were almost nonexistent.

The Revolution of 1905 also gave the Belorussians new hope of building up their national identity. For their position of economic and cultural backwardness, they blamed their neighbors, the Poles and Russians, who had suppressed them continuously since 1569. Nothing could characterize the Belorussian spirit at that time better than the motto of the first Belorussian publishing company founded in 1906, "In our windows also shall the sun shine."[48] In the same year, there appeared in Vilna the first weekly periodical, *Nasha dolia* (Our Destiny). It was shortly suppressed by the Russian authorities for "revolutionary and separatist" tendencies, but was soon followed by *Nasha niva* (Our Land). The latter was the first Belorussian newspaper published with illustrations. During the time it was published, 1906–1915, *Nasha niva* encouraged Belorussian nationalism, yet always maintained a very considerate position toward the other nationalities in Belorussia.

After the Revolution of 1905 the Belorussian Socialist Hramada began to play a leading role in the national revival. In 1906, at its second congress, it worked out an ambitious program which called for not only "cultural autonomy," which it had demanded three years earlier, but also "the federation of all free peoples within the empire."[49] It cooperated closely with the Ukrainian national movement. Its aims were to struggle against Russian autocracy, with its centralization, and against the Polish gentry, who continued to own much of the land in Belorussia even after their own country lost its independence.

During the years 1906–1917, Belorussian literature followed the line of political nationalism directed by the Hramada. Literature was helping to awaken the national consciousness of the people. The Belorussian poets Ianka Kupala and Iakub Kolas, themselves the sons of peasants, acted as the representatives of revolutionary peasant democracy.[50] In their writings during the last decade before the

---

[48] Kolarz, *Russia and Her Colonies*, p. 153.
[49] Vakar, *Belorussia*, pp. 85–86.   [50] *Istoriia BSSR*, 1:586.

Revolution of 1917, they described the sorrow and poverty of the people and reflected the struggle of the Belorussians against national suppression. Ianka Kupala in his 1912 poem "To the King of Heaven and of Earth" thus described Belorussia's sorrow and appeal:

. . . .
Your many nations You have decked with flowers
Their past and future chosen to array,
For us—with foreign[ers'] freedom punish ours—
The past—and even that You took away:

. . . .
Take note! And hear! Wake us, unsheath Your sword,
Send forth Your laws, give righteous justice birth:
Return our Fatherland to us, oh Lord,
If You are King of Heaven and of Earth.[51]

In his writings, as this poem may indicate, Kupala expressed views on Belorussia's future relations with Russia which were more radical than those of the Belorussian Socialist Hramada. From 1914 to 1915, Kupala edited *Nasha niva*. In the works of Kupala and Kolas, Belorussian literature found a true national expression. Their classic positions as poets, writers, and the founders of the Belorussian literary language are comparable to those of Alexander Pushkin and Michael Lermontov in Russian literature.

During the period of Belorussian national revival, a remarkable step forward was made in the field of education. Between 1905 and 1910, the number of pupils in the elementary and high schools increased by 23 percent.[52] This was possible mainly because of the work of the Duma.

When World War I broke out, the agricultural reform in Belorussia was far from finished. Belorussia remained a region of vast estates: in 1915, the state, church, and landlords owned 54 percent of the land. Forty percent of the land was owned by 3,993 landlords.[53] Few of the peasants owned enough land to make a living, and the struggle against the landlords continued. Many Belorussian peasants went to Siberia, where in twenty years (1896–1915), emigrants from Minsk, Mogilev, Smolensk, and Vitebsk provinces of Belorussia made up one-seventh of the settlers from all of Russia.[54]

[51] Quoted from "To the King of Heaven and of Earth," translated by Luba U. Terpak, *Belorussian Review*, no. 3 (1956): 56–57.
[52] *Dokumenty i materialy po istorii Belorussii*, vol. 3, documents nos. 303, 323, pp. 269, 288.
[53] Charviakou, *Za Savetskuiu Belarus'*, pp. 88–89.   [54] Ibid., p. 20.

Historical Background

Many other Belorussians searched for opportunities to go to the United States. Industry in Belorussia began to develop very late and grew very slowly, mainly because there was no regional capital. Competition between the Russian and Polish industries in Belorussia usually resulted in one hindering the development of the other.[55] Because of industrial underdevelopment, the urban population continued to be very small.

The dissatisfaction of the population with internal conditions found its expression in unrest and the destruction of estates at the beginning of the war. Mobilized men felt that their enemies were not the Germans but the landlords. Most of the destruction took place because of dissatisfaction with economic conditions and with the landlords' treatment of the peasants.[56] Large-scale antimilitary disorders broke out in the Senno district of Mogilev province. The mobilized workers and peasants set fire to the Khodtsy estate and destroyed the estates Bykovo, Halishino, and Skrydlovo.[57]

The situation in Belorussia at the beginning of the war was most unhappy. "More than one-half of all the able-bodied men in the Belorussian villages were mobilized and sent to the front."[58] This affected agricultural output; within a year, production decreased sharply and food shortages became acute. Furthermore, with the advance of the Germans in 1915, Belorussia became a battleground, its western half occupied by the German army and its eastern half by Russian troops. Between 1915 and 1917, the civilian population in the major towns of eastern Belorussia was outnumbered by military men stationed there. In Minsk, for example, the population before the war was 110,000; during the war more than 150,000 military men were stationed in the city.[59] The situation in eastern Belorussia was further complicated by the flow of refugees from the area occupied by the Germans. So desperate, in fact, was the situation in Belorussia after three years of war that the February Revolution was greeted with great relief and hope for the future.

[55] Ibid., p. 21.
[56] "Razgrom imeniia 'Iuzefin' kniazia Radzivilla krest'ianami dereven' Glinnoe i Blizhevo Mozyrskogo Uezda" [Destruction of the Estate 'Iuzefin' of the Prince Radzivill by the Peasants from the Villages Glinnoe and Blizhevo or Mozyr District], *Dokumenty i materialy po istorii Belorussii*, vol. 3, document no. 1119, p. 866.
[57] *Istoriia BSSR*, 1:619.   [58] Ibid., p. 625.
[59] "Gubitel'noe vliianie pervoi mirovoi imperialisticheskoi voiny na sostoianie ekonomiki goroda Minska" [The Destructive Influence of the First World Imperialist War on the Economic Condition of Minsk City], *Dokumenty i materialy po istorii Belorussii*, vol. 3, document no. 1047, pp. 816–17.

2.

The Formation of the Belorussian Republic

For centuries, Russia had been one of the most multinational states in the world, and its treatment of the minority nationalities had been less than fair. The fall of the autocracy in the February Revolution of 1917 made the future treatment of internal nationalities a major question. Only the Bolsheviks were prepared to meet the problem, for they, unlike the other parties, had formulated propaganda, if not a policy, on nationalities long before. At the Second Congress of the Russian Social Democratic Party in July 1903, Lenin declared: "We have included in the draft of our Party program the demand for a republic with a democratic constitution that would, among other things, assure recognition of the right of self-determination to all the nationalities contained in the state." He claimed that the Social Democrats would "always combat every attempt to influence national self-determination by violence or by any injustice from without."[1]

Such reassuring statements hardly meant, however, that Lenin was prepared to let the various nationalities within the former Russian Empire secede. He seems to have favored the idea that national disunity and the desire of many nationalities to secede stemmed in part from Great Russian chauvinism and consequent national oppression; if Russian chauvinism toward other nationalities could be eliminated, the nationalities problem could be solved. He stated in his "Speech on the National Question" on May 12, 1917: "All that the Finns want now is autonomy. We stand for giving Finland complete liberty. That will increase their confidence in Russian democracy, and when they are given the right to secede they will not do so."[2]

Formation of the Belorussian Republic

In his writings before the October Revolution, Stalin defined a nation from a historically "scientific" point of view. He believed, or pretended to believe, that the minorities within the Russian Empire were discontented because they did not enjoy liberty of conscience and of movement. He also posed as a firm defender of the nationalities. In "Marxism and the National Question," an article written in 1913, he asserted that "Social-Democracy in all countries proclaims the rights of nations to self-determination. The right of self-determination means that only the nation itself has the right to determine its destiny, that no one has a right to interfere forcibly in the life of the nation, to destroy its schools and other institutions, to violate its habits and customs, to repress its language, nor curtail its right."[3]

In relation to Belorussia, however, the Bolsheviks paid little attention to such policy statements. On the contrary, they treated Belorussia as a Russian province, concentrating their efforts against the national movement and the influence of the Provisional Government. The February Revolution, which had been greeted in Belorussia with great enthusiasm, was followed by a bitter struggle between the Belorussian nationalists and local Bolsheviks, most of whom were Russian soldiers stationed in Belorussia or Party workers sent to conduct propaganda among the troops. The struggle was concentrated around issues relating to the trend the Revolution should follow. The Belorussian nationalists regarded the February Revolution as their final goal. They wanted to cooperate with the Russian Provisional Government in organizing the administration of Belorussia, which would be, they hoped, a part of "the Russian federated-democratic republic."[4] The Bolsheviks, on the other hand, regarded it as a bourgeois revolution which should be followed immediately by a proletarian revolution and subsequently by the establishment of the dictatorship of the proletariat.

Belorussia was in the war zone in 1917. Hundreds of thousands of soldiers were garrisoned in its cities, and Mogilev was the head-

---

[1] Vladimir Lenin, "Natsional'nyi vopros v nashei programme" [The National Question in Our Program], *Sochineniia*, 3d ed. (Moscow, 1929–1939), 5:337.

[2] Idem, "Rech po natsional'nomu voprosu 12 maia, 1917 g." [Speech on the Problem of Nationalities, 12 May 1917], *Polnoe sobranie sochinenii*, 5th ed. (Moscow, 1958–1966), 31:435.

[3] Iosif Stalin, "Marksizm i natsional'nyi vopros" [Marxism and the National Question], *Sochineniia*, 1st ed. (Moscow, 1946–1952), 2:310.

[4] *The Russian Provisional Government, 1917: Documents* (Stanford, Calif., 1961), 1:402.

quarters of the Russian supreme command. Because of Belorussia's geographic position and military importance the Bolsheviks paid close attention to events there. Lacking native Party workers, they sent agitators to spread propaganda in the army and among the civilian population. According to the official *History of the Civil War in the USSR*, "Iakov Sverdlov often summoned the leaders of the Belorussian Bolsheviks to Petrograd and kept them closely informed of the Central Committee's plans and directives."[5] Mikhail V. Frunze was the most notorious of the Bolshevik leaders active in Belorussia after the February Revolution.[6] His activities included undermining and discrediting the Belorussian national movement and attempting to organize a pro-Bolshevik, pro-Russian peasant movement. In the middle of March 1917, the Executive Committee of the Soviet (Council) of Workers' and Soldiers' Deputies in Minsk authorized Frunze, its chairman, to organize a Soviet of Peasant Deputies.[7] A Provisional Peasant Committee was elected which was to establish a Congress of Peasants, eventually to become the Soviet of Peasants' Deputies.[8] M. A. Mikhailov (Frunze's underground name), chief of the civil militia in Minsk, was elected chairman of the committee.[9]

The First Congress of Belorussian Peasants, assembled in Minsk on May 3, elected Frunze chairman and, as expected, passed a resolution providing for the formation of a Soviet of Peasants' Deputies to "go hand in hand with the Soviet of Workers' and Soldiers' Deputies."[10] The Belorussian nationalists replied in an open letter in the *Minskaia hazeta* (Minsk Gazette) on May 4, accusing the leaders of the Peasant Congress, particularly Frunze, of being oriented toward Russia.[11] In addition to taking an antinationalist stand, the congress encouraged peasant uprisings in Belorussia. The landowner

[5] *Istoriia grazhdanskoi voiny v SSSR*, 1st ed. (Moscow, 1935–1960), 2:142.
[6] Mikhail V. Frunze was born in 1885 at Pishpek (now Frunze, capital of the Kirghiz SSR). He joined the Bolshevik Party in 1904 and was sent by the Party to the western front in 1916 to conduct revolutionary activities. After the February Revolution, Frunze worked in Belorussia. See *Bol'shaia sovetskaia entsiklopediia*, 2d ed. (Moscow, 1950–1958), 45:615.
[7] *Kastrychnik na Belarusi: zbornik artykulau i dakumentau* (Minsk, 1927), p. 4.
[8] *Iz istorii ustanovleniia Sovetskoi vlasti v Belorussii i obrazovaniia BSSR: dokumenty i materialy po istorii Belorussii* (Minsk, 1954), vol. 4, document no. 26, pp. 36–37.
[9] Ibid.; and document no. 56, pp. 53–54.
[10] Ibid., document no. 58, p. 55.
[11] *Velikaia Oktiabr'skaia Sotsialisticheskaia Revoliutsiia: khronika sobytii v chetyrekh tomakh* (Moscow, 1957–1961), 1:679.

Chapskii, for example, wrote to the commissar of the Province of Minsk that the peasants considered the resolutions of the congress to be laws compulsory for all citizens and ignored the explanations and decrees issued by the Provisional Government.[12] In his capacity as chief of the local militia, Frunze spent a great deal of time visiting villages and dispensing revolutionary propaganda. Finding many poor peasants who sympathized with Bolshevism, he helped to organize them and supplied them with literature.[13]

Frunze and the other Bolshevik activists in Belorussia were only the executors of Bolshevik agrarian policy. Lenin stated the program succinctly: "Land to the peasants." Iosif Stalin, in his article "The Land to the Peasants," written between March and October 1917, explained Lenin's policy:

> We call upon them to organize and form revolutionary peasant committees . . . , take over the landed estates through these committees, and cultivate the land in an organized manner without authorization. We call upon them to do this without delay, not waiting for the Constituent Assembly and paying no attention to reactionary ministerial prohibitions which put spokes in the wheel of the revolution . . . . Unauthorized cultivation of the landed estates and their seizure by the peasants will undoubtedly "split off" the landlords and their ilk from the revolution. But who would venture to assert that by rallying the millions of poor peasants around the revolution we shall not be awakening the forces of the revolution?[14]

In addition to their activities among the Belorussian peasants, the Bolsheviks paid equal attention to organizing their party. Before 1917 there was no organized Communist Party in Belorussia. At the end of May of that year it was founded by Bolsheviks who had served in the ranks of the Western Army at the time of the February Revolution.[15] Other Bolshevik leaders were then sent to Belorussia by the Central Committee. One of the most notorious of these was Aleksandr Miasnikov,[16] whose role in organizing the Bolshevik

[12] *Iz istorii ustanovleniia Sovetskoi vlasti*, vol. 4, document no. 99, pp. 77–78.
[13] *History of the Civil War in the USSR* (Moscow, 1947), 2:147.
[14] Stalin, "Zemliu krest'ianam" [The Land to the Peasants], *Sochineniia*, 1st ed. (Moscow, 1946–1952), 3:35–36.
[15] Richard Pipes, *The Formation of the Soviet Union: Communism and Nationalism, 1917–1923* (Cambridge, Mass., 1954), p. 74.
[16] Aleksandr F. Miasnikov (Miasnikian was his Armenian name) was born in 1886 to an Armenian family at Nakhichevan' on the river Don. He joined the Bolshevik Party in 1906. He was one of the organizers of the Soviet

Party in Belorussia was identical with Frunze's role in organizing the peasants.[17] At first Miasnikov, together with Frunze, Vilhelm Knorin, and the other Russian Bolsheviks, was not very successful in expanding the Party in Belorussia. In early June 1917 the Bolsheviks had only forty members in the Minsk organization.[18] In early August, in his report to the party's Sixth Congress in Petrograd, Miasnikov proudly stated:

> I am a delegate from Minsk. Our organization was founded not long ago. Previously we cooperated with the compromisers. About twenty to twenty-five days ago we broke away from them and we already have more than five hundred members. Because the front is near, our organization is predominantly military in its composition. We do not have solid ties with the workers. The Mensheviks have approximately 400–500 members. This is predominantly an intelligentsia party. The party of the Bund is strong. The Social Revolutionaries have support in the local town population.[19]

An important role in the work of the Minsk Bolshevik organization was played by the newspaper *Zvezda* (The Star), which began publication in the Russian language on August 8, 1917. Miasnikov, in addition to his other duties, was instrumental in founding this newspaper and became its first editor. Almost every issue featured editorials urging the workers and soldiers to prepare for a struggle.[20] The newspaper also publicized the Leninist slogans for peace, a factor in the declining morale of the army, although the failure of the summer offensive undertaken by the Provisional Government probably contributed more substantially. A rebellion led by the reactionary General Kornilov caused virtual disintegration of the army and certainly was decisive in the speedy growth of the Bolshevik Party everywhere. In Minsk, for example, the Party grew from 2,530 members at the end of August to 28,505 members at the beginning of October.[21] However, the party membership was predominantly Russian and military in composition. "The Bolsheviks had virtually no contact with the Belorussian population."[22]

---

government in Belorussia and of the Belorussian Communist Party. See *Bol'shaia sovetskaia entsiklopediia*, 2d ed., 28:652–53.

[17] Vilhelm Knorin, *1917 god v Belorussii i na zapadnom fronte* (Minsk, 1925), p. 3.

[18] V. K. Shcharbakou, *Kastrychnitskaia Revaliutsyia na Belarusi i belapol'skaia akupatsyia* (Minsk, 1930), p. 20.

[19] *Iz istorii ustanovleniia Sovetskoi vlasti*, vol. 4, document no. 191, p. 136.

[20] *History of the Civil War in the USSR*, p. 146.

[21] Pipes, *Formation of the Soviet Union*, p. 74.

Formation of the Belorussian Republic

After the overthrow of the Russian autocracy, Belorussian nationalists turned their eyes to Petrograd as the new symbol of freedom, equality, and justice. Their movement expanded rapidly, transforming itself into a mass endeavor with clear political goals.[23] Impetus was given by the Congress of the Belorussian Socialist Hramada and other political parties and organizations, which assembled in Minsk on March 25, 1917.[24] Enthusiastic about the great revolution which had brought freedom to Russia, the delegates declared their support of the Provisional Government in its struggle against external and internal enemies and in its defense of freedom for Russia and her people.[25] The congress expressed its determination to fight for the formation of a federal Russian republic in which Belorussia would have the status of an autonomous republic. Later the congress elected and gave executive authority to a Belorussian National Committee, composed of representatives of all the ethnic groups and social classes of the territory,[26] charging it with organizing the administration of Belorussia in collaboration with the Provisional Government.[27]

The National Committee presented demands to the Provisional Government for a permanent regional assembly with advisory authority on local matters, including the right to establish schools using the Belorussian language. "But they had no effect. Apparently Petrograd with some reason put no trust in the National Committee."[28] Despite this discouragement, the Socialist Hramada at its conference in June 1917 voted approval for Socialists to join the coalition cabinet of the Provisional Government. The Hramada also decided to support the continuation of the war, but not the creation of Belorussian national regiments.[29]

An important step in the development of the Belorussian na-

---

[22] Ibid.

[23] J. Mienski, "The Establishment of the Belorussian SSR," *Belorussian Review*, no. 1 (1955): 7.

[24] Strong branches of the Hramada appeared in Moscow, Minsk, Petrograd, and many other cities. During this period, new political parties and organizations were founded, such as the Belorussian People's Hramada, the Belorussian Autonomous Union, the Christian Democratic Union, and others.

[25] *Revoliutsionnoe dvizhenie v Rossii posle sverzheniia samoderzhaviia: dokumenty i materialy* (Moscow, 1957), document no. 712, p. 737.

[26] Pipes, *Formation of the Soviet Union*, p. 73.

[27] *Revoliutsionnoe dvizhenie v Rossii posle sverzheniia samoderzhaviia*, document no. 712, p. 739.

[28] Nicholas P. Vakar, *Belorussia: The Making of a Nation* (Cambridge, Mass., 1956), p. 96. See also *Russian Provisional Government, 1917*, 1:402.

[29] *Velikaia Oktiabr'skaia Sotsialisticheskaia Revoliutsiia*, 2:260.

tional movement was the Second Congress of the Belorussian political parties, held in July 1917 in Minsk. In this, the Socialist Hramada played the major role. The congress, because of its desire to have an organization in which all political parties would be represented, established a Central Rada.[30] At the first session of the Central Rada, which took place in Minsk on August 5–6, the status of this organization was clarified and its position in the Belorussian national movement defined as follows:

> The Rada is the leading organization of the Belorussian national movement. It is composed of deputies sent by all Belorussian organizations and military units which recognize the self-determination of Belorussia, the national language, and the development of national culture. The organizations which joined the Rada are united on the principle of a complete democratization of the social order and transference of the land to the people free of payment.[31]

The Rada's main goal was to achieve agrarian reform modeled after that proposed by the Russian Socialist Revolutionary Party. It excluded the landlords from the right to participate in its activities and elected an Executive Committee of nine who accepted the ideas expressed in the Statute of the Rada:[32] Iazep Liosik, Iazep Dylo, Arkadz Smolich, Paluta Bodunova, Radaslau Astrouski, Platon Halavach, Fabian Shantyr, Kurchevich–Seuruk, and Zmitrok Zhylunovich.[33]

The election of the Central Executive Committee did not bring a radical change in the attitude of the Rada toward the Provisional Government. The Rada simply hoped to obtain the status of an autonomous republic for Belorussia and planned that the Central Executive Committee would be transformed into an autonomous government as soon as the Provisional Government gave its approval.

The October Revolution of 1917 alarmed the Belorussian national government, whose leaders had sincerely sought to cooperate with the Provisional Government. The Provisional Government had

---

[30] The Belorussian word *rada* has identical meaning with the Russian word *soviet*: in English, "council."
[31] *Revoliutsionnoe dvizhenie v Rossii v avguste 1917 goda: dokumenty i materialy* (Moscow, 1959), document no. 345, p. 342.
[32] Pipes, *Formation of the Soviet Union*, p. 74.
[33] *Revoliutsionnoe dvizhenie v Rossii v avguste 1917 goda*, p. 343.

been slow to deal with the nationalities problem and agrarian reform, yet it had tolerated the national movements of various nationalities, thus providing some hope for the future. Its overthrow by the Bolsheviks in Petrograd on November 7, 1917, left only a feeling of insecurity. Eight days later, however, the Soviet government issued a reassuring Declaration of the Rights of the Peoples of Russia. The statement proclaimed the following principles: 1) Equality and sovereignty of the peoples of Russia. 2) The right of the peoples of Russia to free self-determination. 3) Annulment of all the national and national-religious privileges and limitations. 4) Free development of the national minorities and ethnographic groups within Russian territory.[34] To deal with the problem of internal nationalities, the new government created a Commissariat of Nationalities, headed by Stalin. The Declaration temporarily allayed fears in Belorussia, as in other parts of the former Russian Empire, that Bolshevik nationality policy would undergo significant change. There was, however, a feeling that the Bolsheviks did not always keep their promises, and there had been bitter disappointment over the Bolsheviks' negative attitude toward the Belorussian national movement during the period of the Provisional Government. For all that, the Belorussians were prepared to wait and see what the Bolsheviks would do.

They did not have long to wait. When the Soviet government was formed in Petrograd, the Bolsheviks in Minsk, who were already in control of the local Soviet, immediately attempted to take charge of state affairs. For that purpose they established on November 8 a Military Revolutionary Committee (Revkom) as "the supreme organ of power for the whole country and the front."[35] Miasnikov was appointed chairman, and the best-known members were Knorin and Karl Lander.[36] This action awakened the opponents of the Bolsheviks. The Social Revolutionaries and Mensheviks organized a "Committee to Save the Revolution and the Fatherland."[37] This committee was supported by the Belorussian nationalists.[38] Lacking sufficient military strength to seize power, the Bolsheviks decided to abandon the struggle temporarily. They acted as avowed

[34] *Dekrety Sovetskoi vlasti* (Moscow, 1957–1959), 1:40.
[35] Mienski, "Establishment of the BSSR," p. 11.
[36] Knorin, *1917 god v Belorussii*, p. 11.
[37] *Istoriia BSSR*, 2d ed. (Minsk, 1961), 2:59.
[38] *Ocherki po istorii gosudarstva i prava Belorusskoi SSR* (Minsk, 1958), p. 19.

supporters of "Socialist unity" and joined the Committee to Save the Revolution on November 10.[39] The following agreement was the basis for unity:

> The Committee to Save the Revolution, the majority of whose members do not recognize the new government in Petrograd and do not obey it, nevertheless agrees not to send troops from the Western Front for the suppression of the revolutionary movement.[40]

The compromise for "Socialist unity" did not last long. On November 14, at about midnight, an armored train arrived in Minsk to support the Minsk Soviet, and a battalion of the 60th Siberian Rifle Regiment was also dispatched to Minsk.[41] The first Bolshevik coup d'état in Belorussia was accomplished. The Front Committee soon capitulated.[42] Knorin, one of the most prominent Russian Bolshevik leaders in Belorussia at the time of the October Revolution, proudly announced that the Bolshevik revolution in Belorussia was accomplished by the Russians.[43]

To strengthen Soviet authority in Belorussia, the Second Congress of the Representatives of the Soldiers' Committees of the Western Front assembled in Minsk on December 3. The congress chose Miasnikov as its chairman and later elected him commander in chief of the Western Front.[44] He was called the "leader of the revolutionary movement at the front," and was greeted with shouts of "Long live the first elected commander in chief of the Russian People's Army!"[45]

The first meeting of the Executive Committee of the Soviets of Workers', Soldiers', and Peasants' Deputies of the Western Region and the Front took place in Minsk on December 8. N. Rogozinskii was elected chairman of the Regional Executive Committee and the Front Committee. Lander was elected chairman of the Council of People's Commissars.[46] Thus, the foundation was laid for the forma-

---

[39] *Iz istorii ustanovleniia Sovetskoi vlasti*, vol. 4, document no. 340, pp. 248–49.
[40] Ibid.
[41] *Ocherki po istorii*, pp. 20–21.
[42] Mienski, "Establishment of the BSSR," p. 11.
[43] Vilhelm G. Knorin, *Zametki k istorii diktaturi proletariata v Belorussii* (Minsk, 1934), p. 9.
[44] *Istoriia BSSR*, 2:73–74.
[45] *Dokumenty i materialy po istorii Belorussii, 1900–1917 gg.* (Minsk, 1953), vol. 3, document no. 407, p. 302.
[46] *Istoriia BSSR*, 2:74–75.

tion of the Belorussian Soviet Republic, but the word "Belorussia" was not used. After some controversy, the government was named "Soviet of the People's Commissars of the Western Region and the Front."[47] As might be expected from the title, this government was essentially military. "The problem of power was decided only by the army, whose supreme command was not in sympathy with the Belorussian movement."[48] Neither Belorussian military units nor the rank and file of Belorussian workers' and peasants' deputies took part in the establishment of the first Soviet government.[49]

In response to the Bolshevik overthrow of the Provisional Government and the creation of the Belorussian Revkom, the Belorussian Rada[50] approached the people on November 9 with the following appeal:

> In these days we must show that the Belorussian revolutionary democracy, united by suffering, will never permit the storm of disorder to engulf our sacred national cause, "defense of freedom." Unite as a single homogeneous family around the Great Belorussian Rada, rejecting all slogans which bring disharmony.[51]

The Belorussian leaders were clinging, it would seem, to the view that national liberties could be maintained by affirmation. With this in mind, the leaders of the Socialist Hramada, in agreement with the leaders of the other political parties, called for the First All-Belorussian National Congress to discuss the problems created by the Bolshevik coup. This Congress assembled in Minsk on December 28, 1917, and was attended by delegates from the Minsk, Mogilev, Vitebsk, Smolensk, Vilna, and Grodno provinces. The well-known Belorussian nationalist leader, Ales' Burbis, wrote:

> Assembled are 1872 delegates; 716 of them are representatives from the army. At the Congress were: the representatives of the soldiers and sailors of all fronts and fleets, the representatives of the working organizations, the representatives from the towns ... and the representatives of all the political parties including the Bolsheviks.[52]

---

[47] *Iz istorii ustanovleniia Sovetskoi vlasti*, vol. 4, document no. 410, p. 305.
[48] Mienski, "Establishment of the BSSR," p. 11.
[49] E. S. Kancher, *Belorusskii vopros* (Petrograd, 1919), p. 25.
[50] The Central Belorussian Rada and Belorussian Military Rada, in the summer of 1917, united to create the Great Belorussian Rada.
[51] A. Ziuz'kou, *Kryvavy shliakh Belaruskai natsdemakratyi* (Minsk, 1931), p. 55.
[52] Aleksandr Charviakou, *Za Savetskuiu Belarus'* (Minsk, 1927), p. 45.

At the congress were represented not only all social strata of the population, but all ethnographic groups, as well.[53] The debate at this congress revolved around the question of the relationship between Belorussia and the newly created Soviet government in Russia.[54] Although the delegates voted to recognize the Soviet government, they decided against recognizing the Council of People's Commissars of the Western Region and the Front.[55] The Belorussian nationalist leaders who had worked for autonomy under the Provisional Government now turned to the demand for independence for Belorussia. They "decided to create the Belorussian Central Council which was designed to take over power in Belorussia."[56] Because of this decision, the Bolsheviks, using armed force, dispersed the congress during the night of December 30.[57] Nevertheless, the delegates gathered the next day to finish their work, protected by the Minsk railway workers, and elected an Executive Committee. "The leadership of the national movement went underground."[58]

The First All-Belorussian National Congress was dispersed by a military unit acting under the orders of the Council of People's Commissars.[59] Soviet historians have tried to explain this action by arguing that the Belorussian political parties and organizations after the October Revolution endeavored to form a purely nationalist movement.[60] But the main reason for the dispersal, in their view, was that the Belorussian leaders had disregarded a condition for the calling of the congress laid down by Stalin:

> Before the convocation of the All-Belorussian Congress, . . . the representatives of the Belorussian organizations turned for assistance to Comrade Stalin, the Commissar of Nationalities. Having no objections, he set forth necessary conditions for the calling of Congress. These conditions required that the Belorussian leaders should reach an agreement on the matter with the local Soviet organizations. The organizers of the Congress ignored Stalin's conditions and summoned the Congress completely independently.[61]

[53] Mienski, "Establishment of the BSSR," p. 13.
[54] Pipes, "Formation of the Soviet Union," p. 75.
[55] *Iz istorii ustanovleniia Sovetskoi vlasti*, vol. 4, document no. 464, p. 339.
[56] *Istoriia BSSR*, 2:76.
[57] *Byelorussia's Independence Day, March 25, 1918: Documents, Facts, Proclamations, Statements and Comments* (New York, 1958), p. 17.
[58] Mienski, "Establishment of the BSSR," p. 13.
[59] *Iz istorii ustanovleniia Sovetskoi vlasti*, vol. 4, document no. 454, p. 333.
[60] Ibid., document no. 464, p. 339.
[61] Ibid.

The first of the three Soviet governments in Belorussia was established by the Communists with the support of Russian troops on the western front. It remained in power from November 15, 1917, until March 4, 1918. During this period the Bolsheviks dissolved the Minsk City Council and the Minsk Duma,[62] whose functions were taken over by the Minsk Soviet of Workers' and Soldiers' Deputies. Similar action was taken in all other towns occupied by the Soviet army. The authority of the Soviets, however, extended only to the regions occupied by pro-Bolshevik military units.

Meanwhile, the Bolsheviks also tried to put into effect the "Decree on Land," which had been approved by the Second All-Russian Congress of Soviets on November 8, 1917. This decree provided for the abolition of landed proprietorship without compensation and for the confiscation of the land in the following manner:

> The landed estates, as also all appendages, the monasterial and church lands, with all their livestock, implements, farm buildings, and everything pertaining thereto, shall be placed under the control of the Volost' Land Committees and the Uezd Soviets of Peasants' Deputies pending the meeting of the Constituent Assembly. . . . The land of the ordinary peasants and the ordinary cossacks shall not be confiscated.[63]

The Bolsheviks had difficulty in enforcing this decree in an organized manner because the peasants were taking the land without waiting. In addition, the Polish legions under General Dowbor-Musnicki opened a campaign against the Bolsheviks in the fall of 1917. These military units were formed in Russia after March 30, 1917, when the Provisional Government declared by manifesto the formation of an independent Polish state, militarily united with Russia.[64]

The Treaty of Brest-Litovsk, concluded between Russia and the Central Powers on March 3, 1918, left the country divided. The larger part of Belorussia, including the capital at Minsk, was occupied by the Germans. In a memorandum to the German government, the Belorussian Rada protested against the illegality of the treaty.[65]

[62] Ibid., document no. 499, p. 368.
[63] Lenin, "Dekret o zemle" [Decree on the Land], 8 November 1917, *Sochineniia*, 3d ed. (Moscow, 1929–1939), 22:406–07.
[64] Shcharbakou, *Kastrychnitskaia Revaliutsyia*, p. 41; *Polen: Osteuropa-Handbuch* (Cologne, 1959), pp. 6–7.
[65] Mienski, "Establishment of the BSSR," p. 17.

Nevertheless, in the beginning the Germans showed good intentions toward the Belorussian people.[66] The nationalist leaders emerged from hiding and sought to complete the work of the First All-Belorussian Congress, dispersed by the Bolsheviks in December. On March 22 the Executive Committee of the Rada published Decree No. 2, which, in conformity with the resolution of the congress, proclaimed the Belorussian National Republic (BNR).[67] The Rada was to be the supreme authority in the republic until the Constituent Assembly could be elected.[68]

The dream of an independent state was fulfilled when the representatives of the Rada met in Minsk on March 25, 1918, and by a majority of votes declared the independence of the Belorussian National Republic in Decree No. 3:

> A year ago, the peoples of Belorussia, together with all the peoples of Russia, threw off the yoke of Russian tsarism which, taking no advice from the people, had plunged our land into the conflagration of war that ruined most of our towns and villages. . . . Today we, the Rada of the Belorussian National Republic, cast off from our country the last chains of the political dependence that had been imposed by Russian tsarism upon our people. From now on, the Belorussian National Republic is to be a free and independent country. The peoples of Belorussia themselves through their own constituent assembly will decide upon the future relations of Belorussia with other states. . . . Proclaiming the independence of the Belorussian National Republic, the Rada hopes that all liberty-loving people will help the Belorussian people to realize fully their political and state ideals.[69]

By this decree the Rada declared null and void the peace treaty of Brest-Litovsk on grounds that it was negotiated and signed by foreign countries without the participation of Belorussian representatives.[70]

The Germans did not fully support Belorussian and Ukrainian independence. Their only interest in these lands stemmed from their policy of territorial expansion in the East and the desire for economic exploitation of the area.[71] In the meantime, the Germans

---

[66] Shcharbakou, *Kastrychnitskaia Revaliutsyia*, p. 64.
[67] *Za dziarzhaunuiu nezalezhnasts' Belarusi: dakumanty i matar'ialy* (London, 1960), p. 22.
[68] Ibid., p. 23.
[69] Ibid., p. 24.
[70] Ibid.

needed food, and they tried to get it from the Belorussian and Ukrainian peasants by force. As a result, the peasantry became very restless. The repressive measures of the German army in the territories they occupied during the summer of 1918 facilitated the formation of a resistance movement which ultimately benefited the Bolsheviks.

The Rada's attempts to obtain the support of the Allies were also unsuccessful, although Poland, Finland, and the Baltic states received diplomatic and material aid after the defeat of the Central Powers. The restoration of Polish military power, in particular, was viewed with uneasiness by Belorussian leaders. Their apprehensions were later fulfilled when, after the withdrawal of German troops, Belorussia once again became a battlefield—this time between Soviet Russia and Poland. Some of the nationalists, blaming the Allied powers for Belorussia's weakness, began to look for reconciliation with the Bolsheviks.

The defeat of Germany in the fall of 1918 determined its position in the East. In accordance with Point Six of Woodrow Wilson's "Fourteen Points," Germany was to withdraw its forces from the territories of the former Russian Empire. The Soviet Russian government reciprocated with a decree on November 13, 1918, declaring the Peace Treaty of Brest-Litovsk null and void.[72] In the same decree the Soviet government declared that the right of self-determination would be fully recognized for all nations of the former Russian Empire.[73]

Officially the Bolsheviks had begun to reevaluate their attitude toward the Belorussian national movement in December 1917, when the First All-Belorussian Congress assembled in disregard of the Soviet authorities. This convinced the Bolsheviks that they had been wrong in ignoring the movement before the October Revolution.[74] Their mistakes returned to haunt them during their peace negotiations with the Germans at Brest-Litovsk. Trotsky told the Ger-

---

[71] Fritz Fischer, *Germany's Aims in the First World War* (New York, 1967), p. 484; Winfried Baumgart, *Deutsche Ostpolitik, 1918: Von Brest-Litowsk biz zum Ende des Ersten Weltkrieges* (Vienna and Munich, 1966), pp. 42, 281.

[72] *Istoriia Sovetskoi Konstitutsii v dokumentakh, 1917–1956* (Moscow, 1957), p. 166.

[73] Ibid., p. 167.

[74] T. Gorbunov, "Lenin i Stalin v bor'be za svobodu i nezavisimost' Belorusskogo naroda," *Istoricheskii zhurnal*, nos. 2–3 (1944):15–16.

man delegates that Soviet Russia fully maintained its declaration that peoples inhabiting Russian territory had the right of self-determination without outside influence, even to the point of separation.[75] Lev Kamenev, chief Soviet delegate in the last stage of the negotiations, presented a document which reads in part:

> The old frontiers of the former Russian Empire, frontiers established by violence and aggression against the people, and in particular against the people of Poland, have fallen together with Tsarism. The new frontiers of the fraternal union of the peoples of the Russian Republic, and of the peoples which wish to leave its frontiers, must be defined by the free decision of the peoples concerned.[76]

The German reply, delivered by General Hoffman, reminded the Soviet representatives sharply that their words differed from their deeds:

> I would like to state that the Russian delegation demands for the occupied territories the application of the right of self-determination of peoples in a manner and to an extent which its government does not apply to its own country. Its government is founded purely on power, and indeed, on power which ruthlessly suppresses by force all who think otherwise. Everyone with different views is regarded as a counter-revolutionary and bourgeois and simply declared an outlaw. I shall only substantiate my view by two examples. During the night of December 30, the First Belorussian Congress at Minsk, which decided to put into force the right of the Belorussian people to self-determination, was broken up by Maximalists with bayonets and machine guns. When the Ukrainians claimed their right to self-determination, the Petrograd Government sent an ultimatum and endeavored to carry through their will by force of arms.[77]

The conclusion was inescapable: during their first hundred days in power the Bolsheviks had mishandled the Belorussian question; therefore, the Belorussians had rejected the Bolsheviks and declared their independence. Following the peace treaty with the Germans on March 3, 1918, and the declaration of independence of the Belorussian National Republic on March 25, the Bolsheviks began to

---

[75] Judah L. Magnes, *Russia and Germany at Brest-Litovsk: A Documentary History of the Peace Negotiations* (New York, 1919), p. 67.
[76] *Soviet Documents on Foreign Policy, 1917–1941* (London, 1951–1953), 1:31.
[77] Magnes, *Russia and Germany at Brest-Litovsk*, pp. 76–77.

exhibit an interest in Belorussian history and the Belorussian national movement. One conciliatory gesture was the opening of the Belorussian Peoples' University in Moscow in the summer of 1918. Its purpose was to educate students about the history, life, and culture of Belorussia, along with orientation in contemporary national and social revolutionary movements.[78] The best-known Belorussian historians, linguists, and geographers were invited to lecture, among them the distinguished linguist, Professor Efim Karski. The location of the university in Moscow had, of course, political significance. Stalin published an article on December 15, 1918, entitled, "Light from the East," in which he stressed the following:

> Slowly but surely, the tide of the liberation movement is rolling from east to west, into the occupied regions. Slowly, but just as surely, the "new" bourgeois-republican "governments" of Finland, Latvia, Lithuania, and Belorussia are receding into oblivion and making way for the power of workers and peasants. . . . Soviet Russia has never looked upon the western regions as its possession. It has always considered that these regions are the inalienable possessions of the laboring masses of the nationalities inhabiting them, that these laboring masses have the full right to freely determine their political destiny.[79]

The Germans left Minsk on December 9, and the army of the Russian Soviet Federated Socialist Republic occupied it the next day.[80] Most of the members of the BNR Rada left Minsk before the Bolsheviks came. However, "an important fragment of the BNR government—Liosik, president of the Rada, Ihnatouski, secretary of education, and a few others—remained in Minsk in the hope that the Belorussian state might continue with Russian instead of German support."[81] Their hope was realized, at least for a short time. On December 23 the Central Committee of the Russian Communist Party opened a hearing on the question of Belorussia and on the same day decided to create the Belorussian Soviet Socialist Republic.[82] Four days later Stalin met with Party and Soviet leaders from the northwestern regions for discussion of the boundaries of Belorussia, the formation of its new government, and the organization

[78] Efim F. Karski, *Kurs Belorussovedeniia* (Moscow, 1920), introduction.
[79] Stalin, *Sochineniia*, 1st ed., 4:177–78.
[80] *Iz istorii ustanovleniia Sovetskoi vlasti*, vol. 4, document no. 598, p. 428.
[81] Vakar, *Belorussia*, p. 107.
[82] S. P. Margunskii, *Sozdanie i uprochnenie belorusskoi gosudarstvennosti, 1917–1922* (Minsk, 1958), p. 147.

of the Communist Party of Belorussia.[83] As N. V. Kamenskaia stated, "Stalin himself personally selected candidates for the government of the BSSR."[84]

In order to carry out the Party's decision of December 23, the Soviet government directed the Northwestern Regional Committee of the Russian Communist Party to call its sixth conference at Smolensk. At the first meeting, on December 30, the conference changed the name of the party to "Communist Party (Bolsheviks) of Belorussia."[85] Thus, the First Congress of the Belorussian Communist Party was organized on a direct order from Moscow. To Belorussians, however, the most disturbing factor was that a party conference of a Russian region had renamed itself a congress of a Belorussian party. Even the Belorussian Communists were unhappy over this development. They fully realized that as long as the Party in Belorussia remained in the hands of the Smolensk organization they would have little authority. Accordingly, a group of the Belorussian Communist-nationalists requested permission from Moscow to form another, purely Belorussian, Communist Party.[86] Their answer came, not from Moscow, but through the Central Bureau of the newly created Communist Party of Belorussia, which stated flatly that "the majority could not form a faction."[87] Ironically, the majority of the Communists in Belorussia at that time were Russians, and Russians had formed and dominated the Central Bureau itself. They used the word "majority" to refer to the Belorussian people, who composed the majority of the population in the republic.

The first decision of the so-called First Congress of the Belorussian Communist Party was the formation, on December 31, of the Provisional Workers' and Peasants' Revolutionary Government.[88] Zmitrok Zhylunovich was elected head of the government, the congress was ended, and its functions were inherited by the Provisional Government. The first act of this government was a manifesto on January 1, 1919, which announced the formation of the Belorussian SSR.[89] Proclaimed in Smolensk, it consisted of the prov-

[83] Ibid., p. 148.
[84] Quoted in Mienski, "Establishment of the BSSR," p. 21. N. V. Kamenskaia is well known as a recent historian in Belorussia. She is one of the editors of *Iz istorii ustanovleniia Sovetskoi vlasti*, and of *Istoriia BSSR*.
[85] Gorbunov, "Lenin i Stalin," p. 16.
[86] *Istoriia BSSR*, 2:121.
[87] *Kastrychnik na Belarusi*, p. 287.
[88] Ibid., p. 123.
[89] Ibid.

inces of Minsk, Smolensk, Vitebsk, Grodno, and Mogilev. On January 5, the new government moved to Minsk, which thereafter became the capital of the republic.

On February 1 the First All-Belorussian Congress of Soviets assembled for "ratification" of the act proclaiming the Belorussian SSR. Two hundred and thirty delegates attended the congress, all of them Communists except seventeen "sympathizers."[90] Iakov Sverdlov, chairman of the Central Executive Committee of the RSFSR, came from Moscow to address the congress. In his speech of greeting he said, "You more than anyone else suffered from the foreign occupation. But under the heel of triumphant imperialism you continued your work for the establishment of the Soviet system in Belorussia.... We have acquired experience during the last year and we will help you."[91]

As viewed by Soviet historians, the First All-Belorussian Congress of Soviets was a great milestone in the history of the republic. It legally ratified the independence of the proclaimed Belorussian SSR and approved the first constitution.[92] As required by the constitution, it elected a Central Executive Committee of fifty members. Aleksandr Miasnikov was elected chairman of the CEC as well as chairman of the Council of People's Commissars.[93] From the representatives of the national Belorussian groups, the only persons elected were those who joined the local Communist and Soviet organizations. Among them were Aleksandr Charviakou, Zmitrok Charnushevich, I. Lagun, Iazep Adamovich, and others. Zhylunovich failed to be elected.[94]

Since the First All-Belorussian Congress of Soviets had been called into session on orders from Moscow, the Bolshevik leaders immediately approved its "decisions." The ratification of the independence of the Belorussian SSR was approved on February 5, 1919, by the All-Russian Central Executive Committee, and the following note was sent to Minsk:

> In accordance with the principle of a complete and real self-determination of the working peoples of all countries the Presidium of the

[90] S"ezdy Sovetov Soiuza SSR, Soiuznykh i Avtonomnykh Sovetskikh Sotsialisticheskikh Respublik: sbornik dokumentov v trekh tomakh, 1917–1936 gg. (Moscow, 1959–1960), 2:229.
[91] Istoriia BSSR, 2:125.
[92] S"ezdy Sovetov Soiuza SSR, p. 229.
[93] Margunskii, Sozdanie i uprochnenie belorusskoi gosudarstvennosti, p. 155.
[94] Kastrychnik na Belarusi, p. 228.

All-Russian Central Executive Committee recognizes the independence of the Belorussian Soviet Socialist Republic.[95]

Thus, Belorussia in less than two months became a fully sovereign state. It had a constitution in which Russia was not mentioned at all; its independence, ratified by the First All-Belorussian Congress, was approved by the Russian Soviet government; and its territory included almost all its ethnic population. It appeared that even the Belorussian nationalists could not wish for anything better.

But the insincerity of those who gave the orders to create the Belorussian SSR and who loudly proclaimed its sovereignty was revealed when the so-called First All-Belorussian Congress, after performing all these actions, was ordered by Moscow to make a "decision" to unite Belorussia with Lithuania in a state to be known as Litbel.[96] This decision virtually liquidated the Belorussian Republic. Its territory was reduced from five provinces to one (Minsk), which now became a part of Litbel. The other four Belorussian provinces were reabsorbed by the Russian Republic. And the participation of Belorussians in the government of the Lithuanian-Belorussian state was limited to one person.[97] The Belorussians naturally protested such measures. "They resented the fact that Belorussians had been exploited for tactical reasons, and that their republic was being used as a mere device for Soviet expansion."[98] By the time the decision was made to create Litbel, a Soviet-Polish conflict was already under way. The Bolshevik leaders, inspired by the possibility of expanding westward, now hoped to bring Poland under Communist control in the same manner as they had subdued Belorussia. Since most of Belorussia was already under Bolshevik control, it no longer concerned them.

[95] *Iz istorii grazhdanskoi voiny v SSSR: sbornik dokumentov i materialov v trekh tomakh, 1918–1922* (Moscow, 1960–1961), vol. 1, document no. 632, p. 697.
[96] *Kastrychnik na Belarusi*, p. 288.
[97] Mienski, "Establishment of the BSSR," p. 24.
[98] Pipes, *Formation of the Soviet Union*, p. 153.

3.

The Partition of Belorussia

Belorussia, because of its geographic position, has for many centuries been an arena of political, national, religious, and cultural struggle between the Russians and the Poles. Partitions of Poland between 1772 and 1795 decided the outcome of this contest in favor of Russia. From 1795 until 1918, Poland, as a state, did not exist on the map of Europe. A large part of Poland was administered by Russia during this time. The Polish nobles were not deprived of their feudal estates nor of their serfs, whether the latter were Belorussians, Ukrainians, or Poles. But they were deprived of their state symbols and royal court.[1] This hurt the pride of the Poles, whose country once had been strong and had played an important role in European affairs.

During World War I, the Russian government wanted to find a medium of reconciliation with the Poles. To this end, Grand Duke Nikolai Nikolaevich, commander in chief of the Russian forces, in his proclamation of August 14, 1914, promised the Poles autonomy. After the overthrow of the tsar, the Russian Provisional Government recognized the independence of the Polish state.[2] However, at that time Poland was under German occupation, and recognition of its independence had little more than tactical significance.

A radical change in Russian-Polish relations occurred after the evacuation of the German forces from Poland in the fall of 1918, at a time when Russia, Germany, and Austria, being defeated, were faced with internal unrest. Russia, as a matter of fact, was already engaged in civil war. Thus, the collapse of Poland's neighbors gave the Poles an excellent opportunity to revive their state after more than a century. Furthermore, the victorious Western powers were sympathetic to the Poles and assisted them diplomatically and militarily in obtaining independence. The most difficult problem in the

1918–1920 period, however, was the establishment of the Polish frontiers, especially in the east.

President Woodrow Wilson supported the independence of Poland. In the thirteenth of his Fourteen Points, announced on January 8, 1918, Wilson proposed to settle the Polish frontiers in the following way:

> Poland to include indisputable Polish population, and to have "free and secure" access to the sea and to have her independence and integrity guaranteed by the international covenant.[3]

The territory of the Polish state, in accordance with Wilson's proposal, would have been limited by the Polish ethnographic frontiers. The ethnographic Polish state, however, was relatively small. Its eastern frontier before the Mongolian invasion of Russia did not quite reach the Bug River. This did not satisfy the nationalistically minded Polish leaders, who dreamed of the so-called Polish "historical frontiers"—the frontiers of the joint Polish-Lithuanian state which existed between 1569 and 1772.[4] This would be a large commonwealth, as they called it, "from the Baltic Sea to the Black Sea" (*od morza do morza*). They disagreed, however, as to how far Poland should extend its eastern frontier and by what means.

There were two divergent views. One of them, advocated by the National Democrats, whose spokesman was Roman Dmowski, looked toward the creation of a large and centralized state which would include all those areas of the old Grand Duchy of Lithuania "where substantial Polish population, economic interest, and historical tradition had left an imprint of 'Polishness.' "[5] Such a project had considerable appeal to Polish nationalists, who tended to ignore the insoluble problems it would create. To extend the Polish frontier eastward to this extent would annex large parts of Belorussia and the Ukraine where this "substantial Polish population" formed only a tiny minority. The alternative view, advocated by Marshal Jozef

---

[1] James T. Shotwell and Max M. Laserson, *The Curzon Line: The Polish-Soviet Dispute* (New York, [1940s]), p. 2.

[2] Georg von Rauch, *Russland: Staatliche Einheit und Nationale Vielfalt* (Munich, 1953), p. 190.

[3] Harold William Vazeille Temperley, ed., *A History of the Peace Conference of Paris* (London, 1920–1924), 1:193.

[4] Titus Komarnicki, *Rebirth of the Polish Republic: A Study in the Diplomatic History of Europe, 1914–1920* (London, 1957), pp. 441–47.

[5] Piotr S. Wandycz, *Soviet-Polish Relations, 1917–1921* (Cambridge, Mass., 1969), p. 94.

Partition of Belorussia

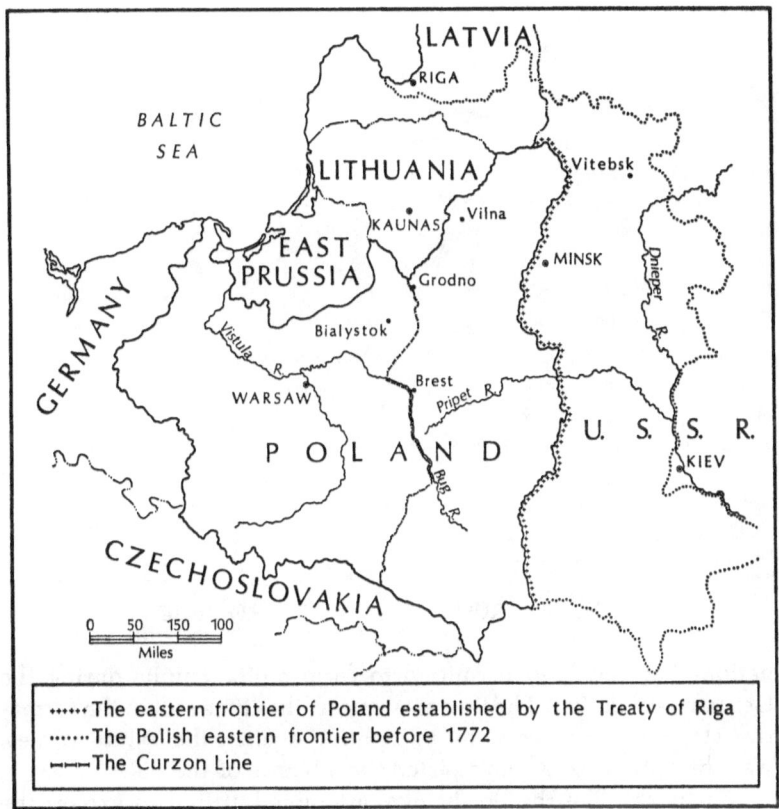

POLAND BETWEEN 1921 AND 1939

Pilsudski's Socialists (also called Federalists), was that the great Polish state could best be achieved by fostering and assisting the movements for self-determination in the areas of the old Grand Duchy of Lithuania and then inviting them to join in a federation with Poland.[6] This was an idealistic conception for restoring the Polish-Lithuanian Commonwealth, and if its advocates had tried sincerely to implement this idea, they might have succeeded in gaining support from the Belorussian, Ukrainian, and Lithuanian peoples. In March 1919, when the Polish armies, led by Pilsudski, started their advance into Lithuania, Belorussia, and the Ukraine, there were practically no military forces to resist them because these

[6] Nicholas P. Vakar, *Belorussia: The Making of a Nation* (Cambridge, Mass., 1956), p. 120; Wandycz, *Soviet-Polish Relations*, pp. 96–97.

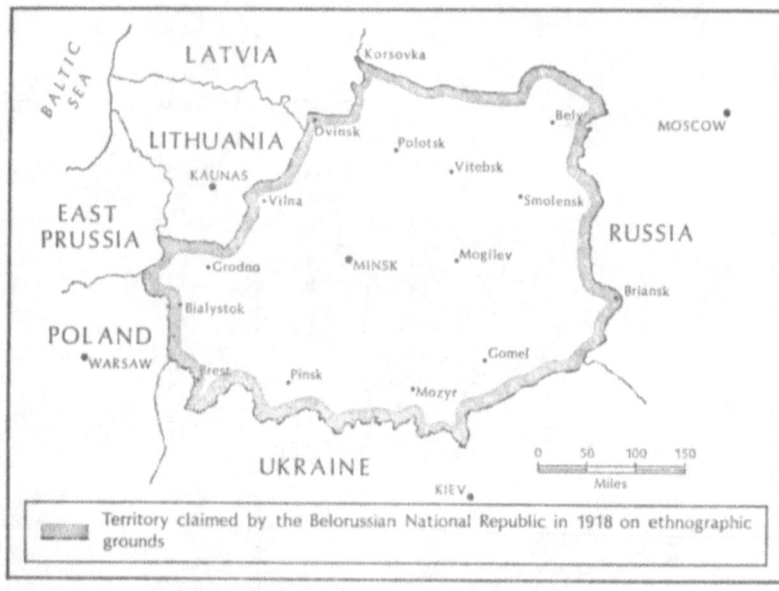

Territory claimed by the Belorussian National Republic in 1918 on ethnographic grounds

THE BELORUSSIAN NATIONAL REPUBLIC

nations had not been permitted to form military units during the German occupation. The Soviet Army, at that time still in the formative stage and weakened by its fighting against the White armies, was the only force which resisted the advance of the Poles.

Pilsudski, like the Bolsheviks, attempted at first to exploit the principle of self-determination as a means of gaining control of the desired territories. After taking Vilna on April 19, 1919, he issued the following proclamation:

> The Polish Army which I lead is bringing you freedom. I want to give the fullest possibility of solving your national and religious problems in your own way, and although guns are still thundering and blood is still flowing in parts of your land, I have no intention of establishing a military occupation.[7]

The Poles appealed to the Belorussians in their native language, promising them freedom and declaring that the future of the country would be decided "by the free will of the people whose rights to self-determination shall in no wise be restricted."[8]

---

[7] Alexandra Pilsudska, *Pilsudski: A Biography by His Wife* (New York, 1941), pp. 292–93.

[8] Vakar, *Belorussia*, p. 109.

The sincerity of the Poles was not questioned at first, and the Belorussians "welcomed the entry of Polish troops and voiced approval of Pilsudski's proclamation."[9] But at the beginning of May, the Sejm (the lower chamber of the Polish Parliament) declared that Belorussia was historically an inalienable part of the Polish Commonwealth, and decreed the complete integration of occupied territories with Poland.[10] Thus, it seemed that Pilsudski's "liberation" meant incorporation. Even Pilsudski's own promises were not kept long. His de facto policy was to occupy the territory and then under the supervision of Polish occupation authorities, to hold a plebiscite for unification of the area with Poland.[11] This policy was applied from the time the Polish army advanced into Belorussian territory. The first decrees of the Polish government for such plebiscites date back to November 28, 1918, when Polish troops occupied the districts of Bialystok.[12] "The Polish settlers in the eastern provinces usually were sending petitions to Warsaw requesting, in the name of the Belorussian people, pure and simple incorporation."[13]

The Council of Ministers of the Belorussian National Republic, in a note of January 2, 1919, to the minister of foreign affairs of the Polish Republic, protested that such plebiscites were equivalent to annexation of Belorussian territory in violation of the sovereign rights of the Belorussian people.[14] The Polish government, despite the protest, continued its policy of expansion and annexation. "By the end of January, 1919, with the support of Marshal Foch, the French and Allied Commander in Chief, a commissar of the Polish Republic appeared in Grodno and began to organize sympathetic elements into a self-defense unit of the Grodno region."[15] In the Grodno region, as in the Bialystok region before, the Poles immediately began to prepare a plebiscite as a legal basis for annexation.

The government of the BNR, in a note to the president of the Paris Peace Conference of February 9, 1919, particularly objected to the Polish claims on Belorussia, claims based on the fact that Lith-

---

[9] Wandycz, *Soviet-Polish Relations*, p. 123.
[10] Richard Pipes, *The Formation of the Soviet Union: Communism and Nationalism, 1917–1923* (Cambridge, Mass., 1954), p. 153.
[11] Mikola Volacic, "The Curzon Line and Territorial Changes in Eastern Europe," *Belorussian Review*, no. 2 (1956), p. 55.
[12] Wiktor Ostrowski, *Spotlight on Byelorussia and Her Neighbours* (London, 1959), p. 55.
[13] Vakar, *Belorussia*, p. 111.
[14] *Za dziarzhaunuiu nezalezhnasts' Belarusi: dakumanty i matar'ialy* (London, 1960), pp. 33–34.
[15] Ostrowski, *Spotlight on Byelorussia*, pp. 55–56.

uania and Belorussia had formed a state union with Poland in the Middle Ages. The note said that the Polish population in Belorussia constituted only a very small percentage of the total population, varying in individual regions from 2 to 10 percent, composed predominantly of Polish landowners and, in the western part of the country, of inhabitants of a few large cities.[16] (Table One shows the ethnic population in five regions of Belorussia.)[17]

Anton Lutskevich, president of the Council of Ministers of the BNR, on May 8, 1919, sent the president of the Peace Conference the following further note of protest:

> Under the banner of the battle against Bolshevism, Polish troops are step by step seizing the territories of the Democratic Republic of White Ruthenia. After having commenced, with the consent of the German Government, by establishing themselves in the Government of Grodno, they have now occupied Vilna, the former capital of the White Ruthenian-Lithuanian State, from which the inhabitants themselves had already driven out the Bolsheviks.
>
> Profiting from the fact that the German authorities had opposed any formation of White Ruthenian regular troops, the Poles without entering into any relations with the local White Ruthenian authorities, are introducing by force of bayonet a Polish civil administration in the White Ruthenian country occupied by them, declaring that Polish officials will organize the election of deputies of the people, who will then express the will of said people.
>
> It is clear that under the pressure of any armed force, there could be no question of a free expression of the sentiments of the people. This has already been proved, moreover, by a noteworthy series of arrests among prominent White Ruthenians without any other reason than for their disapproval of the Polish plans for annexation.
>
> The people of White Ruthenia have already expressed their will in substance at the National Congress of White Ruthenians which met at Minsk, in December, 1917, by proclaiming the Democratic Republic of White Ruthenia, within ethnographic and historic boundaries and by creating a legislative authority embodied in the Council of the Republic and State, represented by the Council of Ministers.

[16] *Za dziarzhaunuiu nezalezhnasts' Belarusi*, p. 37.

[17] According to the census of 1897 (see Usevalad Ihnatouski and A. Smolich, *Belorussiia: territoriia* . . . [Minsk, 1925], p. 9), the total population in these regions was 6,579,600: 73 percent Belorussians; 13.8 percent Jews; 4.7 percent Ukrainians; 4.3 percent Russians; 2.5 percent Poles; and 1.7 percent other nationalities. Quoted in *Istoriia BSSR*, 2d ed. (Minsk, 1961), 1:411.

TABLE ONE

ETHNIC GROUPS AS PERCENTAGES OF THE TOTAL POPULATION
OF BELORUSSIA, 1897

Region	Belorussians and Ukrainians	Russians	Jews	Poles	Lithuanians and Latvians	Others
Mogilev	82.6	3.4	12.1	1.4	—	0.5
Minsk	76.4	3.9	16.0	3.0	—	0.7
Grodno	66.7	4.6	17.4	10.1	0.2	1.0
Vilna	56.0	4.9	12.7	8.2	17.6	0.6
Vitebsk	52.9	13.3	11.7	3.4	17.8	0.9

Source: Census of 1897, in Usevalad Ihnatouski and A. Smolich, *Belorussiia: territoriia* ... (Minsk, 1925), p. 9.

The White Ruthenian Government herewith most emphatically protests to the Peace Conference against the appropriation by the Poles of the civil administration over the White Ruthenian territory occupied by them, as well as against the measures being prepared to make a people terrorized by Polish occupants of its country express "its will" under wholly abnormal conditions.

The Government of White Ruthenia declares that peace in this eastern part of Europe can only be assured by a prompt recognition of all the State organizations, recently formed, and by a just delimitation of the frontiers between them in accordance with the ethnographic principle.

Conversely, the seizure by the Poles of one or another part of the territory of White Ruthenia, even if apparently justified, by the consent of the population (extorted by bayonets) will leave an ever-open wound and will become an untarnished source of violent national contests, which will give re-birth to new Balkans in Eastern Europe.

The Government of White Ruthenia places the responsibility for the possible consequences of such provocating procedure on the part of the Poles, upon the Polish Government.[18]

In April 1919, the Polish army was strengthened by the arrival of General Haller's army, which had been sent back from France with the consent of the Allies.[19] The appearance of this army on the

[18] *Za dziarzhaunuiu nezalezhnasts' Belarusi*, p. 42. Quotation from English text of note.
[19] Pilsudska, *Pilsudski*, p. 285. Jozef Haller was a Polish general and

eastern front in June 1919 enabled Pilsudski to push the Bolsheviks eastward quickly. On August 8, the Poles occupied Minsk, the capital of Belorussia. This gave the Poles more confidence in their victory over the Bolsheviks.

Pilsudski's promises to the Belorussian people were already completely forgotten. Decree No. 8, announced by the Poles on August 20, 1919, said: "In the territory occupied by the Polish army the Polish language is to be considered the official language."[20] The occupied territory of Belorussia was announced to be the "Kresy Wschodnie" (Eastern Provinces) of Poland.[21] The Belorussian and Russian schools were closed, and many of the teachers were arrested. The Polish language was introduced in all offices. Petitions written in the Belorussian or Russian language were not acceptable.[22]

The Belorussian Central Rada refused to support the Polish policy of occupation. At the meeting of the Rada in December 1919, Vatslau Lastouski, who always defended Belorussian independence and whose hostile attitude toward Polish imperialism was well known, was elected prime minister. The Poles arrested Lastouski and several members of his cabinet, while the rest of the Belorussian government went into exile in Kaunas, Lithuania.[23]

The years of Polish occupation (1919-1920) are known in Belorussian history as very hard years. The Polish legionnaires destroyed the village committees and punished their chairmen and members.[24] Many villages, for no particular reason, were burned to the ground. According to an investigating commission, "in only ten volosts of Slutsk district, 323 houses were burned."[25] Such lawless, irrespon-

---

statesman. At the outbreak of World War I, he helped to organize the Polish Legion in the Austrian army and commanded its Second Brigade against the Russians. After the first treaty of Brest-Litovsk (3 March 1918), however, he changed sides and, entering the Ukraine, fought against the Germans until he was forced to flee in May of that year. In September 1918, he took command of the Polish army in France, which had been formed on the initiative of Izvolski, the tsarist ambassador to France, to fight the Germans. In April 1919, he and his army arrived in Poland and joined Pilsudski's forces against the Bolsheviks. See *Bol'shaia sovetskaia entsiklopediia*, 1st ed. (1929-1948), 14:390.

[20] V. K. Shcharbakou, *Kastrychnitskaia Revaliutsyia na Belarusi i belapol'skaia akupatsyia* (Minsk, 1930), p. 101.

[21] *Istoriia BSSR*, 2:142.

[22] I. F. Lochmel', *Ocherki istorii bor'by Belorusskogo naroda protiv Pol'skikh panov* (Moscow, 1940), p. 100.

[23] J. Mienski, "The Establishment of the Belorussian SSR," *Belorussian Review*, no. 1 (1955): 26.

[24] K. Ezavitau, *Belorussy i Poliaki* (Kovno, 1919), p. 33.

[25] Lochmel', *Ocherki istorii*, p. 99.

sible deeds by the Polish legions occurred throughout the occupied area. Belorussia, unarmed, was helpless. The Belorussian poet Ianka Kupala described the second anniversary of the proclamation of independence of the Belorussian National Republic (March 25, 1920) as a death anniversary:

> And on this our anniversary
> The chain is clanking as it had clanked before
> And there and here unrestrainably rages
> The derision and wrath of the executioners.[26]

Kupala and other Belorussian poets and writers such as Iakub Kolas and Zmitrok Biadulia, who at that time were in Soviet Russia, denounced the Polish atrocities and incited the people to open revolt. "The underground Bolshevik organizations formed a whole network of partisan detachments behind the Polish lines."[27] The Pedagogical Institute in Minsk became a center around which began to form a Communist underground movement directed by two young scholars, Usevalad Ihnatouski and I. Karaneuski.[28]

Among the Belorussian native population, the teachers and peasants were the most active in the partisan movement. Vasil' Talash, a peasant from the district of Mozyr, organized a detachment of about 300 men and was particularly successful in fighting the Poles.[29] His participation in the partisan movement found masterly description in Kolas's tale "The Marsh," which became a classic in Belorussian literature.

Poland's right to independence was recognized by the Provisional Government of Russia on March 30, 1917. Soviet Russia, according to Decree No. 698 of the Council of the People's Commissars of August 29, 1918, also recognized the independence of Poland. Article 3 of this decree declared:

> All agreements and acts concluded by the Government of the former Russian Empire with the Governments of the Kingdom of Prussia and the Austro-Hungarian Empire in connection with the partitions of Poland are annulled forever by the present resolution, in view of the fact that they are contrary to the principle of the self-

[26] Quoted in Anthony Adamovich, *Opposition to Sovietization in Belorussian Literature, 1917–1957* (Munich, 1958), p. 45.
[27] *Istoriia BSSR*, 2:144.
[28] Vakar, *Belorussia*, p. 113.
[29] Ibid., p. 145.

determination of peoples and to the revolutionary, legal conception of the Russian nation, which recognizes the inalienable right of the Polish nation to decide its own fate and to become united.[30]

Despite Soviet recognition of Poland, fighting between the Polish and Soviet armies started immediately after the withdrawal of the German army. In this conflict, however, Russia was at a disadvantage because of its continuing struggle against a remnant of the White armies. Primarily because of this, the Soviet government wanted to conclude a peace with Poland. A first message, dated Moscow, December 22, 1919, was addressed by Chicherin, the commissar for foreign affairs, to the Ministry for Foreign Affairs in Warsaw, making a formal proposal for negotiations between Poland and Russia. The Polish government was asked to fix a place and date for the negotiations.[31]

Polish Minister Stanislaw Patek discussed the message with Lloyd George, the British prime minister, on January 26, 1920. Lloyd George said the question of war or peace was for Poland to decide. He added that the "League of Nations would no doubt come to the assistance of Poland if she were attacked by the Bolsheviks within her true Polish boundaries, but she could not expect assistance in holding beyond her ethnological limits."[32] Despite this, the Polish government refused even to consider further the Soviet proposal.[33]

On January 30, the Polish government received a wireless message from Moscow, signed by Lenin, Chicherin, and Trotsky, proposing immediate conclusion of an armistice.[34] Poland, however, did not reply to the Soviet proposals until March 13, when parallel diplomatic notes were dispatched to Russia and the Allied Powers. In its note to Russia the Polish government proposed "to open peace negotiations in Borisov on condition that the Bolsheviks evacuate their troops beyond the Dnieper River, so that a plebiscite might be carried out in these territories."[35] That meant, in effect, that Pilsudski was determined to go on with his plebiscites until all the medieval Lithuanian Duchy could be incorporated into the Polish state.

[30] *Soviet-Polish Relations, 1918–1943: Official Documents* (Washington, D.C., [1940s]), p. 71.
[31] U.S., Department of State, *Papers Relating to the Foreign Relations of the United States, 1920* (Washington, D.C., 1936), 3:370.
[32] Quoted in ibid., p. 376.
[33] *Soviet-Polish Relations*, pp. 72–73.
[34] U.S., Department of State, *Papers Relating to the Foreign Relations of the United States*, p. 370.
[35] Volacic, "Curzon Line," p. 64.

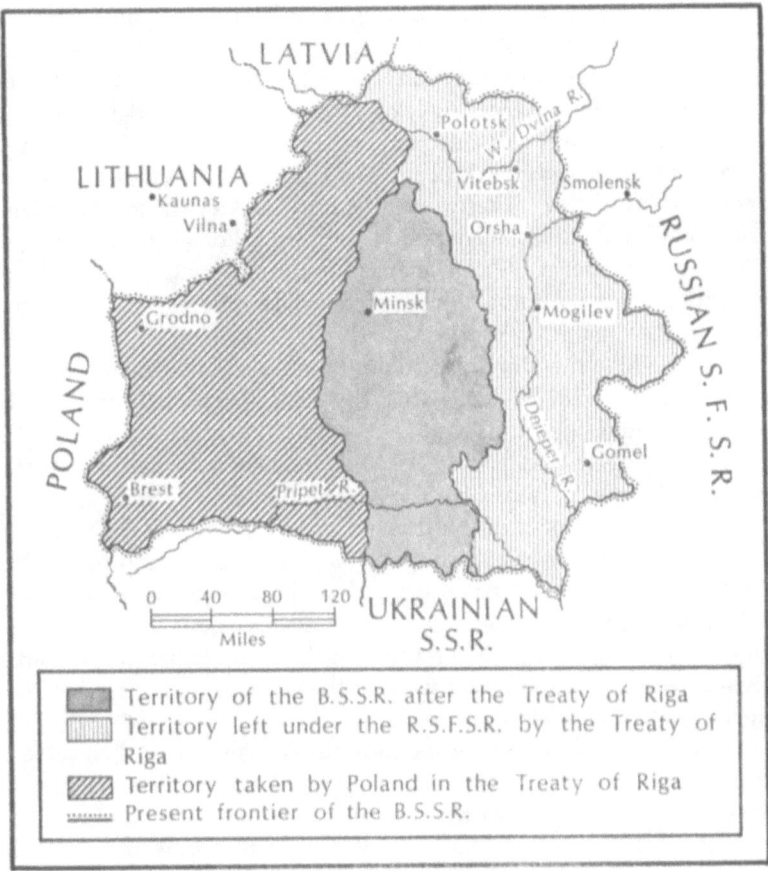

THE PARTITION OF BELORUSSIA, 1921

The Supreme Allied Council rejected the Polish note in a sharply worded reply. The reply referred to the provision in Article 87 of the Versailles Treaty stating that the establishment of the eastern Polish frontiers was within the jurisdiction of the principal Allied Powers. The council added that the idea of a plebiscite was inadmissible under conditions of military occupation.[36] The Bolsheviks also rejected the Polish note, though without stating their reason. It was clear, however, that the Polish note expressed excessive demands at the expense of Belorussia, Lithuania, and the Ukraine.

As explained by the Poles, their desire to rule Lithuania, Belo-

[36] Leszek Kirkien, *Russia, Poland, and the Curzon Line* (London, 1945), p. 26; Komarnicki, *Rebirth of the Polish Republic*, p. 455.

russia, and a large part of the Ukraine was based on a conviction of the "historic mission of Poland as an apostle of liberty and as an outpost of Western Civilization against what they regard as the barbarism of the East."[37] The Poles claimed that the Belorussians and Ukrainians were distinct from the Great Russians and were closer culturally and politically to the Poles. Hence they should be converted into Poles. "They remember how Mickiewicz, a Lithuanian noble with a Belorussian name, writing as a Polish patriot in the Polish tongue, begins 'Pan Tadeusz,' the greatest classic of Polish literature, with the impassioned outburst, 'Lithuania, my country, thou art like health.' "[38]

Meanwhile, the Ukrainian, Belorussian, and Lithuanian delegations in Paris tried to prove that the eastern frontiers of Poland should be along the Bug River.[39] In territorial disputes, of course, it is often an open question as to what is just and what is unjust. Roman Dmowski, leader of the Polish National Democrats, for example, was highly critical of Poland's partition by Russia, Prussia, and Austria.[40] But when the opportunity came for Poland to regain its independence and then to expand at the expense of its eastern neighbors, Dmowski was ready to defend his country's right to a larger percentage of national minorities than Russia previously had. He wanted to partition Belorussia and the Ukraine without regard to their rights as separate peoples.

Some Allied statesmen, especially the British, found themselves in the unhappy position of opposing the Polish claims on many questions involved. They considered it dangerous for Poland to take advantage of Russia's temporary weakness to annex the eastern lands without a free expression of the peoples' wishes. Such action was viewed as not only unjust to Poland's neighbors but a threat to Poland itself, because in the course of time it would bring together the Germans and Russians and they, in turn, might decide for a new and perhaps final partition of Poland.[41] Lloyd George had had firsthand experience with Polish intransigence at the Paris Peace Conference, and later recorded his impressions as follows:

> No one gave more trouble than the Poles. Having once upon a time been the most formidable military power in Central Europe—when

[37] Temperley, *History of the Peace Conference*, 6:234.
[38] Ibid., p. 235.   [39] Volacic, "Curzon Line," p. 58.
[40] Roman Dmowski, *Germaniia, Rossiia i Pol'skii vopros* (Petrograd, 1919), pp. 167, 187.
[41] Temperley, *History of the Peace Conference*, p. 240.

Prussia was a starveling Duchy—there were few provinces in a vast area inhabited by a variety of races that Poland could not claim as being historically her inheritance of which she had been reft. Drunk with the new wine of liberty supplied to her by the Allies, she fancied herself once more the restless mistress of Central Europe. Self-determination did not suit her ambitions. She coveted Galicia, the Ukraine, Lithuania, and parts of Belorussia. A vote of the inhabitants would have emphatically repudiated her dominion. So the right of all peoples to select their nationhood was promptly thrown over by her leaders. They claimed that these various races belonged to the Poles through the conquering arm of their ancestors. Like the old Norman baron, who, when he was asked for the title to his land, unsheathed his sword, Poland flourished the sword of her warrior kings which had rusted in their tombs for centuries.[42]

The government of the Belorussian National Republic headed by Lastouski was in exile at that time in Kaunas, Lithuania. Lastouski himself and most of the members of the Rada stood fast in the claim of independence for Belorussia, opposing both Russia and Poland. They were, however, less bitter about Russia than about Poland, against which they concluded an alliance with Lithuania.[43] The Bolsheviks did not object to the existence of the Lastouski government since most of Belorussia was then occupied by Poland.

On April 26, 1920, Pilsudski's army invaded the Ukraine, and on May 7, took the city of Kiev. The victory was spectacular but short lived. Polish leaders had overestimated their own strength and perhaps underestimated the vigor and tenacity of their opponents. At the time they began their offensive against Soviet Russia, all the White armies (except that of General Wrangel in the Crimea) had already been defeated by the Bolsheviks, who could now concentrate their forces against Poland. By the end of May, the Red Army began a counteroffensive north and east of Borisov on the Belorussian front, and in a few weeks the Poles were falling back all along the front. On July 11, the Red Army took Minsk, and within days the whole of Belorussia was freed from the Poles.[44]

When the Supreme Allied Council met at Spa in July 1920, the Poles were in full retreat. Wladyslaw Grabski, the Polish prime minister, appealed for Allied intervention.[45] The British govern-

---

[42] David Lloyd George, *The Truth about the Peace Treaties* (London, 1938), 1:308–09.
[43] Vakar, *Belorussia*, p. 114.
[44] Ibid.
[45] Temperley, *History of the Peace Conference*, p. 319.

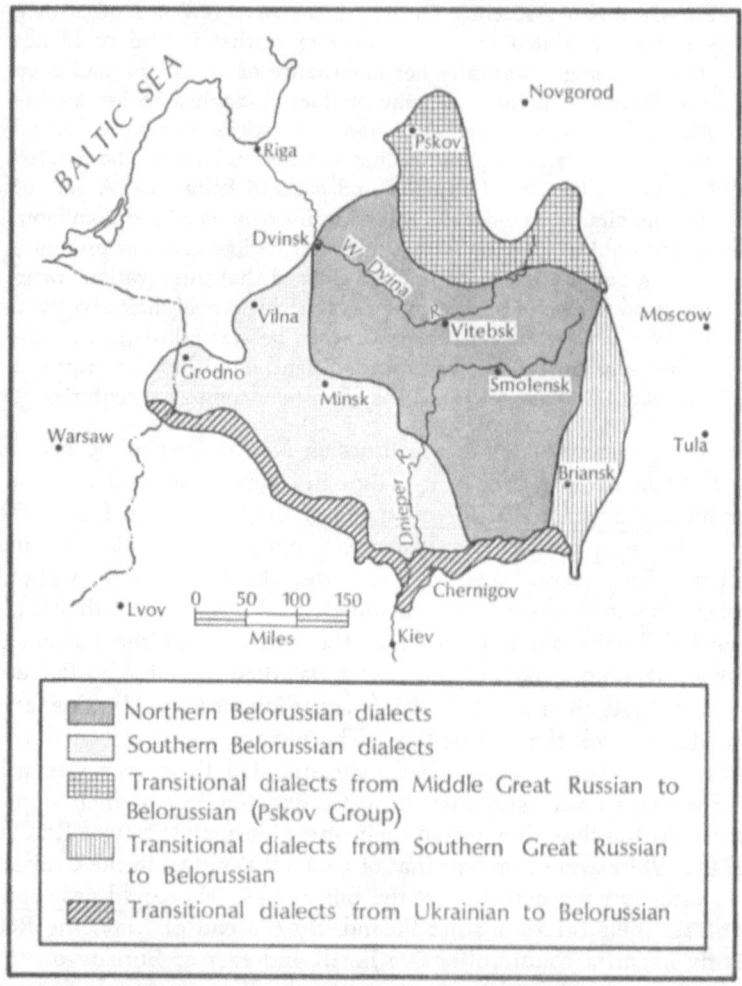

GEOGRAPHICAL DISTRIBUTION OF BELORUSSIAN DIALECTS

ment now expressed moral indignation at the Polish action of the previous February and March. Lloyd George accused the Poles of advancing into Belorussian and Ukrainian territory and asked them to withdraw some 125 miles westward. This would bring them to their "legitimate frontier."[46] When Grabski asked where that frontier lay, the British prime minister indicated what has since been known as the "Curzon Line," named for the British foreign minister,

[46] Shotwell and Laserson, *Curzon Line*, p. 19.

Lord Curzon, who proposed it. It seems to have represented a sincere effort by Lord Curzon to establish an ethnographic Polish eastern frontier.

In the light of later experience, "liberation" by the Red Army might well have reminded Belorussians of the proverbial passage from the kettle into the fire, but Belorussia, and indeed the world at large, had yet to learn the lesson of Communist encroachment. The Belorussians were pleased by their release. In Minsk, July 11 was proclaimed a day of annual celebration, memorializing liberation from the Poles. On July 31, the "independence of the Belorussian Soviet Socialist Republic" was formally proclaimed.[47] The republic was at that time composed of only six districts of the Minsk region. The North-Western territory of Belorussia was handed over to Lithuania on the basis of a treaty concluded in Moscow on July 19. The Soviet government intended to hand over the remainder of western Belorussia to Poland, which, it was hoped, would be a Soviet Poland.[48] With this in mind, creation of a Provisional Polish Revolutionary Committee was proclaimed in Bialystok on July 31. Marchlewski was chairman of the body; Dzerzhinski, Kon, Prochniak, and Unszlicht were its leading members.[49] Thus, the territory of the Belorussian Soviet Socialist Republic was for the second time greatly curtailed because of political considerations. This time a modification of the Curzon line in favor of Poland was intended at the expense of Belorussian territory.

During the days of August 16–18, the Red armies were defeated at the very gates of Warsaw and had to turn back. On their heels the Poles occupied the western part of Belorussia. At the same time, Russia was facing an accumulation of internal difficulties. In the fall, an uprising against the Bolsheviks took place in the Slutsk district of Belorussia. There were also disturbances in the Ukraine and in Russia itself. All this convinced the Bolsheviks that they could not afford another offensive against Poland without jeopardizing the Bolshevik Revolution in Russia. Meanwhile, the Poles decided they had reached the limit of their expansion, and thus both sides were willing to conclude an armistice. Peace negotiations, which began on August 14 in Minsk, continued until March 18, 1921, when the peace treaty between Poland and Russia was finally signed in

[47] *Ocherki po istorii gosudarstva i prava Belorusskoi SSR* (Minsk, 1958), p. 40.
[48] Kirkien, *Russia, Poland, and the Curzon Line*, pp. 34–35.
[49] Wandycz, *Soviet-Polish Relations*, p. 226.

Riga. The treaty represented a grave injustice to the people of Belorussia. The Bolsheviks and Poles ignored the Curzon Line, as well as the aspirations of the Belorussian nationalists, and divided Belorussia between themselves. In accordance with this treaty, more than 40,000 square miles of western Belorussian territory were included in the Polish state.[50] The eastern territory of Belorussia was included in the Russian Soviet Federated Socialist Republic. The center of Belorussia (only six districts of the Minsk region) was left to the Belorussian SSR.

There was no Belorussian representation at the peace negotiations in Riga,[51] a circumstance which thoroughly reveals the hypocrisy and cynicism underlying Stalin's later statement: "A nation has the right freely to determine its own destiny. It has the right to arrange its life as it sees fit, without, of course, stamping on the rights of other nations; that is beyond dispute."[52] The Bolsheviks and the Poles, in their callous parceling out of territory, ignored the very principles of self-determination about which both had talked so much. Ironically, even the treaty itself, in Article 2, states: "The two contracting parties, in accordance with the 'Principle of National Self-determination,' recognize the independence of the Ukraine and White-Ruthenia."[53]

Although the old Polish dream of restoring the borders of 1772 did not materialize, Poland, nevertheless, by the Treaty of Riga extended its eastern border far beyond its ethnographic boundaries.

[50] *Istoriia BSSR*, 2:174.
[51] Volacic, "Curzon Line," p. 67.
[52] Iosif Stalin, *Marksizm i natsional'no-kolonial'nyi vopros* (Moscow, 1937), p. 15.
[53] *Soviet-Polish Relations*, p. 74.

4.

Belorussia & the Formation of the USSR

> Everything changes ... social life changes, and with it the "national question" changes, too. At different periods different classes enter the arena, and each class has its own view on the "national question." Consequently, in different periods the "national question" serves different interests and assumes different shades, according to which class raises it, and when.
>
> Stalin, 1904[1]

The partition of Belorussia gave Soviet Russia a major expansion of territory, yet faced it with a renewed problem of territorial digestion. The recent release of much of Belorussia from Polish bondage gave the Bolsheviks a temporary advantage in popular favor, and the Belorussian Soviet Socialist Republic was speedily reestablished. Nevertheless, there remained an embarrassing dichotomy between the real and the apparent. Real, of course, were Russian military occupation and the rulership by a small minority of predominantly Russian Communists. Still unattained, however, was a convincing semblance of popular government. There had already been two Soviet governments in Belorussia; neither had been very successful nor popularly accepted.

Realizing the numerical weakness of the Communist Party in Belorussia, the Bolshevik rulers resorted to a favorite Party tactic:

unite and conquer. They began negotiations with the left-wing Social Revolutionaries, hoping to establish a coalition government. The Social Revolutionaries agreed to negotiate but proposed to change the definition of government. Instead of the Bolshevik formula of a government of "workers and peasants," they proposed a government of "peasants and workers."[2]

Such a deviation from Party dogma was more than the Communists would accept. Fearing that a coalition government on these terms might result in a democratic government of peasants instead of the "dictatorship of the proletariat" which the party prescribed, they decided to keep firm control in the hands of the Communist Party.[3] To this end, a joint meeting of representatives of the Belorussian and Lithuanian Communist parties and the representatives of the Soviet and trade union organizations of Minsk and the Minsk region took place on July 31, 1920. At this meeting a "declaration proclaiming the independence of Belorussia" was adopted.[4] In accordance with this second proclamation of the independence of the BSSR, complete authority over the administrative affairs of the republic was given to the Military Revolutionary Committee of the Minsk region, which was to function temporarily as a government.[5] The committee was dominated by military men, most of whom were Russians, although Aleksandr Charviakou and Iazep Adamovich, two well-known Belorussian leaders, were members.[6] From that time, Belorussians began to take a more active part in the administration of Belorussia.

Another important event was the Second All-Belorussian Congress of Soviets, which assembled on December 14, 1920, in Minsk. At the congress were 218 delegates: 111 Belorussians, 42 Russians, 36 Jews, 8 Poles, and 21 others. The overwhelming majority of the delegates were members of the Communist Party.[7] First of all, in accordance with tradition, the congress approved an appeal to the

---

[1] Iosif Stalin, "Kak ponimaet Sotsial-Demokratiia natsional'nyi vopros (1904)" [The Social Democratic View of the National Question, 1904], *Sochineniia*, 1st ed. (Moscow, 1946–1952), 1:32.

[2] J. Mienski, "The Establishment of the Belorussian SSR," *Belorussian Review*, no. 1 (1955): 27.

[3] Ibid.

[4] *Istoriia BSSR*, 2d ed. (Minsk, 1961), 2:162.

[5] "Revkomy Belorussii v bor'be za vosstanovlenie i ukreplenie Sovetskoi vlasti letom i osen'iu 1920 goda," *Istoricheskii arkhiv*, no. 3 (1956): 46.

[6] *Istoriia BSSR*, 2:162.

[7] *S"ezdy Sovetov Soiuza SSR, Soiuznykh i Avtonomnykh Sovetskikh Sotsialisticheskikh Respublik: sbornik dokumentov v trekh tomakh, 1917–1936 gg.* (Moscow, 1959–1960), 2:242.

people, declaring that the congress was assembled for the purpose of consolidating the independence of the country.⁸ In the greetings dispatched to the central executive committees of the Russian and Ukrainian Soviet republics, the congress declared that "the basis for the relations between the Belorussian SSR and the Russian Soviet Federated Socialist Republic must be the declaration made by Iakov Sverdlov, the Chairman of the All-Russian Central Executive Committee (Ts.I.K.) and the Council of People's Commissars (Sovnar- and Soldiers' Deputies of Belorussia."⁹

On December 17, the congress approved a project to supplement the constitution of the BSSR adopted at the First Congress of Soviets on February 4, 1919.¹⁰ The congress terminated the administrative authority of the Military Revolutionary Committee and, in compliance with the constitution of the BSSR, formed the highest administrative agencies of the republic—the Central Executive Committee (Ts.I.K.) and the Council of People's Commissars (Sovnarkom).¹¹ Aleksandr Charviakou was elected chairman of both the Ts.I.K. and the Sovnarkom.¹² The latter was composed of the heads of fifteen commissariats. Commissariats essential for independent existence, such as foreign affairs, military affairs, internal affairs, and finances, were included.¹³

With the government of the BSSR securely in Communist hands, the enthusiasm of the Belorussians for independence seemingly caused no disturbance in official circles in Moscow. On the contrary, relations between the BSSR and the RSFSR continued to be very cordial. On January 16, 1921, the two governments concluded an agreement on the basis of mutual recognition of their "independence and sovereignty."¹⁴ Recognition by the RSFSR gave the Belorussian leaders more prestige and increased their belief that a new era had opened in relations between their country and Moscow.

The next important step toward the establishment and consolidation of an independent Belorussian SSR was the Third All-Belorussian Congress of Soviets, which assembled in Minsk on December 21, 1921. In this congress, the Belorussians dominated

⁸ Mienski, "Establishment of the BSSR," p. 28.
⁹ *S"ezdy Sovetov SSSR*, 2:246–47.
¹⁰ *Ocherki po istorii gosudarstva i prava Belorusskoi SSR* (Minsk, 1958), p. 41.
¹¹ Ibid.
¹² *Bol'shaia sovetskaia entsiklopediia*, 1st ed. (Moscow, 1929–1948), 61:195; *Ocherki po istorii*, p. 41.
¹³ *S"ezdy Sovetov SSSR*, 2:251–52.
¹⁴ Mienski, "Establishment of the BSSR," p. 28.

decision-making. All the men elected to the highest governmental positions were Belorussians—Aleksandr Charviakou, chairman of the Council of People's Commissars and commissar of foreign affairs; Iazep Adamovich, commissar of military and internal affairs; Usevalad Ihnatouski, commissar of education; and others.[15]

After the Third Congress, the aim of the Belorussian SSR was to obtain recognition as a sovereign state from Western European countries. This hope was expressed by Vilhelm Knorin, first secretary of the Central Bureau of the Belorussian Communist Party, in an article, "We Want Recognition," published on January 25, 1922. In this article, Knorin revealed an economic motivation:

> The formal juridical recognition of the Soviet Republics by the Western European countries would be a very important fact because it would give an opportunity for the Soviet Republics to use Western European markets and credits and to conduct more normal trade relations with Western Europe. This is essential for the development of our industry and the establishment of agriculture. ... The Soviet Republics have always agreed to make very significant concessions in order to be recognized by Western Europe.[16]

Knorin's article presented the views of the Party and the Belorussian government on the eve of the All-European Economic Conference at Genoa, of which the dominant issue was the renewal of relations between Russia and Europe.[17] Belorussia did not take part in the conference but the supplementary agreement to the Treaty of Rapallo (1922) concluded between Germany and Soviet Russia also applied correspondingly to the relations between the German Reich on the one part and the Soviet Socialist Republics of Ukraine, Belorussia, Georgia, Azerbaijan, and Armenia on the other.[18] This was considered a step forward on the road to more direct relations between Belorussia and Germany.

The year 1920 marked the end of the Civil War in Russia and the beginning of a period of reconstruction. With the change from

---

[15] "Tretii Vsebelorusskii s"ezd Sovetov" [The Third All-Belorussian Congress of Soviets], *Zvezda*, no. 297 (20 December 1921): 1.

[16] Vilhelm Knorin, "My khotim priznaniia," *Zveda*, no. 23 (25 January 1922): 3.

[17] The Genoa Conference of 1922 was the first important international meeting after World War I to which the Soviet Union was invited.

[18] Leonard Shapiro, ed., *Soviet Treaty Series: A Collection of Bilateral Treaties, Agreements, and Conventions, Etc., Concluded between the Soviet Union and Foreign Powers, 1917–1939* (Washington, D.C., 1950–1955), 1:198.

war to peace, a problem arose concerning the interrelationship of various newly established Soviet republics. The traditional Russian policy of maintaining the unity of the territories of the former Russian state was being reconsidered by many political leaders, both Communist and nationalist. The new Russian leaders, who through the years of revolution had at least superficially supported a policy of separation of the borderlands from Russia, now felt that Communist policy toward the nationalities should be modified. Changes, they reasoned, should be made, if only because conditions in Russia had changed. Before, it had been an "autocratic" Russia; now it was a country where all nationalities were "equal." There was need, however, for greater cohesion and centralization of authority among these peers. The ambivalence of this new Communist attitude recalls Aleksandr Herzen's views concerning Poland, expressed in 1859: "Poland, like Italy, like Hungary, has an imprescriptible right to be an independent state. Whether or not we wish a separation of a free Poland from a free Russia, that is another question. No, we do not wish that."[19]

The structuring of the new socialist state was no easy problem, and several practical elements of this problem could not be ignored. In the first place, the world revolution prophesied by the Communists had not materialized, and they had to face a struggle with the capitalist world. For that reason, full diplomatic and military unity among the Soviet republics was an absolute necessity.[20] Unity of the Soviet republics was also as necessary for full economic development as for military security. In the second place, since the Communists retained their international aspirations, it was advisable to dissociate the Communist political system as much as possible from its antecedents in Great Russian statehood.[21] In other words, it was necessary to name the state which would unite all the Soviet republics something other than "Russia." In the third place, there was a fear that any close relationship of this union with the Russian Soviet Federated Socialist Republic would inevitably result in domination by the latter, which had been known for centuries as a most autocratic state. This fear was strengthened by visible evidence; when the problem of unity of the Soviet republics was discussed, the Great Russian nationalists were opposed to any decentralization

---

[19] Aleksandr I. Herzen, "Rossiia i Pol'sha," *Kolokol* (Bell), no. 34 (Geneva, 1887): 95.
[20] Richard Pipes, *The Formation of the Soviet Union: Communism and Nationalism, 1917–1923* (Cambridge, Mass., 1954), p. 265.
[21] Ibid.

and stood on the position of *"edinaia nedelimaia Russia"* (a single and indivisible Russia).[22]

Because of the contradictory characters of the desires involved, the formal joining of the Soviet republics into a union in December 1922 was preceded by a period of bitter debates. Lenin, leader of the Russian Bolsheviks and founder of the first socialist state, was also the first of the Russian Social-Democratic leaders to raise the question of self-determination for the borderlands of Russia. Through more than a decade before the October Revolution, he had persistently defended the right of the borderlands to self-determination. He was highly critical of the Great Russians who aimed "to oppress a greater number of nations than any other people."[23] But in principle the Communists found it unthinkable that any socialist nation should wish to secede from a socialist state. Thus, the dilemma which confronted Lenin after he came to power was "how to reconcile the slogan of national self-determination with the need for preserving the unity of the Soviet State."[24] He found the solution in a subtle semantic twist, replacing the phrase, "right to separate," which he had once used, with the phrase "right to unite."[25] Thus, Lenin became also the first of the Soviet leaders to raise the question of the unity of the Soviet republics. But, according to Lenin, the "liberated people were expected to unite freely into a Union of Soviet Socialist States." In 1917, he wrote, "The proletarian party strives to create as large a state as possible, for this is to the advantage of the toilers; it strives to bring about closer ties between nations and the further fusion of nations; but it desires to achieve this aim not by force, but by a free, fraternal union of the workers and the toiling masses of all nations."[26]

On a proposal by Lenin, the introduction to the Constitution of the RSFSR, adopted in 1918, included a "Declaration of the Rights of the Working and Exploited People," which proclaimed the equality of the people of all nations and all races in the Russian Republic.[27] Lenin wanted the RSFSR to serve as an example for the unification

---

[22] *Ocherki po istorii*, p. 71.
[23] Vladimir Lenin, *Polnoe sobranie sochinenii*, 5th ed. (Moscow, 1958–1966), 31:433.
[24] Pipes, *Formation of the Soviet Union*, p. 108.
[25] Edward Hallet Carr, *The Bolshevik Revolution, 1917–1923* (New York, 1951–1953), 1:364.
[26] Lenin, *Sochineniia*, 3d ed. (Moscow, 1929–1939), 20:123.
[27] *Istoriia Sovetskoi Konstitutsii v dokumentakh, 1917–1956* (Moscow, 1957), p. 14.

of all nations of the former Russian Empire into a "united democratic centralized Soviet state."[28]

Stalin, who was commissar of nationalities, played a major role in the formation of the USSR in 1922. But his attitude toward the problem of nationalities had changed since the October Revolution. On the eve of the Revolution he had written, "The solution of the national problem must be as practicable as it is radical and final, viz.: 1) The right of secession for the nations inhabiting certain regions of Russia who cannot remain, or who do not desire to remain, within the integral framework; 2) political autonomy with the framework of a single integral state, with uniform constitutional provisions for the regions which have a specific national composition and which remain within the integral framework."[29]

After the Provisional Government was overthrown by the Bolsheviks, however, Stalin began to express sharply different views. In his article "The October Revolution and the National Question," published in November 1918, he wrote, "A nation must not be regarded as something self-contained and fixed for all time. Being only part of the general question of the transformation of the existing order, the national question is wholly determined by the conditions of the social environment, by the kind of power in the country, and by the whole course of social development in general."[30] In his next article, "The Policy of the Soviet Government on the National Question in Russia," published in October 1920, Stalin was frankly centralistic:

> The claim of the borderlands to secession from Russia as a form of relationship between the center and borderlands, is to be denied because not only does it contradict the very purpose of the question of establishing links between the center and borderlands, but above all it clashes with the interests of the toiling masses, both of the center and of the border regions. Apart from the fact that the secession of the border regions would undermine the revolutionary might of Central Russia . . . the interests of the working masses indicate that the claim to the secession of the borderlands is, in a given stage of revolution, deeply counter-revolutionary.[31]

As commissar of nationalities, Stalin soon demonstrated his attitude toward the solution of the national problem, and the target

[28] S"ezdy Sovetov SSSR, 3:9.   [29] Stalin, Sochineniia, 3:27–28.
[30] Ibid., 4:155.
[31] Ibid., pp. 352–54.

of action was his native republic, Georgia. Ignoring the fact that the Soviet government had recognized the independence of Georgia and had concluded agreements with it on May 7, 1920, and on February 11, 1921, Stalin sent detachments of the Red Army there to suppress the Menshevik-dominated government.[32]

Stalin supported a centralization of government in Moscow. "At first he built up his People's Commissariat of Nationalities as a centralized organization and then transferred it de facto into a federal government of the autonomous regions and republics of the RSFSR."[33] He made little distinction between the autonomous republics and the nominally independent republics, such as Belorussia and the Ukraine, which he wished to unite within the RSFSR on equal terms with the autonomous republics.[34]

The final phase in the formation of the Soviet Union was mainly the work of Stalin. In 1922, when the unification of the Soviet republics was approaching completion, Stalin was Secretary General of the Central Committee of the Russian Communist Party, and a member of its Political Bureau (Politburo) and Organizational Bureau (Orgburo), as well as chairman of the Commissariat of Workers' and Peasants' Inspection.[35] In addition, he was, of course, still commissar of nationalities.[36] With such a variety of high positions in the Party and the government apparatus, Stalin was a key man.

The formation of the USSR entered its final phase on August 10, 1922, when the Orgburo formed a commission to examine the problem of relations among the Soviet republics.[37] In September, Stalin presented to this commission "a project for the merging of the four Soviet Republics."[38] It was based on the principle of "autonomization" of the sovereign Soviet republics; this meant the entrance of the Belorussian, Ukrainian, and Transcaucasian republics into the RSFSR as autonomous republics.[39] The commission accepted Stalin's project and sent it to the three republics for their consideration. This,

---

[32] Leon Trotsky, *Stalin: An Appraisal of the Man and His Influence* (London, 1947), p. 359.
[33] Pipes, *Formation of the Soviet Union*, p. 248.
[34] Stalin, *Sochineniia*, 4:354.
[35] Pipes, *Formation of the Soviet Union*, p. 266.
[36] In 1923 the Commissariat of Nationalities (Narkomnats) was dissolved because it had completed its fundamental task of preparing the formation of the national republics and regions into a union of republics.
[37] *Istoriia BSSR*, 2:195.
[38] *S"ezdy Sovetov SSSR*, 3:10.
[39] Ibid.

however, revealed sharp divergencies of opinion, and the proposal was rejected by both the Central Bureau of the Communist Party of Belorussia and the party politburos of the Ukraine and Georgia.[40]

Meanwhile, Lenin had been seriously ill and unable to counter Stalin's attempt to reinterpret the slogan of national self-determination. He expressed sharp criticism of Stalin's project, however, in a letter of September 27, 1922, addressed to the Politburo of the Central Committee of the Russian Communist Party. Lenin wrote, "We recognize ourselves as equal with the Ukrainian SSR and the other republics, and together and on equal footing with them, join the new Union, the new federation."[41] Lenin proposed the unification of the other Soviet republics on the principle of complete equality instead of their joining the RSFSR, as Stalin had proposed.[42] He warned the members of the Politburo that "even minor deviation from the principle of equality and the voluntary unification of the republics would lead to the perversion of the idea of the Union by the Great Russian chauvinists."[43]

A commission of the Central Committee of the Russian Communist Party, following Lenin's advice, fundamentally changed Stalin's project. The new project was approved on October 6 by the plenum of the Central Committee.[44] The first article of the new project was phrased thus:

> It is necessary to conclude an agreement among the Ukraine, Belorussia, the Federated Republic of Transcaucasia, and the RSFSR providing for a joining of these republics into a Union of Soviet Socialist Republics with the right for all of them to secede from the Union.[45]

Lenin's project was approved by the central committees of the Belorussian, Ukrainian, and Transcaucasian republics between October and December 1922.[46]

In the face of such an overwhelming display of party unity, Stalin was obliged to retreat. In his report to the Tenth All-Russian Congress of Soviets on December 26, 1922, Stalin said:

> The will of the peoples of our republics, who recently assembled at their congresses and unanimously resolved to form a Union of Re-

---

[40] *Ocherki po istorii*, p. 71.
[41] Quoted in ibid.
[42] *S"ezdy Sovetov SSSR*, 3:11.
[43] *Ocherki po istorii*, p. 72.
[44] *S"ezdy Sovetov SSSR*, 3:11.
[45] *Ocherki po istorii*, p. 72.
[46] *Istoriia BSSR*, 2:196.

publics, is incontestable proof that the cause of amalgamation is pursuing the right lines and that it is based on the great principle of voluntary consent and equality of peoples. Let us hope that by forming our confederative republic we shall be creating a reliable bulwark against international capitalism and that the new confederate state will be another step forward to the amalgamation into a single world Socialist Soviet Republic.[47]

The final step in the formation of the USSR was taken on December 30, 1922, when the First Congress of the Soviets of all republics assembled in Moscow. It was a multitudinous assembly, with 2,214 delegates. The national composition of the Congress was as follows: Russians, 62.5 percent; Ukrainians, 8 percent; Belorussians, 1.1 percent; Caucasian nationalities, 4.5 percent; Jews, 10.8 percent; Turkic nationalities, 5.7 percent; Latvian and Estonian, 3.4 percent; and the representatives of the other nationalities, 4 percent. Ninety-four percent of the delegates were members of the Communist Party.[48] The main task of the congress was to ratify the agreement establishing the Union and to approve "the basic articles of the Constitution of the USSR."

Articles 2 and 7, defining the highest authorities of the newly formed state, are of considerable importance. The former stipulated that the supreme legislative body of the state was the Congress of Soviets of the USSR; during the intervals between sessions of the congress, supreme authority was to be exercised by the All-Union Central Executive Committee (V.Ts.I.K.). The latter stipulated that the executive organ of the All-Union Central Executive Committee was to be the Council of People's Commissars (Sovnarkom). This article also stated that the decrees and decisions of the Sovnarkom of the USSR were to be obligatory in all Union republics.[49]

On the face of things, Lenin's ideas for unity of the republics had prevailed. In fact, however, Lenin's victory remained uncertain. On Stalin's insistence, the commissariats of foreign affairs, military and naval affairs, transport, finances, and post and telegraph were defined as All-Union commissariats, solely under the jurisdiction of the Sovnarkom of the USSR.[50] The fact is that the Sovnarkom was only in theory responsible to the V.Ts.I.K., where the Union republics were represented. In practice, from the very beginning,

---
[47] Stalin, *Sochineniia*, 5:155.
[48] S"ezdy Sovetov SSSR, 3:12.
[49] Ibid., 2:306.
[50] Stalin, *Sochineniia*, 5: 152. The All-Union commissariats have no counterparts in the republics.

it was independent of the V.Ts.I.K.[51] Thus, the Union republics could not influence the work of the Sovnarkom, yet its decrees were compulsory for them.

The decisions of the First All-Union Congress of Soviets left the Union republics dissatisfied. In January 1923, the Ukrainian and Belorussian central executive committees submitted to the drafting commission of the V.Ts.I.K. constitutional projects which were, in effect, a challenge to the whole principle of centralized authority.[52] These projects were rejected, however. Then, Christian Rakovsky, chairman of the Sovnarkom of the Ukrainian SSR, complained that under the proposed constitutional plan, which was patterned on that of the RSFSR, Russia had more than three times as many representatives in the All-Union Soviet as the other three republics taken together.[53] He proposed a new constitutional plan, imitating the Weimar Constitution of the German Reich, under which no single state could have more than two-fifths of the total representation. Stalin rejected all these projects on the ground that the new organ was to be a council not of states but of nationalities.[54] Clearly, Stalin was not disposed to concede any weakening of the hegemony of the RSFSR within the Soviet Union, nor to permit decentralization of power. Even Mikhail Frunze, known for his pro-Great Russian tendencies, voiced some apprehension: "The new USSR might prove to be little more than the old RSFSR writ large, and endowed with enhanced prestige and wide power."[55]

Lenin was unhappy about Stalin's personal behavior and influence in forming the Union. His health did not permit him to attend the First All-Union Congress of Soviets, but while the congress was in session, he wrote a letter on the question of nationalities which he thought might affect the pending decision, also to be discussed at the coming Twelfth Congress of the Communist Party of Russia. The following passages from Lenin's letter indicate his views on the formation of the Union:

> I am, it appears, much at fault before the workers of Russia, for not having intervened with sufficient energy and incisiveness in the notorious question of "autonomization," which is officially called,

[51] Pipes, *Formation of the Soviet Union*, p. 242.
[52] Carr, *Bolshevik Revolution*, 1:399.
[53] Ibid., p. 401. The texts of both the Belorussian and the Ukrainian projects may be found in V. I. Ignatiev, *Sovetskii stroi* (Moscow, 1928), pp. 123–37.
[54] Stalin, *Sochineniia*, 5:278.
[55] Quoted in Carr, *Bolshevik Revolution*, 1:399.

> it seems, the USSR. In the summer, when the question arose, I was ill, and then in the fall, I had great hopes that I would recuperate and have an opportunity to intervene in this question at the October-December plenums. But, in the meantime, I could attend neither the October nor the December plenum dealing with the question, and for this reason it had bypassed me almost entirely. . . . It is said that we needed a single apparatus. From where came such assertions? Is it not from the same Russian apparatus which, as I have pointed out in one of the previous numbers of my diary, was borrowed from Tsarism and only barely anointed with the Soviet chrism. Undoubtedly, we should have waited before taking this measure until we could guarantee that the apparatus would be our own. . . . In such circumstances, it is quite obvious that the "freedom to secede from the union," with which we justify ourselves, will prove to be nothing but a scrap of paper, incapable of defending the minorities of Russia from the inroads of that hundred percent Russian, the Great Russian chauvinist, in reality—the scoundrel and violator, which the typical Russian bureaucrat is. . . . It is necessary to make a distinction between a nationalism of the suppressing nation and a nationalism of the suppressed nation, between nationalism of a big nation and nationalism of a small nation.
>
> Stalin and Dzerzhinski must be held politically responsible for the truly Great Russian nationalistic campaign.[56]

There is much evidence to indicate that, had Lenin's health permitted him to take a more active part in the discussions leading to formation of the USSR, the ultimate structure of the Soviet state might have been different from that which Stalin ultimately gave it. As it happened, however, Lenin's letter did not help the cause of the opposition to Stalin. At the Twelfth Party Congress in April 1923, the opposition tried to reopen questions of overcentralization and the domination of the Union by the RSFSR, but they were helpless because the congress was packed with Stalinists.[57] Stalin presented the national question as less important than the question of international unity of the working class.[58] He also openly defended the dominant position of the Russian Republic in the Union. Stalin's

---

[56] Lenin, *Sochineniia*, 4th ed. (Moscow, 1946–1958), 36:553–59. Lenin's letter "Concerning the Question of Nationalities or about Autonomization" was written on 30–31 December 1922. This letter was frequently mentioned at the Twelfth Party Congress, but it was not published at the time. Asked why it had not been published, L. Kamenev replied that Lenin had given instructions to this effect. In Lenin's Works it first appeared in the fourth edition, published after Stalin's death.

[57] Pipes, *Formation of the Soviet Union*, p. 280.

[58] Stalin, *Sochineniia*, 5: 264.

speech before the Twelfth Congress on April 25 left little room for misunderstanding:

> It is clear to us, as Communists, that the basis of all our work lies in strengthening the power of the workers, and only after that are we confronted by the other question, and a very important one but subordinated to the first, namely, the question of nationalities. We are told that we must not offend the non-Russian nationalities. That is perfectly true. I agree that we must not offend them, but to form out of this a new theory to the effect that the Great Russian proletariat must be placed in a position of inequality in relation to the formerly oppressed nations is absurd. What was merely a figure of speech in Comrade Lenin's well-known letter Bukharin has converted into a regular slogan. Nevertheless, it is clear that the political basis of the dictatorship of the proletariat is primarily and chiefly the central, industrial regions, and not the border regions, which are peasant countries.[59]

Thus, at the Twelfth Party Congress, Stalin for the first time openly opposed Lenin's views on the question of nationalities and demonstrated that he already controlled the Party apparatus.

The Union of Soviet Socialist Republics, officially formed at the First All-Union Congress of Soviets in December 1922, has been since then a highly centralized state dominated by the Russian Soviet Federated Socialist Republic. The reason for the centralization of the Soviet state lies in the concept of the Communist Party itself, which does not recognize decentralization and which represents de facto the highest authority in the USSR. The Communist claim that in the Soviet Union the supreme power belongs to the soviets does not accord with the position occupied by the Communist Party. In reality, the Soviet Union is ruled by one single Communist Party, ruling in the name of the dictatorship of the proletariat. Not the soviets, as the first Constitution of the USSR dictates, but the Communist Party decides domestic and foreign policy. Stalin, in his "Report to the XIV Congress of the All-Union Communist Party of Bolsheviks on the Work of the Central Committee," delivered in December 1925, acknowledged that fact: "The dictatorship of the proletariat is not carried out of its own accord, but primarily by the Party forces under its [the Party's] direction. Without the direction of the Party, the dictatorship of the proletariat would have been impossible in the contemporary conditions of capitalist encircle-

[59] Ibid., pp. 264–65.

ment. I want to say only that in all basic questions of our domestic and foreign policy the directing role belonged to the Party."[60]

The Belorussian Communist Party, through which Moscow controls and rules the BSSR, was organized by the Russians.[61] For all practical purposes, since the beginning of its organization it has been a part of the Russian Communist Party, a fact clearly stated in the resolution of the First Congress of the Belorussian Communist Party, held at Smolensk on December 30–31, 1918.[62] Thus, when the USSR was formed four years later, the Central Committee of the Russian Communist Party was directing the Belorussian Communist Party, just as it directs the Party organizations of the other Russian provinces. The formation of the USSR did not alter the relationship of the Communist Party of Belorussia to the Russian Communist Party. This was so because the Party pretended to be a nongovernmental organization; therefore changes in the soviets had no effect on the structure of the Party.

It is true, however, that three years after the USSR was formed the Russian Communist Party of Bolsheviks renamed itself the All-Union Communist Party of Bolsheviks.[63] This was, of course, only another name for the same party. This new name, it was hoped, would be more appealing to Communists in the non-Russian republics.

The Central Committee of the Russian Communist Party achieved a subordination of the Belorussian Communist Party only after a period of struggle against the Belorussian Communists, led by Zmitrok Zhylunovich, who resisted Moscow's hegemony.[64] The Belorussian Communists were against the centralization of the party generally and against the domination of the Party of Belorussia by the Russians particularly.[65] They failed, however, to regain control over their own party. The Central Committee of the Russian Bolsheviks put an end to the dispute.[66] This experience

[60] Ibid., 7:343–44.
[61] Boris Kirillovich Markiianov, *Bor'ba Kommunisticheskoi Partii Belorussii za ukreplenie edinstva svoikh riadov v 1921–1925 gg.* (Minsk, 1961), p. 16.
[62] Ibid.; *Bol'shaia sovetskaia entsiklopediia*, 2d ed. (Moscow, 1950–1958), 4:492.
[63] B. N. Ponomarev, ed., *Politicheskii slovar'*, 2d ed. (Moscow, 1958), p. 268.
[64] Evgenii Iosifovich Bugaev, *Vozniknovenie bol'shevistskikh organizatsii i obrazovanie Kommunisticheskoi Partii Belorussii* (Moscow, 1959), p. 242.
[65] Mienski, "Establishment of the BSSR," p. 22; *Kastrychnik na Belarusi: zbornik artykulau i dakumentau* (Minsk, 1927), pp. 286–87.
[66] Bugaev, *Vozniknovenie bol'shevistskikh organizatsii*, p. 242.

convinced the Russians that the Belorussian Communists, if left to proceed without the guidance and control of Moscow, inevitably would renew their demand for decentralization of the Party apparatus. To prevent this, Moscow adopted the practice of selecting a non-Belorussian Communist as First Secretary of the Central Committee of the Belorussian Communist Party. The Secretary's duties were then, and are now, to control the Party in Belorussia and thus to assure the All-Union Central Committee and its Politburo that their program is carried out in the Belorussian SSR.

5.

Belorussia under the New Economic Policy

> Let us retreat and reorganize
> anew, but on a firmer basis,
> before we are utterly defeated.
> Lenin, 1921[1]

At the end of the Civil War, Belorussia was on the verge of total economic chaos. Its transportation system was completely paralyzed after six years of war and revolution; its industry, underdeveloped as it was before the war, had practically ceased to exist. Agricultural production dropped to less than 50 percent of the prewar level.[2] In addition to this, forced requisitions of agricultural products and mass political terror, enforced by the Cheka, the Communist Security Police, stimulated unrest in Belorussia, as in many parts of Russia. During 1920–1921, a series of peasant uprisings took place, the most serious of which was that in Tambov Province under the leadership of Antonov. Most alarming of all, from the Communist viewpoint, was a revolt by the sailors of the Red Navy in Kronstadt, who had previously been the chief supporters of the Bolshevik revolution. To placate the peasantry and to save the socialist revolution from threatened disaster, the Soviet government introduced, in the spring of 1921, a New Economic Policy (NEP). It called, even in the face of grumbling among the more dogmatic Communists, for drastic change.

The new policy was most of all the work of Lenin, who in it demonstrated once again his genius for masterly maneuvering in critical situations. It is an excellent example of strategic retreat. The Bolsheviks had employed the tactic before, in concluding the Treaty of Brest-Litovsk with Germany, in order to survive during the Revolution. They now employed it to keep themselves in power. The NEP was a retreat on a broad front, from the perilous battle line of unyielding Marxist idealism to the safer realities of the marketplace.

Lenin's shrewdness had led the Bolsheviks to power in a country where the working class, in whose name power was taken, was a small minority. However, with the same shrewdness, he now saw that only flexibility of policy could save Russia from the threat of a new civil war. As internal unrest spread throughout the country, he foresaw that "only agreement with the peasantry can save the Revolution in Russia."[3] Lenin urged the party to "try to satisfy the demands of the peasants who are dissatisfied, discontented, and legitimately discontented."[4] In his "Report on the Political Activities of the Central Committee," delivered to the Tenth Congress of the Russian Communist Party on March 8, 1921, Lenin presented his reasons for the introduction of the NEP:

> While concentrating all our attention on restoring our economy, we must bear in mind that we have before us the small tiller of the soil, the small proprietor, the small producer, producing for commodity circulation, until the restoration of large-scale industry is achieved. But this restoration cannot be achieved on the old basis: it is the work of many years, not less than a decade, and in view of the ruined state of our country perhaps even longer. Meanwhile, for many years we shall have to deal with these small producers as such, and the free trade slogan will be inevitable.[5]

The first important concession to the peasantry was "the abandonment of the policy of forced requisition in favor of a fixed tax in kind, which left the peasants free to dispose of such surpluses as remained after the tax assessment had been met."[6]

Secondly, with the adoption of the NEP, party organizations were instructed to devote their energies to the task of peaceful reconstruction. At the same time, the government ordered the Cheka

---

[1] Vladimir Lenin, *Sobranie sochinenii*, 1st ed. (Moscow, 1920–1923), 18, pt. 1:372.
[2] *Ocherki po istorii gosudarstva i prava Belorusskoi SSR* (Minsk, 1958), p. 6.
[3] Vladimir Lenin, *Sochineniia*, 3d ed. (Moscow, 1929–1939), 26:238.
[4] Ibid., p. 239.
[5] Lenin, *Sobranie sochinenii*, 1st ed., 18:119.
[6] Merle Fainsod, *Smolensk under Soviet Rule* (Cambridge, Mass., 1958), pp. 7–8.

to handle the people carefully. In campaigning to collect the tax, the Cheka was ordered

> [to] avoid administrative pressure on the population and make only a minimum of arrests of people who do not pay, for this will reflect poorly on the mood of the masses, undermining the foundation of the political well-being of the *uezd*. Do not sentence to imprisonment those who do not pay, except in the case of millers. Treat the poor peasants with the most skillful diplomacy. Make the wealthiest people carry the main tax burden.[7]

The agricultural practices of the NEP were warmly greeted in Belorussia. Immediately after the introduction of the NEP, the Belorussian government enforced the "Leninist Decree on Land," whereby nationalized land was distributed among the small peasants. In the spring of 1921 alone, the Belorussian peasants received 2,160,000 acres. About 54,000 acres were also given to the state farms (*Sovkhozes*).[8] In general, as a result of the distribution of landed estates in Belorussia, the peasants enlarged their landownership to 14,850,000 acres, or 28 percent more than they had before the Revolution.[9]

The New Economic Policy was not limited to economic questions and the diminution of the role of the Cheka. It also introduced a certain element of liberalism into the administration of the Soviet state. Within the Party ranks, for instance, with the introduction of the NEP, a certain degree of democracy was tolerated. Furthermore, the NEP included certain concessions to education and national culture in general. All these concessions in administration enabled the leaders of the BSSR to raise, first of all, the question of reclaiming the territories with predominantly Belorussian-speaking population which were included in the RSFSR. Their views agreed with the Leninist nationality policy, which "required a consideration of the people's language, economy, culture, and customs at the time of building the Soviet national statehood."[10]

First, in 1923, the Belorussian Sovnarkom appealed this question to the Russian Council of Labor and Defense. At the request of the

[7] Quoted in ibid., p. 43.
[8] M. E. Shkliar, *Kommunisticheskaia Partiia (bol'shevikov) Belorussii v period perekhoda na mirnuiu rabotu po vosstanovleniiu narodnogo khoziaistva, 1921–1925 gg.* (Minsk, 1950), p. 28.
[9] *Istoriia BSSR*, 2d ed. (Minsk, 1961), 2:187.
[10] *Ocherki po istorii*, p. 65.

THE BELORUSSIAN S.S.R. BETWEEN 1921 AND 1939

Belorussian government, the question was also discussed at the Party conferences of the Gomel, Smolensk, and Vitebsk regions, which were included in the RSFSR. These conferences approved resolutions favoring efforts to include Belorussian ethnographic districts in the Belorussian SSR.[11] The appeal and resolutions were considered by the Central Executive Committee of the USSR, whose first decision concerning this question was made on March 3, 1924.

[11] J. Mienski, "The Establishment of the Belorussian SSR," *Belorussian Review*, no. 1 (1955): 31.

This resulted in the first expansion of the Belorussian SSR by the inclusion of a number of districts from the Gomel, Smolensk, and Vitebsk regions. This addition enlarged the territory of the BSSR from 20,310 square miles to 43,000 square miles, while the number of inhabitants was raised from 1,500,000 to 4,172,000.[12]

This decision by the V.Ts.I.K. was followed by a gathering of the Fourth All-Belorussian Extraordinary Congress of Soviets in the same month, at which Mikhail Kalinin, chairman of the V.Ts.I.K., expressed his regret at the suppression of the Belorussians under the tsarist government and wished the Belorussians success in forming their state and maintaining brotherly relations with the Russians and the other peoples of the Soviet Union.[13]

Finally, in December 1926, two more districts of the Gomel region were added. The number of inhabitants of the Belorussian SSR now reached five million.[14] Even after these additions, however, large Belorussian ethnographic territories still remained outside the borders of the republic. The national composition of the population in 1926 is shown in Table Two.

During the period of the New Economic Policy (1921–1928), the Belorussian government devoted much attention to improving the work of the soviets (councils). An important measure in this direction was the periodic elections to village and town soviets.[15] The first decree of the Belorussian Ts.I.K. on the conduct of elections was issued in October 1922. In the beginning, however, a great majority of the people distrusted the soviet authorities and consequently refused to take part in the elections. Often the local soviet authorities were elected, in fact, by a small minority of the population. The presidium of the V.Ts.I.K., therefore, on December 29, 1924, decreed that elections to the soviets were to be annulled if less than 35 percent of the eligible voters took part, or if there were complaints about irregularities in the conduct of the elections.[16] In the first half of the 1920s, many elections were annulled for these reasons. The population's interest in the soviet authorities gradually grew, however, and they began to take a more active part in elections. For instance, in the elections held in 1927, 46.3 percent of

[12] *Ocherki po istorii*, p. 66.
[13] *Chetvertyi vsebelorusskii chrezvychainyi s"ezd Sovetov rabochikh, krest'ianskikh, i krasnoarmeiskikh deputatov: stenograficheskii otchet* (Minsk, March 1924), p. 9.
[14] Mienski, "Establishment of the BSSR," p. 31.
[15] *Istoriia BSSR*, 2:215.
[16] *Sobranie ukazanii BSSR za 1922 god*, no. 10:131.

TABLE TWO

NATIONAL COMPOSITION OF THE POPULATION OF THE BSSR ACCORDING TO THE CENSUS OF 1926

Nationality	Rural Population Number	%	Urban Population Number	%	Total Population Number	%
Belorussians	3,684,441	89.10	332,860	39.26	4,017,301	80.62
Jews	66,897	1.60	340,162	40.12	407,059	8.19
Great Russians	251,603	6.10	132,203	15.60	383,806	7.70
Poles	77,833	1.86	19,665	2.32	97,498	1.96
Latvians	10,869	0.25	3,192	0.37	14,061	0.28
Lithuanians	4,745	0.11	2,118	0.25	6,863	0.14
Ukrainians	27,263	0.70	7,418	0.87	34,681	0.69
Germans	4,757	0.11	2,318	0.26	7,075	0.15
Gypsies	2,198	0.05	168	0.02	2,366	0.05
Estonians	716	0.02	251	0.03	967	0.02
Tartars	558	0.01	2,219	0.38	2,777	0.07
Others	3,530	0.09	4,256	0.52	7,786	0.13
TOTAL	4,135,410	100.00	846,830	100.00	4,982,240	100.00

Source: *Prakticheskoe razreshenie natsional'nogo voprosa v BSSR* (Minsk, 1927), 2:12.

the village population and 62.4 percent of the town population participated.[17] The Belorussian people were beginning to think of the word soviet as a symbol of the right of the people to make decisions on local issues through discussions, consultations, and elections.

The Belorussian government wanted members representing all social classes to be elected to the soviets. In the elections to the town soviets, for instance, out of 1,718 members chosen throughout the republic in 1925, 756 were workers, 218 Red Army men, 129 peasants, 57 craftsmen and artisans, and 412 state employees.[18] Of course, these figures indicate that not all social classes were represented equally. Nevertheless, equality of representation was the aim of the government. The members of the village soviets, including their chairmen, were usually local people. With governmental encouragement, there was also an increase in the number of middle-class peasants among those elected to the soviets. In 1924, for instance, 74 percent of the members of the village soviets were from

[17] *Ocherki po istorii*, p. 147.
[18] *Istoriia BSSR*, 2:201. No information is available on the remaining 146 members.

this class. By 1925, their number had risen to 81 percent, and in 1926 to 87 percent.[19] The agricultural aspect of the New Economic Policy was oriented toward this group.

The Belorussian Ts.I.K., constitutionally the highest authority in the republic, was periodically elected through indirect elections. In these elections, too, the Soviet government desired a more or less proportional representation of every social class and population group. For instance, in 1926, fifty-one workers, fifty peasants, thirty-five state employees, and three craftsmen and artisans were elected to the Ts.I.K.[20]

Belorussians composed 80.62 percent of the total population in the BSSR in 1926.[21] The rest were Jews, Russians, and others. Because there were several minority nationalities in the republic, the Belorussian government wanted as many of them as possible to be proportionally represented in the local and central soviets. Among the members of the local soviets elected in 1926–1927, the nationalities were represented as shown in Table Three. By comparison with

TABLE THREE

PERCENTAGES OF NATIONAL GROUPS ELECTED TO BELORUSSIAN LOCAL SOVIETS IN 1926–1927

Local Soviets	Belorussians	Russians	Jews	Poles	Others
Village soviets	92.3	1.5	2.3	2.4	1.5
Town soviets	52.0	12.0	30.0	2.3	3.7
District soviets	79.2	5.8	11.2	1.4	2.4

Sources: Aleksandr Charviakou, *Za Savetskuiu Belarus'* (Minsk, 1927), p. 74; *Prakticheskoe razreshenie natsional'nogo voprosa v BSSR* (Minsk, 1927), 2:14.

Table Two, it can be seen that the members elected in the village, town and district soviets followed closely the national composition of the population. A comparison of Table Four with Table Two, however, shows that the Belorussians were underrepresented in the central soviet institutions, especially in the courts and economic bureaus. This disproportion stemmed, in all likelihood, from a comparative lack of professionally educated men among the Belorussians, especially in law and economics.

[19] *Sobranie ukazanii BSSR za 1925 god*, no. 9:74.
[20] *Istorii BSSR*, 2:201.
[21] See Table Two, p. 67.

TABLE FOUR

NATIONAL COMPOSITION OF EMPLOYEES OF THE CENTRAL
SOVIET ADMINISTRATIVE INSTITUTIONS OF BELORUSSIA
IN 1927, IN PERCENTAGES

Institutions	Belorussians	Russians	Jews	Poles	Others
Administrative	51.3	18.0	24.8	0.1	5.8
Economy	30.8	13.0	49.3	0.2	6.7
Courts	26.3	21.1	42.1	—	11.5
Agriculture	59.5	24.1	10.1	—	5.3

Source: *Prakticheskoe razreshenie natsional'nogo voprosa v BSSR* (Minsk, 1927), 2:13.

As can be seen from Table Five, about four-fifths of the members elected to the town and village soviets of the BSSR in 1926 and 1927 were non-Party members. More important, however, during the period of the New Economic Policy, non-Party members composed a majority even among the officials of most of the commissariats. As late as 1930, non-Party employees were in the majority in such important commissariats as those of education, agriculture, and finance, as can be seen from Table Six. Of course, these commissariats were headed by men who were officially members of the Party. In the 1920s, however, most of them were National Communists, some of whom shared the views of the Belorussian National Democrats. Among these men should be mentioned Anton Balitski, commissar of education, and Zmitrok Pryshchepau, commissar of agriculture. This perhaps explains why Party members were in the minority.

TABLE FIVE

PARTY AFFILIATIONS OF MEMBERS ELECTED TO BELORUSSIAN
VILLAGE AND TOWN SOVIETS IN 1926 AND 1927

Affiliation	1926		1927	
	Number	%	Number	%
Communist Party	1,678	8.9	2,127	11.1
Communist Youth Organizations (Komsomol)	1,800	9.5	1,977	10.3
Non-Party members	15,424	81.6	15,069	78.6

Source: *Ahliad dzeinastsi Savetu Narodnykh Kamisarau i Ekanamichnae Narady BSSR: zbornyia matar'ialy za II-kvartal 1926–1927 hodu* (Minsk, 1927), p. 82.

TABLE SIX

PROPORTIONS OF PARTY AND NON-PARTY MEMBERS AMONG
EMPLOYEES OF BELORUSSIAN COMMISSARIATS OF EDUCATION,
FINANCE, AND AGRICULTURE, 1930

Commissariat	Number of Employees	Party Members Number	%	Komsomol Members Number	%	Non-Party Members Number	%
Education	63	24	38.1	2	3.2	37	58.7
Finance	122	25	20.5	2	1.6	95	77.9
Agriculture	186	24	12.9	2	1.1	160	86.0

Source: *Sluzhachyia dziarzhaunaha i kaaperatyunaha apparatu BSSR* (Minsk, 1930), p. xvi.

During the first half of the 1920s, the Communist Party of Belorussia remained very small, and its members were predominantly Russian by nationality. Altogether, there were only 6,157 members and candidates of the Communist Party in Belorussia in 1922,[22] 72 percent of whom were Russian.[23] In 1925, the Party was still small, having only 7,691 members and 4,972 candidates. Of this number, Belorussians represented about 45 percent.[24] In the second half of the decade, the number of Communists in Belorussia grew rapidly. In July 1928, there were already 31,713 members and candidates. Belorussians composed 54.3 percent of the total number; Jews, 23.7 percent; Russians, 14.0 percent; and all other nationalities in the BSSR, 8 percent.[25] Thus by the end of the NEP period, the Belorussians had become a majority, although a slight one, in the ranks of the Communist Party. Presumably the Party was becoming more appealing to the local population. On the whole, however, the Communist Party of Belorussia continued to be the weakest among those of all the Union republics.[26]

In the first half of the 1920s, the Belorussian government was preoccupied with establishing the basic legal foundations of the state. It was necessary to find a medium of reconciliation between

---

[22] *Vseobshchaia perepis' chlenov RKP(b), 1922 g.* (Moscow, 1922), p. 9.
[23] *Belorussia*, Subcontractor's Monograph HRAF-19 (New Haven, Conn., 1954–1955), p. 160.
[24] Ibid., p. 60.
[25] *Belorusskaia SSR v tsifrakh: k desiatiletiiu sushchestvovaniia BSSR, 1919–1929* (Minsk, 1929), p. 30.
[26] Merle Fainsod, *How Russia Is Ruled* (Cambridge, Mass., 1953), p. 219.

the Socialist interests of the state and the private interests of the people, and to pass laws which would be in accord with the New Economic Policy. There were many difficulties. First of all, the BSSR, like the other Union republics, was lacking in experience and deficient in lawyers—both vital elements in drafting sound statutes. There were, moreover, no definite limits on how far ideological reconciliation should go or how long the New Economic Policy would continue.

The Belorussian leaders, however, did not want to enter very deeply into ideological discussions; the need, first of all, was to solve immediate problems. With this in mind, the Seventh All-Belorussian Congress was assembled in May 1925. One of the major tasks of the congress was the adoption of a new constitution, in accordance with the First Constitution of the USSR, adopted in January 1924. The Ukrainian and Transcaucasian republics had adopted their constitutions quickly. The Belorussian Republic, however, failed to adopt its new constitution until 1927.

The cause of the delay was ideological quibbling, of the very sort which Belorussian leaders had earlier hoped to avoid. A draft of the constitution, prepared by a special commission, defined the Soviet state as the "dictatorship of the proletariat, realized by the proletariat and the laboring peasants."[27] The Party, however, considered this definition incorrect because it misinterpreted the "dictatorship of the proletariat." From the Party's ideological point of view, the dictatorship of the proletariat is "a special union of the proletariat and the laboring peasants in which the proletariat plays a leading role."[28]

Because of the ideological "mistakes" contained in the draft, it was first rejected, then rewritten; it was finally adopted in 1927.[29] The article of the adopted constitution defining the dictatorship of the proletariat affirms that "in the Soviet State there are two classes —the working class, which is realizing its dictatorship, and the laboring peasantry, which is rendering support to the working class."[30]

[27] *Ocherki po istorii*, p. 131.
[28] B. N. Ponomarev, ed., *Politicheskii slovar'*, 2d ed. (Moscow, 1958), p. 173.
[29] *Ocherki po istorii*, p. 131. From the type of criticism of the first constitutional project, it is clear that it was rejected by the Party. Nevertheless, one must point out also that the government appointees continued to reject the Party's views for three more years. Such a dispute between the government and the Party was impossible in the 1930s.
[30] Ibid., p. 132.

The adoption of the new constitution did not spell complete defeat for the Belorussian leaders, who continued to struggle for constitutional equality of the peasants with the workers in administering the state, and for improving the work of the Soviets. With this in mind, the Belorussian Ts.I.K. and Sovnarkom adopted a decree on December 22, 1927, "for the reorganization and simplification of the Soviet apparatus and also for widening the authority of local officials." Only the functions of general administration, planning, and control were left to the central government. All other executive functions were decentralized and handed over to local officials.[31]

The Belorussian government paid great attention to the necessity of "people overcoming their mistrust of the law, which had been inherited from the tsarist government, and educating them in the spirit of respect for the Socialist legality."[32] With this in mind, they wished to improve the qualifications of the judges and to bring the agencies of justice closer to the people.[33]

Under the NEP, the Belorussian Sovnarkom took an active part in the work of the All-Union Sovnarkom. On many occasions the drafts of laws of the All-Union Sovnarkom were accepted only on certain conditions or were rejected completely. In 1926, for example, of seventy-two drafts of laws proposed by the All-Union Sovnarkom, the Belorussian Sovnarkom agreed to thirty-six without any comment, but accepted nineteen others only on condition that their own corrections and additions be accepted by the All-Union Sovnarkom. Seventeen of the projects were rejected completely, the most important of which was the Statute of the Academy of Sciences of the USSR. The Belorussian Sovnarkom rejected this project for the following reasons:

1) The project of the Academy does not recognize other nationalities in the territory of the USSR except Russian.

2) It can be seen from the list of the institutions proposed that the Academy of Sciences would be preoccupied exclusively with the study of the development of Russian culture, without paying any attention to the study of the cultures of other peoples which as yet are little known.

[31] Ibid., p. 144.
[32] *Istoriia BSSR*, 2:201.
[33] *Ahliad dzeinastsi Savetu Narodnykh Kamisarau i Ekanamichnae Narady BSSR: zbornyia matar'ialy za IV-kvartal 1925–1926 hodu* (Minsk, 1926), p. 97.

3) The method of selecting the members of the Academy does not give opportunities for the Union republics to introduce members to the staff of the Academy who had made themselves known because of their scientific work in other Union republics.

The Sovnarkom of the Belorussian SSR states that the above-mentioned draft ... could not be accepted because if the All-Union Academy were administered by this statute, it would be not an All-Union but a Russian Academy of Sciences.[34]

The fact that the Union republics had to consider and could even reject laws proposed by the All-Union government before they were passed indicates the considerable voice they had in the administration of the USSR under the NEP.

The Belorussian SSR began to develop its agricultural program in 1923, when the first land code was approved by the Second Session of the Ts.I.K. This code was based on the principles declared in the fundamental legislative acts of the Belorussian SSR and RSFSR. All land was declared the property of the state and offered for use to the peasants with the understanding that they would cultivate it by their own labor.[35]

The Belorussian land code differed in some aspects from the Russian. Before the revolution, communal use of the land had scarcely existed in Belorussia; thus the new Belorussian land code, in enumerating the forms of landownership, did not recognize the communal one.[36]

For a short time after expansion of the Belorussian state in 1924, two land codes were in effect—that of 1923 in the old districts, and that of the RSFSR in the districts transferred from the Russian Republic. It was therefore necessary to work out a new land code which would be effective for all of Belorussia. The awaited code, approved on September 1, 1925, established only the individual form of landownership, rather than communal use of the land, as in Russia. It also recognized the *pasiolak* (small village settlement) as the most satisfactory form of landownership in Belorussia.[37]

[34] Ibid.
[35] *Ocherki po istorii*, p. 96.
[36] Ibid., p. 97.
[37] *Istoriia BSSR*, 2:205. In Belorussia, as in the southern part of Russia, especially the Ukraine, many villages were large. Consequently, some pieces of land owned by the farmers individually were located far from their homes. This, of course, was very impractical. In the early 1920s, the Belorussian gov-

As to collective farms, the Belorussian government adhered to a decision made at the Second All-Belorussian Congress of Soviets in December 1920, and expressed in Article 29 of "The Thesis of the Agrarian Problem":

> Aiming at the organization of the collective farms, the Soviet government would, nevertheless, not permit any forced actions against the wide mass of the toiling peasantry. The Soviet government, however, would assist the voluntary formation of collective farms, providing them with the necessary area of land and helping them economically.[38]

This mild decision caused little strain, for few peasants chose to join the collective farms. Throughout the period of the NEP, the number of such farms remained very limited. In 1925, for instance, only 121,000 acres, 0.79 percent of the total agricultural land in the BSSR, were under collective farming.[39] Consequently, the government devoted most of its energy to helping the individual farmers raise the productivity of their farms by improved methods of agriculture. Farmers who achieved the best crops were specially rewarded.[40] The government also periodically sponsored an All-Belorussian Congress of Farmers. The government wanted to discover and study the best agricultural achievements by individual farmers or by whole *raions* (districts).[41]

The Commissariat of Agriculture, headed by Zmitrok Pryshchepau, sponsored delegations of farmers to Holland, Denmark, and other West European countries to observe the most modern farms there.[42] The government also extended enthusiastic support to schools which offered agricultural training. On August 21, 1925, by a decree of the Ts.I.K. and the Belorussian Sovnarkom, the Belo-

---

ernment popularized the idea of splitting these large villages into small farm settlements so that the farmers could have their land as close to their homes as possible. These settlements were called *pasiolki* (plural of *pasiolak*). The land in a *pasiolak* was owned by the farmers individually. It had nothing in common with the Russian *obshchina* (commune).

[38] *S"ezdy Sovetov Soiuza SSR, Soiuznykh i Avtonomnykh Sovetskikh Sotsialisticheskikh Respublik: sbornik dokumentov v trekh tomakh, 1917–1936 gg.* (Moscow, 1959–1960), 2:258.

[39] *Istoriia BSSR*, 2:220.

[40] *Ocherki po istorii*, p. 123.

[41] *Zbornik zakonau i zahadau rabocha-sialianskaha uradu Belaruskai SSR* (Minsk, 1924–1938), 12:276.

[42] U. Hlybinny, *Dolia Belaruskai kul'tury pad Savetami: dosledy i matar'ialy*, ser. 2, no. 68 (Munich, 1958): 47.

russian Institute of Agriculture and Forestry was merged with the Gorki Institute of Agriculture, becoming the Belorussian State Academy of Agriculture.[43] Within the next ten years the academy was considerably expanded, with new student dormitories, a theater, a student union, and other facilities. About 60 percent of the students had state assistantships.[44]

In undertaking agricultural reforms, the Commissariat of Agriculture gave preference to the creation of new farmsteads, a reform the peasants eagerly welcomed. By September 1929, 40.1 percent of the total land under cultivation in Belorussia was already in farmsteads.[45] The peasants moving from villages to farmsteads were helped by the state, both by long-term loans and by freedom from some taxation.[46]

The agricultural reforms of the NEP were successful in arresting the downward trend of the Belorussian agricultural economy. By 1924, 6,175,647 acres were under cultivation, 81,000 acres more than in prewar times.[47] Also a reflection of improvement was a sharp decline in the number of peasants officially categorized as "poor." Before the Revolution in Belorussia, the poor peasants composed 67.7 percent of the total number of farmer-peasants; in 1927, they were only 26 percent. Concomitantly, the number of middle-class peasants increased from 21.3 percent in 1914 to 65 percent in 1927. In the latter year the kulaks composed 9 percent of the total number of farmers.[48]

The trend toward improvement of agricultural conditions af-

[43] *Ahliad dzeinastsi Savetu Narodnykh Kamisarau i Ekanamichnae Narady BSSR: svodnyia matar'ialy za II-kvartal 1925–1926 hodu* (Minsk, 1926), p. 58.
[44] Ibid.
[45] *Ocherki po istorii,* p. 123.
[46] *Istoriia BSSR,* 2:208, 244, 245.
[47] Ibid., p. 208.
[48] *Ocherki po istorii,* p. 187. At the end of the Civil War, all landed estates and the lands of the Church were distributed among the poor farmers and farm-laborers. In distributing the land, a general principle was that the farmers could own only as much land as they could cultivate without help from outside their families. Because of this limitation, after the Civil War none of the farmers had much land. The amount of land owned by the individual farmers in Belorussia during the 1920s differed in various villages and districts, depending on the quantity of land available and the number of farmers there. Generally, however, the farmers who were classified as poor had less than 10 acres, the middle-class farmers had between 10 and 25 acres, and the kulaks had more than 25 acres. Otherwise, the poor were considered those who could not produce enough for their needs, the middle-class farmers were those who produced enough or more than they needed, and the kulaks were prosperous farmers.

fected the whole Soviet Union. Stalin, in his "Political Report of the Central Committee to the 15th Congress of the All-Union Communist Party" on December 3, 1927, was optimistic:

> We have figures on the increase in income of the peasant population. Two years ago, in 1924–1925, the income of the peasant population amounted to 3,548 million rubles; in 1926–1927, this income grew to 4,792 million rubles, i.e., it increased 35.1 percent; whereas the peasant population during this period of time increased only 2.38 percent. This is an indubitable indication that material conditions in the countryside are improving.[49]

The role of industry in the national economy of Belorussia before the Revolution was very insignificant. Heavy industry was especially underdeveloped. In 1913, the heavy industry of the regions now included in the BSSR produced only 0.88 percent of the industrial production of Russia, while the population of these regions composed 3.6 percent of Russia's total population.[50] Or, to express the ratio differently, the production of heavy industry per capita in Belorussia before the Revolution was less than one-fourth of the per capita production of Russia as a whole.

During the Civil War, Belorussia was twice subjected to foreign occupation—in 1915–1918 by the Germans, and in 1919–1920 by the Poles. Not counting those in the western regions of Belorussia, 480 industrial enterprises were destroyed and the rest were put out of order.[51] It was, therefore, a very difficult task to renew the development of industry. The government decided, however, to try with all possible means to use the remaining factories and raw materials of the republic.[52] Limited availability of materials severely restricted the project; through the period of reconstruction, more than 50 percent of all industrial production was in the woodmaking, paper, and food industries. Table Seven indicates the relative economic contributions of various industries in the Belorussian SSR during 1924–1927.

Great aid to the recovery of the Belorussian economy in general and of industry in particular was rendered by small private enterprises. These enterprises had been nationalized during the

---

[49] Iosif Stalin, *Sochineniia*, 1st ed. (Moscow, 1946–1952), 10:316.
[50] *Ocherki po istorii*, p. 113.
[51] *Promyshlennost' BSSR: itogi i perspektivy* (Minsk, 1928), p. 14.
[52] The basic raw materials in the republic at that time were agricultural products and lumber.

TABLE SEVEN

PRODUCTION OF INDUSTRIES IN BELORUSSIA, 1924–1927,
IN PERCENTAGES

Industry	Value of Gross Production in % of Total		
	1924–1925	1925–1926	1926–1927
Silicates	6.6	6.5	7.1
Metals	6.7	6.3	6.8
Wood	17.8	25.2	25.5
Chemicals	6.5	6.6	5.9
Food	17.9	17.5	15.4
Leather and shoes	7.4	7.8	9.0
Textiles	3.4	5.1	5.2
Paper	23.7	18.0	16.1
Others	10.0	7.0	9.0

Source: *Promyshlennost' BSSR v diagramakh i tablitsakh* (Minsk, 1928), p. 3.

years of the Revolution and Civil War. At the beginning of the NEP period, they were returned to their former owners or to the producers' cooperatives (industrial artels) for a fixed term, with the provision that rental was to be paid, depending on the output of the enterprise, and they were promised freedom from nationalization.[53] At the end of 1925, the gross output of private and cooperative enterprises in the BSSR was thirty-nine million rubles, at a time when the gross output of state industry was only thirty-two million rubles,[54] 45 percent of the total industrial output. In the same year, the socialized sector of industry in the USSR as a whole yielded 81 percent of the total industrial production.[55]

To the recovery of the Belorussian national economy, private and cooperative trade contributed far more significantly than did state-directed trade, as is shown in Table Eight. These figures indicate clearly that, between 1923 and 1926, state trade was at a standstill and private trade was declining rather rapidly, while cooperative trade achieved a steady growth. These trends continued after 1926. In 1928, when the New Economic Policy was terminated, cooperative trade in Belorussia was dominant. Had the NEP remained in effect, the Belorussian economy would almost certainly have progressed toward freedom from direct state control.

[53] Fainsod, *Smolensk under Soviet Rule*, p. 8.
[54] *Istoriia BSSR*, 2:204.   [55] Stalin, *Sochineniia*, 10:297.

TABLE EIGHT

COMPARATIVE VOLUME OF STATE, COOPERATIVE, AND
PRIVATE TRADE IN THE BSSR, 1923–1926, IN PERCENTAGES

Type of Trade	1923–1924	1924–1925	1925–1926
State	19.9	22.7	22.0
Cooperative	26.3	39.1	46.6
Private	53.8	38.2	31.4

Source: *Istoriia BSSR*, 2d ed. (Minsk, 1961), 2:210.

In 1926, industrial output of the BSSR reached the prewar level. The rate of industrial recovery only slightly surpassed the rate of agricultural recovery. As can be seen from Table Nine, industry grew under the NEP, but its growth was comparatively slow. By the end of the period, industrial production in the republic had not reached the All-Union level. While in 1926–1927 the Belorussian share of industry in the gross output of the national economy was 28.6 percent, in the Soviet Union as a whole it was 38 percent.[56]

The Belorussian government was far from happy to see the republic lagging behind the other Union republics in industrial development. Mikola Haladzed, chairman of the Belorussian Sovnarkom, made the following complaint at the plenary meeting of the Presidium of the USSR State Planning Committee on December 31, 1927:

> Conditions in our republic, as seen from statistics, are tragic. At this time, while in the USSR the growth of industrial production is planned to be raised to 54 percent of the total national output and the point of departure is 42 percent, we do not have very favorable conditions in our republic.... They say that Belorussia borders on the capitalist countries and the first stroke from capitalist Europe and the counterrevolution may always be expected on Belorussia; and, therefore, it is not wise to spend a lot of money on developing the industry of Belorussia. I believe that such a consideration is wrong and even harmful.[57]

The Belorussian government did not, as a matter of fact, insist on building up the heavy industry of the republic. It did, however,

[56] Stalin, *Sochineniia*, 10:296. See also Table Eight, above.
[57] *Perspektivy razvitiia narodnogo khoziaistva BSSR* (Minsk, 1928), pp. 34–35.

TABLE NINE

RELATION BETWEEN INDUSTRIAL AND AGRICULTURAL PRODUCTION
IN THE BELORUSSIAN NATIONAL INCOME, 1923–1927,
IN PERCENTAGES

	1923–1924	1924–1925	1925–1926	1926–1927
Agriculture	73.4	74.2	72.7	71.4
Industry	26.6	25.8	27.3	28.6

Source: Aleksandr Charviakou, *Za Savetskuiu Belarus'* (Minsk, 1927), p. 66.

desire more help from the central government for more intensive development of their light industry, which would help facilitate agriculture.

Despite the failure of Belorussian industry to match the pace of development in the other Union republics during the NEP period, its progress was, on the whole, impressive. In addition, several other aspects of the economic recovery were both satisfactory and promising. The industrial development of the republic permitted, and even demanded, the undertaking of an extensive program of building new highways and railroads and improving the old. A great deal was done during the last years of the NEP period in drainage of the marshlands, which made up 10.3 percent of the territory of the Belorussian SSR.[58] All in all, the Belorussian people had much reason to hope for a better future.

[58] *Doklad Soveta Narodnykh Komissarov BSSR Sovetu Narodnykh Komissarov SSR* (Minsk, 1926), p. 10.

6.

A Golden Age of Belorussian Culture

The New Economic Policy of the 1920s represented more than concessions to the peasantry, restoration of a limited system of private enterprise, and a temporary political reconciliation with the local nationalists. It aimed also at a realization of the policy of nationalities by making concessions to the minority nationalities of the USSR for the development of their national cultures. Taking advantage of these concessions, the Belorussian leaders began at once to build up the cultural and educational institutions of the republic. In 1921, they founded the Institute of Belorussian Culture (Inbelkult) as a scientific research center to study Belorussian culture in all its aspects.[1] There was a feeling that the Belorussian language, now the official language of the republic, was inadequate because it had been nearly out of literary use since the sixteenth century. Hence, the main goal of the Institute was perfection of the Belorussian literary language.[2] A further project was the organization of scientific expeditions to study the country. In 1923, for instance, the Institute organized ethnographic investigations and archaeological excavations.[3] Research of this sort was something new, for the tsarist government had never been interested in studying Belorussia. Another task of the Institute was the study of Belorussian history and culture. At the very start, this study laid a foundation for the development of Belorussian nationalism, for its principal motivation was ethnic pride—a belief that the Belorussians were of pure Slavo-Baltic descent. The Russians, on the other hand, were considered an ethnic miscellany of Slavs, Finns, and Tartars.[4]

One argument advanced in favor of Belorussian nationalism was that for centuries there had been differences between the political backgrounds of the Belorussian and the Russian peoples. "Ancient Belorussia, it was said, was an early home of democratic and social equalitarian ideas, in contrast to the great social class divisions which were to be found in Byzantinized and Mongolized Muscovy."[5] While Russia was under the direct or indirect influence of the Mongols, Belorussia was a part of the Grand Duchy of Lithuania, in which the Belorussian culture was dominant. In the sixteenth century, when Russia, not yet recovered from Mongolian suppression in the preceding centuries, was going through a period of terror during the reign of Ivan IV, Belorussia lived in freedom and enjoyed an advanced state of cultural development, and the two great codes of law of the Grand Duchy of Lithuania were written in the Belorussian language.[6] Belorussian historians, studying their country's past, found many distinguished men who had made great contributions to the development of its civilization. Two of these especially should be mentioned. Frantsishka Skaryna, born in Polotsk in 1490, was known as the most educated and enlightened man of his time. He translated many books, including the Bible, into the Belorussian language, and was the first to print books in Belorussian.[7] Symon Polotski (1629–1680) was a talented poet and scientist. In his poems, he opposed Polish domination of Belorussia and called for a union of the Belorussian and Russian peoples.[8] After the Civil War of 1917–1920, his idea of a union between these two peoples having materialized, he became a symbol for good Belorussian-Russian relations.

[1] A. Balitski, "Instytut Belaruskai Kul'tury," As'veta, no. 3 (1927): 6.
[2] Ibid.   [3] Ibid., p. 7.
[4] *Belorussia*, Subcontractor's Monograph HRAF–19 (New Haven, Conn., 1954–1955), p. 155. The question of the Slavo-Baltic origin of the Belorussian people had received considerable attention in the works of such scholars as A. Liavdanskii, *Nauchnye izvestiia Smolenskogo Gosudarstvennogo Universiteta* [Scientific Information of the Smolensk State University] vol. 3 (Smolensk, 1927?); M. K. Liubavskii, *Ocherki istorii Litovsko-Russkogo gosudarstva do Liublinskoi Unii vkliuchitel'no*, 2d ed. (Moscow, 1915).
[5] *Belorussia*, p. 157.
[6] *Bol'shaia sovetskaia entsiklopediia*, 1st ed. (Moscow, 1938), 37:114; Constantine R. Jurgela, *History of the Lithuanian Nation* (New York, 1948), p. 222.
[7] I. S. Kravchenko and I. E. Marchenko, *Belorusskaia SSR* (Moscow, 1956), p. 18.
[8] Ibid., p. 19. Symon Polotski took an active part in defending the idea of unity between the Belorussian and Russian peoples during the Russian-Polish War (1648–1654). After the occupation of Polotsk by Polish troops, he had to leave his home town and seek refuge in Moscow. Living there until the end of his life, he continued his social-cultural activities and in many aspects made important contributions to the development of Russian culture.

The New Economic Policy brought with it a reconciliation between the Communist Party and local nationalism, which now was encouraged by the Communists. The Communists in the national republics and regions were instructed to get along with the local nationalists. The purpose of this amiability was revealed by Stalin at the Fourth Conference of the Central Committee of the Russian Communist Party with the Responsible Workers of the National Republics and Regions, June 9–12, 1923. His instructions also contained a warning:

> A Communist in the borderlands must keep in mind that he is a Communist; therefore, in his activities he must adapt himself to local conditions, making necessary concessions to the local nationalists who want to and could work loyally within the limits of the Soviet system. This does not exclude, but, on the contrary, presupposes a systematic ideological struggle for the principles of Marxism and for a real internationalism, and against a deviation towards nationalism. Only in such a way will it be possible to eliminate local nationalism and bring to the side of the Soviets a wide stratum of the local population.[9]

The Belorussian nationalists, however, many of whom were already members of the Party, were not afraid of being eliminated in an ideological struggle with the Moscow Communists, and eagerly continued their work of reconstructing the republic.

The era of concessions to Belorussian culture and education impressed Belorussian nationalists abroad. Even the members of the government-in-exile of the Belorussian National Republic, who viewed the Bolshevik system of government with complete hostility, were tempted by the notion that the BSSR could, by intensified cultural reassertion, transform itself into a truly democratic state.[10] The government in Minsk, for its part, was eager to impress its old opponents abroad and to persuade them to return. For this reason, in the winter of 1924, Zmitrok Zhylunovich, a well-known Belorussian political and national leader during the formation of the BSSR, went to Prague to negotiate with the leaders of the BNR.[11]

These leaders, and Belorussian national leaders generally, were

---

[9] Iosif Stalin, *Sochineniia*, 1st ed. (Moscow, 1952), 5:294.

[10] Vladimir I. Seduro, "Belorussian Culture and Totalitarianism," *Proceedings of the Conference of the Institute for the Study of the History and Culture of the USSR* (New York, 20–22 March 1953), p. 85.

[11] Nicholas P. Vakar, *Belorussia: The Making of a Nation* (Cambridge, Mass., 1956), p. 144.

much displeased that the All-Union Constitution of 1924 had retained for the All-Union center such important commissariats as the army, foreign affairs, post and telegraph, and transport.[12] It was difficult for them to accept such extensive control by the central government over the Union republics. Nevertheless, other aspects of Soviet policy eventually persuaded them to accept a reconciliation with the Communists. The idealistic basis of their conversion was persuasively described by Aleksandr Tsvikevich, a former premier of the BNR, in his article, "The Berlin Conference," published in 1926:

> In the Soviet Union a unity of the working class has been consolidated so that its supreme authority is not Moscow and not the Russian people but the class of workers and peasants of all those nationalities who joined this union. The class of workers and peasants represents a power which stands above the Soviet Union and in this power every nation of the Soviet Union identifies itself. The principle of the Soviet State does not know the strong or the weak. It knows only the laboring people.[13]

Many other members of the BNR apparently felt the same way. Tsvikevich, for instance, wrote that "it looks as if all of us felt that there in the East, including Soviet Belorussia, together with tremendous destruction, in a fog of the bloody struggle, the real truth is shining through."[14]

After meeting with the Soviet representatives in Prague, Vatslau Lastouski, prime minister of the BNR government-in-exile, called a conference of his cabinet in Berlin, October 12–16, 1925, to decide whether they should continue their activities or give them up, that is, surrender their authority to the government in Minsk. The "result of this conference was the liquidation of the government of the BNR and the recognition of Minsk as the only center of the national and state regeneration of Belorussia."[15]

After the Berlin conference, such political and cultural Belorussian leaders as Lastouski, Tsvikevich, V. Zhylka, M. Horetski, Frantsishak Aliakhnovich, and several others returned to Minsk,[16] where they were received with honor and given positions in the educational and cultural branches of the government. As a further to-

[12] A. Tsvikevich, "Berlinskaia Konferentsyia," *Polymia*, no. 4 (1926): 91.
[13] Ibid., pp. 91–92.
[14] Ibid., p. 87.
[15] Ibid., p. 83.
[16] Seduro, "Belorussian Culture," p. 85.

ken of its magnanimity, Moscow secured the release of leaders of the Belorussian national movement from Polish jails and concentration camps.[17] Among them were the former Belorussian deputies to the Polish Sejm.[18] Thus, by the end of 1925, all the leaders of the Belorussian national movement abroad had given up their active opposition to the Bolsheviks and were ready to collaborate with them in the development of Belorussian national culture.

Immediately after the Civil War, cultural and educational establishments, including schools in the Belorussian language, began to appear. However, an active and planned Belorussification began only when the Second Session of the Central Executive Committee of the BSSR, on July 15, 1924, drew up a plan of practical measures for carrying out the national policy in general, and Belorussification in particular.[19] Among other things, this plan stipulated that all administrative, cultural, and educational institutions should use Belorussian in their offices as the official language of the republic.[20] Generally, under "Belorussification," in a broad interpretation of this word, the following aims should be understood:

1) Introduction of the Belorussian language in the elementary, secondary, and advanced schools.

2) Introduction of Belorussian as an official language in the Party, soviet, trade union, cooperative, and other organizations of the BSSR.

3) Use of the Belorussian language by all town and village populations.

With no objection from Moscow, the Communist Party supported these aims. A plenum of the Central Committee of the Belorussian Communist Party in July 1924 approved a program defining the Party's national policy. This program emphasized that Belorussian was to be spoken by all citizens. The Communists, it was said, must set the example.[21]

Vilhelm Knorin, First Secretary of the Belorussian Communist

[17] *Interpeliatsyi Belaruskikh Paslou u Pol'ski Sejm, 1922–1926: zbornik dokumentau ad panskikh hvaltakh, katavan'niakh i zdzekakh nad sialianami i rabochymi u Zakhodniai Belarusi* (Minsk, 1927), pp. 337–82.

[18] Vakar, *Belorussia*, p. 145.

[19] *Prakticheskoe razreshenie natsional'nogo voprosa v Belorusskoi Sovetskoi Sotsialisticheskoi Respublike* (Minsk, 1927), 2:12.

[20] H. Niamiha, "Education in Belorussia before the Rout of 'National Democracy,' 1917–1930," *Belorussian Review*, no. 1 (1955): 45.

[21] U. Hlybinny, *Dolia Belaruskai kul'tury pad Savetami: dosledy i matar'ialy*, ser. 2, no. 68 (Munich, 1958): 20.

Party during the NEP period, even identified Belorussification as one aspect of the revolutionary mission. In 1928 he commented, "Inasmuch as the Socialist Revolution caught the Belorussian Republic in a period of incomplete bourgeois-democratic renaissance, and inasmuch as the national-liberating problem of this period had not been accomplished, it is the task of the proletariat to develop to the fullest extent all truly revolutionary-democratic aspects of the renaissance."[22]

With the return of the Belorussian cultural and political leaders from abroad in 1925, progress in Belorussification was accelerated; by 1927, it was already completed in several of the highest institutions of the government. The extent of official use of the Belorussian language by early 1927 is shown in Table Ten. The success of Belorussification in the lower administrative institutions was even greater, because the proportion of native Belorussians there was somewhat higher.[23]

TABLE TEN

EXTENT OF BELORUSSIFICATION IN THE BELORUSSIAN GOVERNMENT BY FEBRUARY 1, 1927

Governmental Institution	Percent of Belorussification
Central Executive Committee (Ts.I.K.)	100
Council of People's Commissars	100
Commissariat of Education	100
Commissariat of Agriculture	50
Commissariat of Internal Affairs	30
All other commissariats	30–50

Source: Aleksandr Charviakou, *Za Savetskuiu Belarus'* (Minsk, 1927), p. 73.

A great deal was also done toward the Belorussification of army units from Belorussia, which was now obliged to contribute troops to the Red Army. A military school had been opened in Minsk to prepare commanders for these units, and by 1927 a Belorussian infantry division had been formed,[24] with formation of other divisions

[22] Vilhelm G. Knorin, "Ab rashaiuchykh 'drobiaziakh' u vialikim pytan'ni," *As'veta*, no. 3 (1928). Knorin compares the Belorussian national renaissance in 1917 to the Czechoslovak renaissance in 1848–1849.
[23] Ibid., p. 73.
[24] Ibid., p. 74.

TABLE ELEVEN

DEVELOPMENT OF SCHOOLS IN THE BSSR, 1924–1928

Type of School	Year	Total Number of Schools	% of Increase
Public (four years)	1924–1925	3,774	—
	1927–1928	5,163	36.8
Seven-year	1924–1925	253	—
	1927–1928	308	21.7

Source: Iu Erafeiau, "Suprats' vialikadziarzhaunaha shavinizmu u kul'turnym budaunitstve," *Kamunistychnae vykhavan'ne*, no. 5 (1931):9.

under way. The Revolutionary Military Council (Revvoensovet) of the USSR, in response to a petition of the Belorussian government, on October 20, 1926, renamed the Western Military Region the Belorussian Military Region,[25] since it was composed mainly of the territory of the BSSR.

The renaissance in Belorussian cultural development under the New Economic Policy had a great effect on education. Before World War I, Russia was backward in education. In European Russia in 1897, only 299 out of every 1,000 persons of all ages were literate.[26] During the years of war and revolution, many schools in Belorussia were destroyed. In reestablishing an educational system, the republic thus faced a very difficult problem. But the men inspired by the Belorussian national revival were devoted to education and were spiritually prepared to lay the foundations for universal education. Among these men were Professor Usevalad Ihnatouski, first people's commissar of education; Anton Balitski, deputy and later successor to Ihnatouski;[27] Iazep Liosik, a distinguished linguist; Professor Mitrafan Dounar-Zapolski; Aleksandr Krutalevich, a mathema-

[25] *Ocherki po istorii gosudarstva i prava Belorusskoi SSR* (Minsk, 1958), p. 137. The Revvoensovet was formed on 6 September 1918 as the central military executive organ of the Russian Soviet Republic. It served as an embodiment of collective control over the Military and Naval Commissariat, which was renamed the Commissariat of Defense on 15 March 1934; the Revvoensovet was then abolished. John Erickson, *The Soviet High Command: A Military-Political History, 1918–1941* (New York, 1962), pp. 36, 366; Dimitri Fedotoff White, *The Growth of the Red Army* (Princeton, 1944), p. 358.

[26] *Sluzhachyia dziarzhaunaha i kaaperatyunaha apparatu BSSR* (Minsk, 1930), p. xxxi.

[27] In 1922, when the Institute of Belorussian Culture was organized, Ihnatouski was appointed president and Balitski replaced him as commissar of education.

TABLE TWELVE

GROWTH OF SCHOOLS FOR ADULTS IN THE BSSR, 1925–1928

Type of School	1925–1926		1926–1927		1927–1928	
	Number of Schools	Number of Students	Number of Schools	Number of Students	Number of Schools	Number of Students
For liquidation of illiteracy	1,034	26,267	1,297	40,776	1,484	45,723
For general adult education	59	9,218	95	12,276	161	13,437

Source: *Belorusskaia SSR v tsifrakh: k desiatiletiiu sushchestvovaniia BSSR, 1919–1929* (Minsk, 1929), p. 75.

tician, Efim Karski, an internationally known linguist; and many others.[28] In 1925 they were joined by many other intellectuals returning from abroad.

Such rapid progress was made in education that compulsory elementary education (four years) was introduced in the republic by a decree of the Belorussian Central Executive Committee and the Council of People's Commissars on April 7, 1926.[29] The expansion of educational facilities is shown in Table Eleven. The new schools were built rapidly, not only because of the state's interest in education, but because of the people's interest, as well. Many people in rural areas labored without pay to build these schools.[30]

The government also undertook to stamp out illiteracy among adults. A session of the Central Executive Committee in 1923 decided to eliminate illiteracy among the adult population before the tenth anniversary of the October Revolution.[31] In order to achieve this, evening schools for illiterate and semiliterate adults were organized throughout the republic.[32] The growth of such schools can be seen in Table Twelve. In three years, 1926–1929, 300,000 adults of the Belorussian SSR became literate.[33]

There was also an expansion of professional-technical schools.

[28] Niamiha, "Education in Belorussia," p. 41.
[29] *Ocherki po istorii*, p. 133.
[30] Z. Stiapura, "Shto zroblena u haline useahul'naha navuchan'nia u BSSR za 1926–1927 navuchal'ny hod?" *As'veta*, nos. 5–6 (1927): 7.
[31] *Ocherki po istorii*, p. 108.
[32] *Istoriia BSSR*, 2d ed. (Minsk, 1961), 2:225.
[33] *Ocherki po istorii*, p. 133.

These schools were built to fill the need for qualified leaders in industry, agriculture, medicine, education, and other fields. They were known variously as professional schools (*tekhnikumy*), vocational schools (*profshkoly*), factory workshop schools (*fabzauchi*), school workshops (*uchebnye masterskie*), trade union courses (*profkursy*), and workers' high schools (*rabfaki*).[34] The increase in these facilities is shown in Table Thirteen.

TABLE THIRTEEN

DEVELOPMENT OF PROFESSIONAL EDUCATION IN THE BSSR, 1925–1928

Type of School	1925–1926		1926–1927		1927–1928	
	Number of Schools	Number of Students	Number of Schools	Number of Students	Number of Schools	Number of Students
Professional schools	29	4,906	32	5,151	30	5,276
Vocational schools	36	3,353	30	3,286	34	3,922
Factory workshops	7	441	15	1,088	13	1,009
School workshops	7	516	7	561	8	616
Trade union courses	15	1,331	6	525	14	1,276
Workers' high schools	3	882	4	845	6	1,018

Sources: *As'veta*, no. 8 (1928): 25; *Belorusskaia SSR v tsifrakh* (Minsk, 1929), p. 74.

Before the Revolution, there was no institution of higher learning in the territory of Belorussia. The Belorussian State University was founded in 1921 to serve as a center for the development of higher education in the republic and for the preparation of experts in education, state administration, medicine, and other fields. Despite

[34] The most prominent of these schools were the *tekhnikumy*. They provided a general education on the secondary school or junior college level, depending on the type of school. In addition, they provided professional education in technical fields, agriculture, medicine, education (elementary school teachers), and other fields. Students with a seven-year education were admitted. The course of study was from three to five years, depending on the specialization provided.

material difficulties, such as a lack of buildings and scientific equipment, the university developed into a noteworthy institution of higher learning before its fifth anniversary. In those five years, it graduated 273 high school teachers, 130 lawyers, 125 economists, and 170 medical doctors. At the beginning of the 1927–1928 academic year there were already 2,672 students at the university.[35]

By the time the New Economic Policy was terminated in 1928, Belorussia had four institutions of higher learning: the Belorussian State University in Minsk, the Communist University in Minsk, the Belorussian Agricultural Academy in Gorki, and the State Veterinary Institute in Vitebsk. In 1928 they had a combined total of 504 professors and 4,632 students.[36] In addition, there was a Belorussian Academy of Sciences in Minsk.[37] Although such facilities were inadequate for a country with a population of five million, the fact that seven years earlier none of these institutions had existed shows that the republic had made great progress in higher education during the NEP period. These achievements served as the basis for a later, more intensive expansion. In 1931, compulsory seven-year education was introduced in the towns and the workers' settlements.[38] In that year, Belorussia had 32 institutions of higher learning, with 11,000 students, and 104 professional schools, with 20,000 students.[39]

About one-fifth of the total Belorussian population during that period was composed of other nationalities. In accordance with current Soviet policy these minority nationalities were entitled to have their own national schools, and so they did, as shown in Table Fourteen. As can be seen by comparison with Table Two, the percentage of elementary schools for the minorities was a little below the percentage of the minority nationalities in the population of the republic. This was so mainly because in the villages and small towns the minority groups were too small to justify having their own schools.

Departments to prepare teachers for the Jewish and Polish secondary schools were established at the Belorussian State University.

[35] Hlybinny, *Dolia Belaruskai Kul'tury*, p. 25.
[36] *Belorusskaia SSR v tsifrakh: k desiatiletiiu sushchestvovaniia BSSR, 1919–1929* (Minsk, 1929), pp. 70, 99.
[37] *Prakticheskoe razreshenie natsional'nogo voprosa*, p. 76. In July 1927, the Belorussian Council of People's Commissars approved a new code of the Institute of Belorussian Culture, identical with the code of the All-Union Academy of Sciences.
[38] *Ocherki po istorii*, p. 133.
[39] *Itogi vypolneniia pervogo piatiletnego plana razvitiia narodnogo khoziaistva BSSR* (Minsk, 1933), p. 84.

TABLE FOURTEEN

NATIONAL COMPOSITION OF SCHOOLS IN THE BSSR IN THE
1926–1927 SCHOOL YEAR

Type of School	Belorussian		Jewish		Russian		Polish		Other	
	Number	%	Number	%	Number	%	Number	%	Number	%
Elementary (four years)	4,190	85.3	147	3.0	407	8.4	125	2.6	31	0.7
Seven-year	197	66.6	53	18.2	32	11.0	11	3.8	1	0.4

Source: *Belorusskaia kul'tura*, no. 1 (1928):14.

In addition, there were one Polish and three Jewish teachers' schools (pedagogical tekhnikums) preparing teachers for Jewish and Polish elementary schools.[40] In other ways, Jews and Poles were given opportunities to develop their national cultures, such as special sections in the Institute of Belorussian Culture which conducted scientific research in the culture, language, literature, and history of these people.[41]

At the beginning of the NEP period, preference in education was given to the children of workers and poor peasants. However, as time passed and the material conditions of the people improved, these preferences gradually became unimportant. People of all classes, except "enemies of the Socialist state," were given opportunities for education.[42] The social origin of students in the higher educational institutions and professional schools between 1926 and 1929 is shown in Table Fifteen. As can be seen, the percentage of workers' children was gradually growing in all educational institutions except the vocational schools, while the percentage of peasants' children in all but the vocational schools was gradually declining. It should be remembered, of course, that during this period the working class was growing and the number of farmers was decreasing.

The Belorussian language served as the most important foundation for the development of Belorussian culture during this period, and most of the newspapers, magazines, and books were published in this language.[43] Besides older Belorussian poets and writers, such

---

[40] *As'veta*, no. 8 (1928): 10.
[41] Aleksandr Charviakou, *Za Savetskuiu Belarus'* (Minsk, 1927), p. 81.
[42] In the late years of the NEP, preference was given to students with better academic records over those with proletarian social background.

TABLE FIFTEEN

SOCIAL ORIGINS OF STUDENTS IN BELORUSSIAN HIGHER AND
PROFESSIONAL SCHOOLS IN THE 1926–1929 SCHOOL YEARS

Vocational Schools		Workers' High Schools		Technical Schools		Higher Educational Institutions	
Workers	Peasants	Workers	Peasants	Workers	Peasants	Workers	Peasants
1926–1927							
29.3	4.3	41.7	58.3	14.8	49.6	14.6	49.9
1927–1928							
24.7	46.3	59.9	26.6	22.5	14.2	15.8	44.5
1928–1929							
28.6	47.5	66.2	30.9	33.1	47.0	27.0	43.5

Source: *As'veta*, no. 8 (1928): 44.

as Ianka Kupala, Iakub Kolas, and Zmitrok Zhylunovich, there appeared many young poets and writers who had received their education after the October Revolution. There were several literary associations, such as Polymia (Flame), BAPP (The Belorussian Association of Proletarian Writers), Maladniak (Undergrowth), Uzvyshsha (Elevation), and others.[44] Maladniak alone had a membership of 500 writers and poets.[45]

The senior Belorussian poets and writers, such as Kupala and Kolas, who had been critical of the October Revolution and Bolshevik violence, changed their views during the period of the New Economic Policy. Kolas finished writing his long and brilliant poem "Novaia ziamlia" (The New Land) before the renaissance of the Belorussian national and cultural development had reached its summit.[46] The theme of the poem was the peasants' desire to have land and to live on the farmstead instead of in the village. It was just what they were now achieving, and for this reason the poem was hailed as a prophecy of the renaissance which promised to restore human dignity to the Belorussian people.[47]

---

[43] Ibid., p. 10. In Minsk in 1923, four newspapers and seventeen journals were published in Belorussian.
[44] Ibid., p. 11; Seduro, "Belorussian Culture," p. 85.
[45] Seduro, "Belorussian Culture," p. 85.
[46] "The New Land" was published in 1922, and the renaissance of the Belorussian national and cultural development reached its summit in 1926–1927.
[47] It has to be pointed out that during the period of the NEP the clergymen and all those who were considered to belong to the "exploiting class"

Ianka Kupala kept silent for several years after the Civil War. He condemned the October Revolution when it happened, and now doubted that the Bolsheviks could bring liberty and freedom to his native land. However, by 1926 his earlier doubts were yielding to hope for a better future. He broke his silence, and in his poem "There Is, You See," published in 1926, he proudly declared his love of freedom and his and the Belorussian people's readiness to fight for it. The following passages illustrate the poet's acknowledgment of freedom during the years of the renaissance:

> There are still, you see, in me songs,
> Full of hope and life—
> However constricted the world may be for them
> They will burst into the world from their non-existence
> . . . .
> There is still, you see, in me the faith
> In my free native people,
> Which in need will come out
> With an axe in the drive for freedom.[48]

From a wider viewpoint, the peaceful absorption of diverse nationality groups into the Soviet Union was a major triumph of Communist policy. In Belorussia the effect of the NEP was one of great improvement. There was a sense of freedom which, if in the main illusory, had nonetheless sufficient substance to permit self-respect, national enterprise, and hope for the future. The Belorussian nationalists and the Communists had been able to unite in a common cause—the peaceful reconstruction of their war-battered country. Within the concept of the NEP, nationalism and communism were compatible, and under the NEP aegis the Belorussians were able to enter into a pursuit of their national identity. If the locus of power remained in Moscow, it was only vaguely so; during this period the relationship between the Russian and the Belorussian people was friendly and cooperative, in sharp contrast to the subjugation and suppression of the tsarist era. Harsher times, however, were ahead.

---

before the October Revolution were oppressed but were not so persecuted as after termination of the NEP.

[48] Quoted in Anthony Adamovich, *Opposition to Sovietization in Belorussian Literature, 1917–1957* (Munich, 1958), p. 78.

7.

Collectivization & Industrialization

> *Every intelligent Socialist will agree that Socialism cannot be imposed upon the peasantry by force, and we can rely only on the force of example and on the mass of the peasants' assimilating living experience.*
>
> Lenin, 1918[1]

Great diversity of opinion existed among the leaders of the Communist Party of Russia with regard to the New Economic Policy when it was introduced. The old Bolshevik leaders, such as Grigory Zinoviev and Lev Kamenev, who later became known as the leaders of the Left-Wing Opposition, considered the NEP a great and dangerous concession to the peasantry and to private enterprise generally. Other Bolshevik leaders, such as Nikolai Bukharin and Aleksei Rykov, later known as the leaders of the Right-Wing Opposition, accepted the NEP as the policy of the Soviet government for many years to come.

It is difficult to define Stalin's view on the NEP when it was introduced at Lenin's insistence. During Lenin's lifetime, Stalin seldom dared to disagree with him. But during the first three years after Lenin's death, when Stalin was struggling for power against the Zinoviev-Trotsky bloc, he continued or pretended to act as a firm supporter of the NEP. He adopted this attitude in order to appear as a friend of the peasants generally and even of the more prosperous peasants, who were considered anti-Socialist elements and were classified as kulaks. For this reason some members of the Left-Wing called him "the Tsar of the Kulaks."[2]

However, as was revealed later, Stalin turned to the support of the peasants in order to gain the support of Bukharin, Rykov, and other Bolsheviks in his struggle against the Left Opposition. For the same reason, he wanted the support of the Union republics; he therefore accused the "Lefts" of a wrong attitude toward the bourgeois-democratic and loyal elements in the republics.[3]

Stalin's real aim was to eliminate both oppositions within the Communist Party. To accomplish this, he adopted the policy of "divide and conquer." Having eliminated the Left Opposition in 1927, he moved then against the Right Opposition—his last opponents. The stage for conflict was set by disagreements over the policy toward the peasants and the method and tempo of industrialization. Realizing the strength of the Right, Stalin took measures against it very carefully. To weaken its power, he began removing from high governmental positions in the Union republics those national leaders who supported the policy of the Right. Thus, in June 1927, Iazep Adamovich, chairman of the Council of People's Commissars of the Belorussian SSR, was removed from his post[4] on Stalin's order, because he was in sympathy with the New Economic Policy and "opposed Moscow's new colonial methods of administration toward the Belorussian SSR."[5] The strength of the Right Opposition in Belorussia was weakened further when, on August 31, 1929, Anton Balitski, commissar of education, and on September 14, 1929, Zmitrok Pryshchepau, commissar of agriculture, were removed from their posts.[6] Soon after, they were arrested by the GPU (State Political Administration—the Communist security po-

[1] Vladimir Lenin, "Doklad o deiatel'nosti Soveta Narodnykh Kommissarov 24 ianvaria 1918 goda" [A Report on the Activities of the Council of People's Commissars on 24 January 1918], *Sochineniia*, 3d ed. (Moscow, 1929–1939), 22:207.

[2] Boris Souvarine, *Stalin: A Critical Survey of Bolshevism* (New York, 1939), p. 438. The Zinoviev-Trotsky bloc advocated an immediate offensive against the kulaks. Stalin, however, considered their policy a "dangerous adventure." See Stalin, *Sochineniia*, 1st ed. (Moscow, 1946–1952), 12:167.

[3] Stalin, *Sochineniia*, 5:310.

[4] *Zbor zakonau i zahadau robocha-sialianskaha uradu Belaruskai Satsyialistychnai Savetskai Respubliki*, no. 22 (Minsk, 1927): 247–48.

[5] Eugen von Engelhardt, *Weissruthenien: Volk und Land* (Berlin, 1943), p. 175.

[6] U.S., Congress, House, Select Committee on Communist Aggression, *Communist Takeover and Occupation of Byelorussia* (Washington, D.C., 1955), p. 14.

lice).[7] The same practice was followed in the other Union republics.

Stalin's next and final move on the road to eliminating the Right Opposition was directed against its leader, Nikolai Bukharin. A plenary meeting of the Central Committee, which assembled November 10–17, 1929, and which was dominated by the Stalinists, "excluded Bukharin, as an ideologist of the Right-Wing Opposition," from the Politburo of the Central Committee of the All-Union Communist Party.[8] This spelled the defeat of the Right Opposition, and the former terrorist became a dictator.[9]

Many early Bolsheviks who had initiated the Revolution and who later fought for a form of Socialist democracy opposed Stalin openly, but they failed and were eliminated from power. Most of those who survived were men of lesser importance who did not try to oppose Stalin. Instead, together with the new men whom Stalin brought into the administration, these state and party bureaucrats flattered Stalin and encouraged his ambitions. The Soviet press began calling him *"Velikii vozhd' partii"* (great leader of the Party). From that time on, Stalin was de facto ruler of the Soviet Union, even though his official position was General Secretary of the Party's Central Committee, not head of the government.

After eliminating the Right Wing in the fall of 1929, the ambitious dictator relentlessly pushed through a program of industrialization and collectivization of agriculture which caused more casualties than the February and October revolutions together. "The cruelest offensive made itself felt first in the country district."[10] Collectivization, like every other obligation imposed on the people of the Soviet Union, was supposedly a "voluntary" act, in direct contradiction to the state plan. The plan, adopted by the All-Union Central Committee on January 5, 1930, divided the regions of the USSR into three groups and set dates for completion of collectivization for each group.[11]

---

[7] H. Niamiha, "Education in Belorussia before the Rout of 'National Democracy,' 1917–1930," *Belorussian Review*, no. 1 (1955): 620; Englehardt, *Weissruthenien*, p. 175. A decree of February 1922 abolished the Cheka, the first Communist Security Police, but established in its place the GPU.

[8] *Kommunisticheskaia Partiia Sovetskogo Soiuza v rezoliutsiiakh i resheniiakh s"ezdov, konferentsii i plenumov Ts.K., 1898–1960*, 7th ed. (Moscow, 1954–1960), 2:489.

[9] Yves Delbars, *The Real Stalin* (London, 1953), pp. 52–54.

[10] Souvarine, *Stalin*, p. 521.

[11] *Kommunisticheskaia Partiia Sovetskogo Soiuza*, 2:665.

The first group included the principal grain-growing areas.[12] Collectivization there, according to this plan, should be completed in the fall of 1930, or, at the latest, by the spring of 1931. Collectivization in the secondary grain-growing regions should be basically completed in the fall of 1931, or by the spring of 1932. Finally, in the third group (the non-grain-growing regions), the process of collectivization could be extended to 1933.[13] The Belorussian SSR, according to this plan, was included in the third group.[14]

Under the Stalinist system, the Union republics had to do their best to fulfill the plans adopted by the Central Committee and the government authorities. The leaders in the Union republics, depending on their progress in fulfilling these plans, were rewarded or punished. With this in mind, the Central Committee of the Belorussian Communist Party decided, on January 8, 1930, to complete the collectivization of the individual farms before the end of 1931, two years earlier than originally scheduled.[15]

Party decisions for forced collectivization directly contradicted Lenin's ideas on the voluntary building of collective farms. In his "Report Delivered to the Tenth Congress of the Central Committee of the RKP (b)" on March 15, 1921, Lenin said, "Only a material base, technique, the employment of tractors and machinery in agriculture on a mass scale, and electrification on a mass scale, can solve the problem of the small farmer and make his whole mentality sound, so to speak."[16] Lenin's views were based on the principle that industry should be built first so that it could adequately supply the collective farms with the necessary farm machinery. In the meantime, the peasants should be better educated. Krynitski, secretary of the Belorussian Central Committee, attempted to present Lenin's opinion on collectivization at the sixteenth conference of the Party in April 1929.[17] But the majority at the conference were supporters of Stalin.

As previously noted, collectivization of agriculture in the BSSR progressed very slowly. Until the Fifteenth Party Congress in December 1927, which adopted the policy of industrialization and

[12] The Lower and Middle Volga and the North Caucasus.
[13] *Kommunisticheskaia Partiia Sovetskogo Soiuza*, 2:665.
[14] *Ocherki po istorii gosudarstva i prava Belorusskoi SSR* (Minsk, 1958), p. 117.
[15] *Istoriia BSSR*, 2d ed. (Minsk, 1961), 2:270.
[16] Lenin, *Sochineniia*, 3d ed., 26:239.
[17] *Shestnadtsataia konferentsiia VKP(b): stenograficheskii otchet* (Moscow, 1962), p. 160.

collectivization, there had been almost no progress at all. In 1924, there were 378 collective farms; in 1925, 414; in 1926, 380; and in 1927, 416.[18] The rate of collectivization continued to be slow during the first two years after the Fifteenth Party Congress, until the Party began to force the pace. Table Sixteen indicates that rapid and forced collectivization began in the fall of 1929, that is, after the November plenary meeting of the Central Committee.[19] Between October 1, 1929, and January 1, 1930, the percentage of collectivized

TABLE SIXTEEN

PROGRESS OF COLLECTIVIZATION IN THE BSSR FROM THE FIFTEENTH PARTY CONGRESS TO THE BEGINNING OF FORCED COLLECTIVIZATION

Date	Number of Collective Farms	Number of Collectivized Individual Farms	% of Individual Farms Collectivized
October 1, 1928	994	8,499	1.1
June 1, 1929	1,013	10,644	1.4
October 1, 1929	1,713	25,830	3.8
January 1, 1930	2,414	165,300	20.9

Source: *Istoriia BSSR*, 2d ed. (Minsk, 1961), 2:269.

individual farms grew from 3.8 to 20.9 percent. Forced collectivization was intensified after the decisions of the All-Union and Belorussian central committees in January 1930. By the end of that month, the proportion of collectivized farms reached 38.3 percent.[20]

The peasants offered firm resistance to both "voluntary" (in theory) and "forced" (in practice) collectivization. The more prosperous peasants, the kulaks, were made scapegoats.[21] By a February

[18] *Kalhasy BSSR: papiaredniia vyniki absledvan'niau kalhasau u 1928 i 1929 hadokh* (Minsk, 1929), p. 8.

[19] At this meeting the Right Opposition was defeated and forced collectivization began.

[20] *Istoriia BSSR*, 2:270.

[21] There were no landlords left in the Belorussian SSR after the October Revolution. After the Civil War, their land was partitioned among the poor peasants. Differences in prosperity among the individual peasants during the NEP period were caused not so much by the amount of land the peasants had as by their relative industry and skill in farming. Generally the more prosperous peasants, those who produced more than they needed for their own use, were referred to as kulaks. Officially, peasants who employed hired labor

1, 1930, decree of the Central Executive Committee and of the Sovnarkom of the USSR, the property of the kulaks was confiscated and transferred to the collective farms.[22]

Most of the native soviet officials in Belorussia were in sympathy with the kulaks[23] and regarded them as the hardest-working farmers. Under the New Economic Policy the Bolsheviks themselves had encouraged the peasants to work on modernization of their farms and had rewarded the best farmers.[24] Now they were treating them as the worst criminals. Why? The kulaks did not want to join the collective farms, it was true, but the government had declared that it was building the collective farms on a voluntary basis. Nevertheless, the middle-class peasants were forced to join the collective farms under "the threat of being accused as kulaks, and . . . deprived of their citizenship."[25] There were many cases of "exceptionally rude, hideous, criminal treatment of the people by local officials."[26] Those sent by the Party from the towns to "persuade" the peasants to join the collective farms especially distinguished themselves by their cruelty, and middle-class Belorussian peasants were arrested and exiled for refusing to comply.[27]

On March 2, 1930, in response to a number of alarming signals concerning collectivization, and by a decision of the All-Union Central Committee of the Party, Stalin's article "Dizzy from Success" was published.[28] In it Stalin wrote:

> It is a fact that, by February 20 of this year, fifty percent of the peasant farms throughout the USSR had been collectivized. This means that by February 20, 1930, we had overfulfilled the five-year plan of collectivization by more than one hundred percent. . . . But successes have their seamy side, especially when they are attained with comparative "ease"—"too easily" so to speak. Such successes sometimes induce a spirit of vanity and conceit: "We achieve anything!" . . . The successes of our collective-farm policy are due,

---

during sixty or more working days per year before forced collectivization were classified as kulaks. Some of these "kulaks" were not necessarily prosperous, since the definition would also apply in the case of a peasant who was sick or for another reason was forced to use outside help.

[22] *Ocherki po istorii*, pp. 128–29.
[23] Interview with a former Belorussian collective farmer.
[24] Merle Fainsod, *Smolensk under Soviet Rule* (Cambridge, Mass., 1958), p. 250; interview with a former Belorussian collective farmer.
[25] *Kommunisticheskaia Partiia Sovetskogo Soiuza*, 2:699.
[26] Ibid.
[27] *Ocherki po istorii*, p. 126.
[28] *Istoriia Vsesoiuznoi Kommunisticheskoi Partii (bol'shevikov): kratkii kurs* (Moscow, 1938), pp. 294–95.

among other things, to the fact that it rests on the voluntary character of the collective-farm movement and on taking into account the diversity of conditions in the various regions of the USSR. The collective farms must not be established by force.[29]

The publication of Stalin's article was followed by a decision of the Central Committee on March 14 "concerning the distortion of the party line in the collective farm movement." Two paragraphs of this decision are of particular interest in relation to Stalin's divorce of theory and practice.

> 1) The practice of forced methods of collectivization, observed in many instances, should be ended. At the same time, it is necessary to continue further unyielding work to attract the peasants into the collective farms.
>
> . . . .
>
> 7) To stop categorically the practice of closing the churches in an administrative manner, fictitiously covered by the "voluntary desire of the people". . . . Those guilty of mocking tricks with regard to the religious feelings of the people must be severely punished.[30]

Point one is an excellent example of Party "doublethink." "Should be ended" is contradicted immediately; obviously "further unyielding work" among the reluctant peasants could mean only a continued exercise of force. Point seven is equally meaningless, for there was no attempt to stop the persecution of the clergy and the closing of the churches. In no instance in Belorussia did the Soviet authorities punish those guilty of "mocking tricks with regard to the religious feelings of the people." "Hundreds of churches, Orthodox and Catholic, and synagogues were barbarously ruined."[31] By the middle of the 1930s, nearly all organized religious activities in Belorussia had been liquidated. "Most of the closed churches were turned into clubs, theatres, anti-religious museums, storage rooms, etc.; some were demolished."[32]

Publication of Stalin's article was followed by disintegration of the collective farms in Belorussia.[33] The peasants, willing to clutch

[29] Stalin, *Sochineniia*, 12:191–93.
[30] *Kommunisticheskaia Partiia Sovetskogo Soiuza*, 2:670–71.
[31] U.S., Congress, House, *Communist Takeover and Occupation of Byelorussia*, p. 17.
[32] *Belorussia*, Subcontractor's Monograph HRAF–19 (New Haven, Conn., 1954–1955), p. 196.
[33] Interview with a Belorussian writer.

at any straw of hope, chose to accept Stalin's article as a condemnation of those who had forced the people onto the collective farms. In this they were thoroughly mistaken. Stalin was aware, beyond question, that collectivization was being forced upon an unwilling peasantry. It was convenient, however, to blame local officials for violating the "voluntary" principle of collectivization and thus to preserve an appearance of the innocence of the central government. Stalin himself would hardly have lifted a finger to halt this brutal process, nor did he do so.

The peasants, unaware of Stalin's duplicity, began to leave the collective farms, thinking that the local officials who had terrorized them could now do nothing against them. They were speedily disillusioned. After many of the collective farms were broken up, GPU investigators appeared in the villages and started asking questions about the deserters. Mass prosecutions followed, designed to force the peasants back onto the collective farms.[34] The people spontaneously revolted in various districts of Belorussia. One of the more extensive uprisings took place in Beshankovichy district in March 1930. In response to persecution by the secret police, the village Zastaryn'ne in the Hankovichy Village Soviet revolted and was joined by the neighboring villages. The peasants, armed with axes, pitchforks, and hunting rifles, took control of the district center. Storming the building of the security police, they captured the chief of police and, as a measure of their fury, cut off his right hand with an ax.[35] This uprising was suppressed by the militia and security police units sent to Beshankovichy from the provincial center, Vitebsk. Vasil' Harkavy, leader of the uprising, and many others were executed. The other peasants who had taken part in this uprising were sent to concentration camps.[36]

The Party blamed the local soviets for the failure of collectivization. The village soviets, it was said, had not fulfilled their basic task in socialist reconstruction of agriculture, and thus had "failed to act as the organs of the dictatorship of the proletariat."[37] A joint plenary meeting of the Central Committee and the Central Control Commission of the All-Union Communist Party, in a resolution of December 21, 1930, made the following declaration: "In order to

[34] Iurka Stukalich, "Kvitneiuts' na ikh mahile viarhini," *Bats'kaushchyna*, no. 18 (1 May 1955): 1.
[35] Ibid.
[36] Ibid.
[37] *Istoriia Sovetskoi Konstitutsii v dokumentakh, 1917–1956* (Moscow, 1957), p. 615.

achieve a reorganization of the soviets, they should, in their work, learn to rely on the new activists of the masses and first of all on the shock-workers of the factories and the collective farms."[38] In accordance with this declaration, the chairmen and deputies of the village soviets which had failed to enforce collectivization were to be removed from office and new men were to be elected.[39] Instead, however, these "new men" were appointed by the Party.[40] As a result, there were increased numbers of industrial workers among the deputies of the village soviets in 1930–1931. During the same period, the proportion of workers among the chairmen of the village soviets increased from 7.3 to 19.5 percent and the proportion of Party members from 55.1 to 73.2 percent.[41] Among the chairmen of the village soviets were many Russian "shock-workers" who had been sent to Belorussia to complete collectivization.[42]

The ruthlessness of this browbeating of the local soviets calls to mind once again discrepancy, so frequently to be observed in Party affairs, between theory and practice. This same Party plenary meeting, with regard to the new elections, piously declared: "In electing the soviets, care should always be taken to carry out and further develop Lenin's policy of nationalities."[43] In practice, the Party was sending members from Russia to Belorussia and installing them in the chairmanships of the village soviets and in other key positions.[44] These Russian shock-workers were generally Party members,[45] and distinguished themselves by their cruelty. They neither knew nor wanted to know local conditions. Their only interest was to follow Moscow's orders to achieve total collectivization. Consequently, mass arrests and brutality were their usual procedures. At the meetings of the peasants, they emphasized repeatedly that "Moscow does not believe in tears," and their actions demon-

[38] *Kommunisticheskaia Partiia Sovetskogo Soiuza*, 3:91.
[39] *Istoriia Sovetskoi Konstitutsii*, p. 615.
[40] Interview with a Belorussian writer.
[41] *Istoriia BSSR*, 2:264.
[42] *Ocherki po istorii*, p. 124.
[43] *Kommunisticheskaia Partiia Sovetskogo Soiuza*, 3:90.
[44] The shock-workers were sent from the RSFSR to the Belorussian and the other Union republics temporarily. They were usually used as agitators in the crucial times of building the collective farms. However, some of them were temporarily appointed chairmen of the village soviets or as other officials in the local administration. These were the cases in which the local people occupying these positions had failed in collectivization. (Interview with a Belorussian writer.)
[45] *History of the Communist Party of the Soviet Union* (Moscow, 1960), p. 448.

strated this. By force, they did succeed in speeding up collectivization in Belorussia. This was a period when, by decision of the "*raitroika*," many individual farms were liquidated.[46] Soviet historians blandly acknowledge that the organization of collective farms in the BSSR was accomplished with "the help of the brotherly Russian Soviet Federated Socialist Republic."[47]

When Emil Ludwig, a prominent German author, interviewed Stalin on December 13, 1931, the rule of terror in the collectivization of farms was at its peak. Having this in mind, Ludwig questioned Stalin thus: "It seems to me that a considerable part of the population of the Soviet Union stands in fear and trepidation of the Soviet power, and the stability of the latter rests to a certain extent on that sense of fear. I should like to know what state of mind is produced in you personally by the realization that it is necessary to inspire fear in the interests of strengthening the regime."[48]

Stalin told Ludwig that he was mistaken in thinking the Soviet Union was ruled by terror. He added that "the Soviet government could not have stayed in power for fourteen years if it ruled by methods of intimidation and terrorism."[49] To which Ludwig replied, "But the Romanovs held on for 300 years."[50]

Two years later, Stalin openly admitted how he had built the collective farms. In this article "Work in the Village," published in 1933, he wrote: "There is not, nor has there ever been in the world, such a powerful and authoritative government as our Soviet government. There is not, nor has there ever been in the world, such a powerful and authoritative party as our Communist Party. No one prevents us, nor can anyone prevent us, from managing the affairs of the collective farms in a manner that suits the interests of the collective farms, the interests of the state."[51]

Despite Stalin's terrorism, Belorussia remained far behind the other Union republics in collectivization. On July 1, 1934, in the USSR as a whole, 71.4 percent of the individual farms were col-

---

[46] Fainsod, *Smolensk under Soviet Rule*, pp. 242, 247. The *raitroikas* were formed in March 1930. Their task was to direct the process of collectivization. They consisted of three top men of the district administration, the first secretary of the Party committee, the chairman of the soviet executive committee (ispolkom), and the head of the local GPU.
[47] *Ocherki po istorii*, p. 124.
[48] Quoted in Stalin, *Sochineniia*, 12:109.
[49] Ibid.
[50] Ibid., p. 110.
[51] Stalin, *Voprosy Leninizma*, 11th ed. (Moscow, 1947), p. 408.

lectivized, as against 55.1 percent in the BSSR.⁵² Agricultural collectivization in Belorussia was completed only in 1937, four years later than called for in the 1930 plan.⁵³ The Belorussian people suffered more than any other group in the USSR, except the Ukrainians, with whom they shared a common fate in resisting Stalin's policy in practice.⁵⁴ In Belorussia in 1927, 9 percent of the peasants were classified as kulaks,⁵⁵ and all kulaks were transported, together with their families, beyond the Urals to the Arctic regions.⁵⁶ Many middle-class peasants who refused to join the collective farms faced the same fate.⁵⁷ Their number can be estimated at about 3 to 6 percent of the total number of peasants. Thus, all together, about 12 to 15 percent of the Belorussian peasants were deported to concentration camps far removed from their homes.⁵⁸ How many of them survived? There has not as yet been anything about them in the Soviet press. Nor did Khrushchev blame Stalin for this crime in his 1956 "secret speech." The GPU records alone hold the secret of how many peasants, in addition to those transported to Siberia, were arrested, murdered, or executed.

When forced collectivization began, the Bolshevik agitators promised a "prosperous and happy life" in the collective farms after a short period of time. Events proved the opposite. The best peasants were "liquidated" and the management of the collective farms was entrusted to the poorest, who had been unable to handle their small individual farms. Consequently, from the very beginning, almost everything went wrong. As a result of bad and inefficient farming, and also of a resentful indifference, the food situation rapidly deteriorated. "By mid-1932, the food situation bordered on desperation."⁵⁹ The government, for its part, cared little or nothing about the food situation in the rural areas. The state officials, as a matter

---

⁵² *Istoriia BSSR*, 2:315; see also Stalin, *Sochineniia*, 13:323.
⁵³ *Istoriia BSSR*, 2:339.
⁵⁴ The Belorussian and Ukrainian republics bordered the "Western Capitalist World" and parts of their territories were included in Poland. Moscow was thus especially suspicious of espionage, diversion, etc., in these areas. This fitted Stalin's mentality. Therefore, collectivization was enforced more ruthlessly in these two republics than in the others.
⁵⁵ *Ocherki po istorii*, p. 121.
⁵⁶ Souvarine, *Stalin*, p. 522; Fainsod, *Smolensk under Soviet Rule*, p. 250.
⁵⁷ *Kommunisticheskaia Partiia Sovetskogo Soiuza*, 2:699.
⁵⁸ In 1929, when forced collectivization started, the population of the BSSR was a little over five million. The rural population made up about 75 percent of that number.
⁵⁹ Fainsod, *Smolensk under Soviet Rule*, p. 261.

of fact, were far more interested in fulfilling plans for delivery of agricultural products to the state. Most of all, the peasants who did not want to be collectivized suffered. The amount of produce which was supposed to be delivered to the state was quite large,[60] and peasants often could not fulfill their quotas, even if they delivered to the state all they produced. In this case, the "grain and potato requisitions" followed.[61] Little or nothing was left to the peasants.

Thus, the peasants, themselves producers of food, had to buy in order to eat. But the bread and other food items which were made of their plundered grain could not be bought in the state food stores because the food was rationed and the peasants did not have ration cards. This meant they had to buy on the black market. Between 1931 and 1934, prices of agricultural products on the black market in Belorussia were very high. In early August 1932, for example, a pud (35.2 pounds) of wheat flour cost from seventy to eighty rubles, a pud of rye flour, sixty rubles, and a pud of potatoes, from twenty to thirty rubles.[62] It must be noted, however, that a new crop was harvested in August, and this lowered the prices on the black market. Even so, the peasants, whose wealth consisted of agricultural products which were confiscated by the state, could not buy much and were destined to go through several years of famine.

The village teachers and other local employees who did not have ration cards and whose salaries were low found themselves in an extremely difficult position, too. The monthly salary of an elementary school teacher in a village was from seventy to eighty rubles, the salary of a nurse from forty-five to fifty rubles.[63]

In Belorussia, the period 1931–1933 was the most severe. There are no Soviet statistics on how many people in Belorussia died of starvation during these years, but those who lived there estimate the number of dead at between 3 and 5 percent of the total population.[64] The principal victims of starvation were the peasants who resisted collectivization, older people, people of low income in the towns, and children.[65]

Potatoes, chaff, and horse-sorrel saved many lives in Belorussia

---

[60] Interview with a former Belorussian collective farmer.
[61] Fainsod, *Smolensk under Soviet Rule*, p. 252.
[62] Ibid., p. 262; interview with a former Belorussian collective farmer.
[63] Fainsod, *Smolensk under Soviet Rule*, p. 262; interview with a Belorussian teacher.
[64] Interview with a former Belorussian collective farmer.
[65] Ibid.

in the springs and early summers of those years. In the Ukraine, the situation was even worse.[66] In the early summers of 1932 and 1933, many Ukrainians moved to Belorussia and joined in this subsistence diet; thus a large number succeeded in saving their lives.[67]

The tragedy of the millions of people of the Soviet Union during the time of collectivization even now remains to a large extent unknown in the outside world, for the Soviet press never disclosed the terrible sacrifices of human life. On the contrary, while people were dying from starvation, the Soviet press continued to write about the happy life on the collective farms. The top Soviet officials, as usual, directed such distortions of reality. The peasants, for example, had not yet recovered from starvation when, in his "Report to the Seventeenth Party Congress on the Work of the Central Committee of the VKP(b)" on January 26, 1934, Stalin said, "With the disappearance of kulak bondage, poverty in the countryside disappeared. Every peasant, whether a collective farmer or an individual farmer, has now the opportunity to live a human existence."[68] Stalin began at that time to play the role of "father of the people." He declared, "Life has become better, comrades. Life has become more joyful." This seems the ultimate in cynicism.

Stalin built the collective farms by force, in direct violation of Lenin's principle that "Socialism cannot be imposed on the peasantry by force." After living under Stalin's terror, some people in Belorussia, as in the other republics, still retain the belief that "were Lenin alive, he would have allowed free trade and eased our lot; afterward he would have instituted a shift toward collectivization—not by force, but by consent and persuasion."[69]

Of course, no positive proof can be found for any theories of what might have been. This theory, however, is based on the differences between the personalities of Stalin and Lenin. Stalin used terror in building the collective farms, largely because of his personal ambitions, his thirst for power, and his personal cruelty. His power rested not on his popularity as a leader but on force. Lenin, on the other hand, was much more popular among the people. His

[66] Descriptions of the famine in the Ukraine in 1931–1933 are given in the following books: Dmytro Solovei, *The Golgotha of the Ukraine* (New York, 1953); F. Pigido, *Visim mil'ioniv: 1933—i rik na Ukraini* (Winnipeg, 1951). There are many other sources on this famine.
[67] Interview with a Belorussian writer.
[68] Stalin, *Sochineniia*, 13:334.
[69] Quoted in Fainsod, *Smolensk under Soviet Rule*, p. 248.

authority as the leader of the Communist Party and the Soviet state rested more on personal prestige than on the use of force. And Lenin was much more broad-minded and humane than Stalin. He might have realized that the great surplus of laborers in the countryside could be more useful for the expansion of industry as free men than as slaves in concentration camps. Post-Stalin development in the Soviet Union proves this point of view correct.

8.

The Liquidation of Belorussian Nationalism

> *Tyranny is a system which chooses bad men for its friends. Tyrants love to be flattered, and nobody with the soul of a freeman can ever stoop to that; a good man may be a friend, but at any rate he will not be a flatterer.*
>
> Aristotle[1]

The idea has always prevailed among the leaders of the Bolshevik section of the Russian Social Democratic Labor Party (RSDRP) that the party should be monolithic in its unity and that any weakness of will or disobedience to Party discipline on the part of the individual members should not be tolerated. Lenin, as a leader of the Bolsheviks, wanted Party members not only to obey Party discipline but also to show their devotion to the Communist cause. Those who did not follow these requirements were to be expelled from the Party. In the introduction to his work *What Is to Be Done*, published in 1902, Lenin wrote: "A party's struggle lends it strength and vitality. The best proof of the weakness of a party is in the diffusiveness and the blurring of clearly defined boundaries. A party becomes stronger by purging itself."[2] Since that time the purges of the Communist Party have become a chronic phenomenon.

The first purge after the end of the Civil War was conducted in 1921, a year of transition from war to peaceful reconstruction. Many members of the Party who had been useful in the Revolution and the Civil War could not be tolerated in a time of peace. "Altogether, nearly 170,000 persons, or about 25 percent of the total membership, were expelled from the Party as a result of this purge."[3]

The first purge of the Communist Party of Belorussia, conducted between August 15 and October 25, 1921, removed 1,495 members, about 25 percent of the total membership.[4] According to an official Party statement, "from the Party were expelled rascals, bureaucrats, dishonest or wavering Communists, and Mensheviks at heart."[5] During Lenin's time, however, those expelled from the Party usually were left free.

During the period of the New Economic Policy (1921–1928), there were no Party purges. But the change of policy from the NEP to swift industrialization and collectivization left many Party members dissatisfied. In Belorussia most Party members supported the NEP and consequently stood against Stalin's methods of enforcing economic change. This was why the Belorussian Communists were accused of being "National Democrats" (Natsdems) "or influenced by them."[6]

The signal for the purge of 1929–1931 was given at the Sixteenth Party Conference, which met in Moscow, April 23–29, 1929. The resolution of the conference called for the "purging of the ranks of the Party in order to free it from all non-Communists and thereby to make it more homogeneous."[7] As a matter of fact, this purge was to be directed primarily against the followers of Nikolai Bukharin and Aleksei Rykov, former leaders of the Right-Wing Opposition, which had the support of an overwhelming majority of the top Belorussian Party and government officials. But for Stalin and his followers this was not enough. They wanted also to attack the Belorussian National-Democrats. With this aim, in the fall of 1929, several contradictory accusations were advanced against the Belorussian Natsdems.

The Communist-controlled press started by attacking Poland.

[1] *The Politics of Aristotle*, translated with notes by Ernest Barker (Oxford, 1950), p. 288.
[2] Vladimir Lenin, *Polnoe sobranie sochinenii*, 5th ed. (Moscow, 1958–1966), 6:1.
[3] *Istoriia Vsesoiuznoi Kommunisticheskoi Partii (bol'shevikov): kratkii kurs* (Moscow, 1938), p. 247.
[4] *Istoriia BSSR*, 2d ed. (Minsk, 1961), 2:184.
[5] *Istoriia VKP(b)*, p. 247.
[6] Boris K. Markiianov, *Bor'ba Kommunisticheskoi Partii Belorussii za ukreplenie edinstva svoikh riadov v 1921–1925 gg.* (Minsk, 1961), p. 64.
[7] *Shestnadtsataia konferentsiia Vsesoiuznoi Kommunisticheskoi Partii (bol'shevikov): stenograficheskii otchet, 23–29 aprelia 1929 g.* (Moscow, 1962), p. 662.

It was said that "bourgeois Poland is a first vanguard, a first step in an attempt to destroy the Soviet Union."[8] The activities of the Belorussian national leaders in Poland were criticized. Anton Lutskevich and Radaslau Astrouski, who had not returned from Poland to Belorussia in the 1920s were especially subjected to attack.[9] This was, of course, the beginning of an attempt to uncover an underground organization in Belorussia and to tie its activity to those of the Belorussian national organizations in Poland. For a time the security police failed. In the fall of 1929 and the first half of 1930, the Soviet press, contrary to the aims of the security police, continued its accusations of the Belorussian Natsdems for their cooperation with the Provisional Government in Petrograd after the February Revolution of 1917.[10] Thus, while the police wanted to accuse the Belorussians of lack of loyalty to Soviet Russia, the press was accusing them of too much loyalty to Russia between the February and October Revolutions. It was repeatedly stated that the Belorussian Natsdems had placed great hope in the Provisional Government and had not demanded the independence of Belorussia. In truth, on the contrary, they wanted to have a united Russia. "If Russia was to be a bourgeois country, the Belorussian Natsdems wanted it to be a strong country."[11]

In March 1930, the trial of the "Union for the Liberation of the Ukraine" (*Spilka Vyzvolennia Ukrainy*) was staged. After this trial "there was a suspicion that the GPU was preparing a similar action in Belorussia."[12] It proved true. All those arrested in June 1930 were charged with belonging to an underground counterrevolutionary organization called the "Union for the Liberation of Belorussia" (*Saiuz Vyzvalen'nia Belarusi*, abbreviated as SVB), although the security police have never proved the existence of such an organization.[13] "It was invented by the GPU, which did not even take the trouble to invent a different name for the alleged Belorussian underground organization."[14]

At the end of November 1930, the press announced the discovery of another "conspiracy." Among the accused were Vatslau Lastouski,

[8] *As'veta*, nos. 11–12 (1929): 25.
[9] Ibid., p. 28.
[10] A. Ziuz'kou, *Kryvavy shliakh Belaruskai natsdemokratyi* (Minsk, 1931), p. 8.
[11] Ibid., p. 64.
[12] Anthony Adamovich, *Opposition to Sovietization in Belorussian Literature, 1917–1957* (Munich, 1958), p. 160.
[13] Ibid., p. 163.
[14] Ibid.

Iazep Liosik, Stsiapan Nekrashevich, and Aleksandr Tsvikevich.[15] It was stated that the "conspirators had striven to take Belorussia away from the path of Socialist reconstruction and direct it to the path of restoration of capitalism."[16] Among other epithets, they were branded "enemies of the people," "spies of a foreign power," and "bourgeois nationalists."[17] Now it remained only for the GPU to find an "effective and representative" leader for the SVB and then to stage a big trial of the Belorussian Natsdems similar to that in the Ukraine in March. The GPU choice fell on Professor Usevalad Ihnatouski, president of the Belorussian Academy of Sciences and a distinguished historian, "but he committed suicide rather than face the platoon of executioners."[18] After his death, there were no other attempts to "find" the leader of the alleged SVB, and there was no big trial of the Belorussian Nationalists. Most of them were arrested and condemned to imprisonment, exile, or death without trial.

During the purges of 1929–1931 in Belorussia, a primary target was the People's Commissariat of Education. It had directed all educational and cultural activities in the republic, and consequently most of the Belorussian national intelligentsia was concentrated there. First of all, in January 1930, *As'veta* (Education), a periodical published by the commissariat, was renamed *Kamunistychnae vykhavan'ne* (Communist Upbringing). This change was explained by the editorial board in the following way: "Our periodical *As'veta* is given another name. It is not accidental. In this period of developed class struggle, the old name has become outdated. The old name did not properly convey our class attitude toward education."[19] The programs and the textbooks were criticized as being designed "to implement counterrevolutionary nationalist ideas."[20] In 1929–1930, nearly all textbooks were eliminated, either because their authors had been arrested or because of their unsuitability for the period of "Socialist reconstruction." Altogether, fifty-four textbooks were prohibited, including even those in mathematics.[21]

---

[15] *Kamunistychnae vykhavan'ne*, no. 12 (1930): 14–15.
[16] *Mataryialy da spravazdachy uradu X z'ezdu Savetau BSSR* (Minsk, 1931), p. vi.
[17] Nicholas P. Vakar, *Belorussia: The Making of a Nation* (Cambridge, Mass., 1956), p. 147.
[18] Ibid.
[19] *Kamunistychnae vykhavan'ne*, no. 1 (1930), introduction.
[20] Ibid., p. 7.
[21] Ibid., p. 59.

Among the most distinguished men in education who became victims of the first Stalinist purge were, in addition to Ihnatouski, Anton Balitski, commissar of education; Uladimir Picheta, rector of the Belorussian State University; and Vydra, director of the Institute for Retraining Soviet Educators.[22] Many professors at the universities were purged, too. Among them, an especially high percentage were of Belorussian nationality. Thus, at the end of this purge, "the Belorussians comprised only 15 percent of the professional staff of the higher educational institutions of the Belorussian SSR."[23]

The first Stalinist purge in Belorussia also affected former members of the government of the Belorussian National Republic, who had left Belorussia in 1918 and then had returned in 1924 to help build a Belorussian "free country." The former prime minister of the BNR, Vatslau Lastouski, then Permanent Secretary of the Belorussian Academy of Sciences, and the former minister of the BNR, Aleksandr Tsvikevich, then president of the Belorussian Red Cross, died in prison.[24] Most of those purged were accused of belonging to the "counterrevolutionary organization of Belorussian bourgeois Nationalists called SVB,"[25] and were subject to immediate arrest and prosecution without formal trial.[26]

The fate of these innocent people, who had done so much in the field of education and culture, lends a certain retrospective irony to Lenin's article "To the Rural Poor," written in 1903. In it Lenin had declared, "The Social Democrats demand that the police be deprived of the power to imprison everyone without trial. The officials must be severely punished for arbitrary arrests. To prevent them from violating the law, the officials must be chosen by the people; and everyone must have the right to lodge a complaint against any official, directly or indirectly, in a court."[27] What Lenin had demanded before the Revolution with regard to human rights and liberty was realized to some extent during the period of the New Economic Policy. But Stalin eliminated this achievement. The rights

[22] *Zbor zakonau i zahadau rabocha-sialianskaha uradu Belaruskai Satsyialistychnai Savetskai Respubliki* (Minsk, January 1931), no. 1, part 1:6; and Vakar, *Belorussia*, p. 149.

[23] H. Niamiha, "Education in the Belorussian SSR and Communist Doctrine," *Belorussian Review*, no. 3 (1956): 83.

[24] Vakar, *Belorussia*, p. 146; *Kamunistychnae vykhavan'ne*, no. 12 (1931): 14.

[25] *Iz istorii bor'by Belorusskogo naroda za Sovetskuiu vlast' i pobedu sotsializma* (Minsk, 1957), p. 140.

[26] Those expelled from the Communist Party in 1921 were not prosecuted.

[27] Vladimir Lenin, *Sochineniia*, 3d ed. (Moscow, 1929–1939), 5:292.

and liberty of Soviet citizens since that time have become much more limited than they were before the Revolution.

The period between 1929 and 1934 was one of struggle between Belorussian nationalism and Great Russian chauvinism. This struggle, as a matter of fact, was inaugurated by Stalin's letter, "The National Question and Leninism," written in reply to Comrades Meshkov, Koval'chuk, and others, and published on March 18, 1929. In it Stalin wrote:

> You so lightly confuse and lump together diverse periods in the development of the revolution and fail to understand that the changes in the character and tasks of revolution in the various stages of its development give rise to corresponding changes in the character and aims of the national question.... It is apparent from your letter that you do not approve of this policy of your party. That is because, firstly, you confuse the new Socialist nations with the old bourgeois nations, and do not understand that the national cultures of our new Socialist nations are in content Socialist.[28]

This letter was interpreted by the Great Russian chauvinists to mean that the national question had lost its validity and therefore should be forgotten.[29]

The Belorussians, however, stubbornly resisted this planned reversal of the policy of permitting cultural autonomy to the various nationalities. The Central Committee of the Communist Party of Belorussia joined the nationalists in defense of the earlier Leninist policy on the national question. A plenary meeting of the Central Committee in October 1930 said concerning nationality policy, "Great Russian chauvinism is expressed in the denial of the existence of the Belorussian nation and of the Belorussian language."[30] The Belorussians through 1929–1931 had insisted that Lenin was against the bourgeois content of a culture but not against its form.[31] The Belorussian press of this time continued to support the thesis that "Lenin stood for a culture, national in content, during the period of the dictatorship of the proletariat."[32] They pictured "Great Rus-

[28] Iosif Stalin, *Sochineniia*, 1st ed (Moscow, 1946–1952), 11:350–54.
[29] *Kamunistychnae vykhavan'ne*, nos. 9–10 (1930): 83.
[30] *Rabochii*, no. 291 (13 December 1931): 3.
[31] *Kamunistychnae vykhavan'ne*, no. 5 (1931): 4.
[32] P. [pseud.], "Na barats'bu z vialikadzharzhaunym kontrrevaliutsyinym shavinizman. Za Leninskuiu natsyianal'nuiu polityku" [To Fight against the Great Russian Counterrevolutionary Chauvinism. For Lenin's Policy of Nationalities], *Kamunistychnae vykhavan'ne*, no. 5 (1931): 3.

sian chauvinism as the main enemy of the Leninist national policy in general and of Belorussification in particular."[33]

The struggle was unequal, and the Belorussian Central Committee was able to make only one more strong stand on the national issue in a December 1931 decision which declared, "the slogan stating that National-Democracy appears to be at the present time a main danger is incorrect. It contradicts the decision of the Twelfth Party Congress of the RKP (b) and the Sixteenth Congress of the VKP (b). The Communist Party (Bolsheviks) of Belorussia immediately after this congress adopted a decision that at this time Great Russian chauvinism is the main danger."[34]

Stalin's second purge was conducted in 1933–1934. In his greeting on the "Fifteenth Anniversary of the GPU," on December 20, 1932, Stalin wrote, "I wish them success in the difficult task of eradicating the enemies of the dictatorship of the proletariat! Long live the GPU, the bared sword of the working class!"[35] Following Stalin's guidance, a joint plenary meeting of the Central Committee (Ts.K.) and the Central Control Commission (Ts.K.K.) of the All-Union Communist Party adopted, on January 12, 1933, the following resolution:

1) The joint plenary meeting of the Ts.K. and the Ts.K.K. favors the decision of the Politburo of the Ts.K. regarding the purge of the Party ranks during 1933.

2) The joint plenary meeting of the Ts.K. and Ts.K.K. entrusts the Politburo of the Ts.K. and the Presidium of the Ts.K.K. with organizing the purge in such a manner that it will ensure an iron proletarian discipline in the party by eliminating from the party ranks all unreliable, unstable, and "hang-on-the-party" elements.[36]

A commission composed of three members was appointed to conduct a purge in Belorussia: Nikolai Kirillovich Antipov, chairman; I. A. Lychev; and Praskoviia Fedorovna Sakharova. All three were Russians.[37]

[33] *Rabochii*, no. 296 (20 December 1931): 1.
[34] Ibid., no. 302 (27 December 1931): 2.
[35] Stalin, *Sochineniia*, 13:158.
[36] *Rabochii*, no. 11 (14 January 1933): 3.
[37] Ibid., no. 117 (30 May 1933): 3. Antipov was born in 1894 in the Russian province of Novgorod. At the time of appointment he was chairman of the Ts.K.K. of the VKP(b) and a deputy chairman of the People's Commissariat of Workers' and Peasants' Inspection (RKI). Lychev was born in 1885, in the Russian province of Samara. In July 1932 he was appointed chairman of the

Predictably, in conducting the purge of the Belorussian Communist Party during the summer and fall of 1933, this commission discovered that Belorussian nationalism had survived the first purge and was still dangerous. In December 1933, Antipov reported:

> Belorussian organizations have spent a great deal of energy in a struggle against Great Russian chauvinism. . . . However, comrades, the commission uncovered predominantly Belorussian nationalism. . . . In the People's Commissariat of Education were people who did not care about the Party directives and pursued their own nationalist policy. During the purge of the cell of the KP(b) of Belorussia at the People's Commissariat of Education, the commission found that, until this very time, the school section has not paid sufficient attention to the study of the Russian language.[38]

Accordingly, the principal victims of the purge of 1933–1934 were once again the staff of the Commissariat of Education, faculty members of the university and the institutes, and teachers in the secondary and elementary schools.[39] Purging, for example, the Party cell at the Higher Pedagogical Institute in Minsk in the fall of 1933, the Commission found the following shortcomings: "Individual communists of the Higher Pedagogical Institute have lost their class vigilance. They do not study one another and the individual non-Party students."[40] In other words, the Party members had failed to spy upon one another. Stalin, who was well along toward becoming a tyrant in the early 1930s, knew well that a "tyranny is never overthrown until men can begin to trust one another."[41]

In the summer of 1933, the Party announced the discovery of a "Belorussian National Center" which was charged with seeking the establishment of an independent Belorussian Democratic Republic. The Center, it was reported, had been receiving its instructions from Belorussian organizations in Vilna, Poland.[42] This announcement was followed by the arrest of the members of the Belorussian

---

Ts.K.K. of the KP(b) of Belorussia. Sakharova made her career in the Moscow Party organization. At the time of her appointment she was a member of the Party Board of the Ts.K.K. of the VKP(b).

[38] Nikolai K. Antipov, "Chistka sdelala KP(b) Belorussii eshche bolee sil'nym i splochennym otriadom VKP(b)," *Rabochii*, no. 235 (28 December 1933): 3.

[39] Ibid., no. 256 (22 November 1933): 2. See also *Zbor zakonau i zahadau rabocha-sialianskaha uradu BSSR*, no. 19 (27 May 1933).

[40] *Rabochii*, no. 256 (22 November 1933): 2.

[41] *Politics of Aristotle*, p. 289.

[42] Walter Kolarz, *Russia and Her Colonies* (New York, 1952), pp. 155–56.

Hramada, most of whom had been in Polish jails a few years earlier but had been freed by the Bolsheviks in exchange for some Polish citizens arrested in the Soviet Union.[43] Their treatment was inhumane. "The former deputies to the Polish Sejm, Ihnat Dvarchanin and Iazep Hauryliuk, for example, who had barely lived through their beating by the Polish police, were now shot as 'Polish spies.' Symon Rak-Mikhailouski was killed by guards on his way to jail."[44] Altogether, ninety-six well-known Belorussians—statesmen, educators, and writers—who had left the western part of Belorussia in the 1920s because of Polish national suppression and had come to the Belorussian SSR, were shot in prisons or liquidated in concentration camps.[45] In 1933, during the summer and fall, 38,568 members and 14,624 candidates of the Communist Party of Belorussia were subjected to loyalty checks. A systematic investigation was made of 37,244 members and 13,093 candidates; 6,002 members and 3,767 candidates were expelled from the Party.[46]

At the end of the second purge, the Belorussian national and cultural leadership was almost completely destroyed. "Thus, reorganization of the Belorussian educational system in 1933 along RSFSR lines found Belorussia without teachers or administrative personnel who could adequately undertake leadership of the system."[47] The textbooks for the Belorussian schools were rewritten and, by decree of the Belorussian Council of People's Commissars of August 26, 1933, "changes and simplifications in Belorussian grammar and orthography" were made.[48] In this decree, the Belorussian National Democrats were accused of "intending to tear away the Belorussian literary language from the language of the Belorussian working masses and of thus creating an artificial barrier between the Belorussian and the Russian languages."[49] Thus, the aim of the reform of Belorussian grammar was to bring the Belorussian literary language closer to Russian.

The second purge, in fact, broke Belorussian national resistance.

[43] Adamovich, *Opposition to Sovietization*, p. 169.
[44] Vakar, *Belorussia*, p. 146.
[45] Wiktor Ostrowski, *Spotlight on Byelorussia and Her Neighbours* (London, 1959), p. 18.
[46] *Rabochii*, no. 285 (28 December 1933): 2. These figures are taken from the "Report of Antipov at a joint plenary meeting of the Ts.K.K. of the KP(b) of Belorussia on the result of the purge."
[47] *Belorussia*, Subcontractors Monograph HRAF-19 (New Haven, Conn., 1954-1955), p. 184.
[48] T. P. Lamtsiou, *Belaruskaia hramatyka* (Minsk, 1935), p. 67.
[49] Ibid.

Even the Central Committee of the Belorussian Communist Party was forced to reconsider its previous stand on the policy of nationalities. At its December 1933 plenary meeting, the Central Committee openly admitted that "at this time, local Belorussian nationalism is the main danger."[50] Thus, the question as to which deviation had been more dangerous—Great Russian chauvinism or Belorussian local nationalism—was answered. The Belorussian and Ukrainian nationalists were made the primary scapegoats. Belorussia, as a Union republic, lost its position as "an equal among equals" in the Union. Since the end of 1933, it has never been adequately represented in the Central Committee of the All-Union Communist Party or in the Supreme Soviet.[51]

For example, at the Seventeenth All-Union Party Congress, which assembled in January 1934, out of 1,227 delegates, 19 were from Belorussia.[52] Thus, the Belorussian delegates comprised 1.6 percent of the total number of delegates at the congress. Statistically, the Communist Party of Belorussia was represented proportionally, since at the time there were 44,423 Party members and candidates in Belorussia, making up 1.6 percent of the 2,700,000 Party members and candidates in the USSR.[53] On the other hand, the people of the Belorussian Republic comprised 3.27 percent of the total population of the Soviet Union.[54]

The most important point, however, is who made up the Belorussian delegation at the Seventeenth Party Congress. Most of them were Russians, including all three members of the Central Commission for the purge.[55] Furthermore, Antipov was elected the only member to the Central Committee of the VKP(b) from Belorussia.[56] In other words, he was sent from Russia to purge the Communist Party of Belorussia and, at the Seventeenth Party Congress, was chosen to represent Belorussia in the Central Committee.

While Stalin was consolidating his dictatorship, the Soviet government passed a number of decrees which acted to enslave Soviet citizens. The first of these was the decree of the Central Executive

[50] *Kamunistychnae vykhavan'ne*, nos. 3–4 (1934): 18.
[51] The Supreme Soviet was elected for the first time in 1937.
[52] *Semnadtsatyi s"ezd Vsesoiuznoi Kommunisticheskoi Partii (bol'shevikov) 26 ianvaria–10 fevralia 1934 goda: stenograficheskii otchet* (Moscow, 1934), pp. 681–701.
[53] Merle Fainsod, *How Russia Is Ruled* (Cambridge, Mass., 1953), p. 223.
[54] Ibid., p. 229.
[55] *Semnadtsatyi s"ezd*, pp. 681–701.
[56] Ibid., p. 680.

Committee and the Council of People's Commissars of the USSR on August 7, 1932, "concerning the preservation of state property." It stipulated the death penalty for theft of Socialist property, including the property of the collective farms.[57] Thus, a starving person who gleaned a few sheaves of rye or wheat from a field or stole a few vegetables produced by his own labor was subject to capital punishment.[58]

In December 1932, the obligatory interior passport for the entire population was introduced. "Nobody could move or stay twenty-four hours away from home without the visa of the GPU."[59] Introduction of the passport affected most of all the peasants who were dissatisfied with intolerable conditions on the collective farms and wanted to move to town, for now they could not move. At an earlier date, Lenin had vigorously denounced almost identical conditions prevailing before the Revolution. In his "To the Rural Poor," published in 1903, he wrote:

> What does it mean to be free to move from place to place? It means that the peasant must be free to go where he pleases, to move wherever he wants, to choose for himself the village or the town he prefers, without having to ask for permission. It means that passports must be abolished in Russia, too. In foreign countries passports were abolished long ago. . . . The Russian peasant is still the serf of the officials to such an extent that he is not free to move to a town, or free to settle in a new district. The minister issues orders that the governors should not allow unauthorized settlement! The governor knows better than the peasant what is good for the peasant! The peasant is a child who dares not move without authority! Is this not serfdom, I ask you?[60]

[57] *Istoriia Sovetskoi Konstitutsii v dokumentakh, 1917–1957* (Moscow, 1957), p. 72.
[58] 1932–1934 were the years of starvation. The peasants suffered more than the urban population.
[59] "Postanovlenie Ts.I.K. i SNK ob ustanovlennii edinoi pasportnoi sistemy po Soiuzu SSR i obiazatel'noi pripiske pasportov, 31 dekabria 1932 goda, No. 84, St. 516" [Decree of the Central Executive Committee and the Sovnarkom about the Introduction of the Unified Passport System in the USSR and about the Compulsory Registration of the Passports, Passed on 31 December 1932, No. 84, Article 516], *Sobranie zakonov i rasporiazhenii raboche-krest'ianskogo pravitel'stva Soiuza Sovetskikh Sotsialisticheskikh Respublik, izdavaemoe upravleniem delami Soveta Narodnykh Komissarov Soiuza SSR i STO* (Moscow, 1924–1949), part 1 (microprint, Indiana University Library). The passport was a potentially incriminating document which indicated the social origin of the bearer, his occupation, place of living, and family attachment—all data necessary for eventual prosecution.
[60] Lenin, *Sochineniia*, 3d ed., 5:293.

Under Stalin, living conditions among the peasants were far worse than they had been under the tsar. "Happy life" on the collective farms, as it was described in official government publications, was popularly known as the "second serfdom of the Bolsheviks," or in Russian, *Vtoroe Krepostnoe Pravo bolshevikov*, abbreviated VKP(b), the same initials as the All-Union Communist Party of Bolsheviks.

The condition of the workers, in whose name the Communist Party ruled, was not much better than that of the peasants. A decree passed by the Ts.I.K. and the Sovnarkom of the USSR on November 15, 1932, "On Dismissal from Work for Absence from Work without a Valid Reason," provided for the firing of workers with deprivation of their right to use food-cards.[61] Who had the right to define this "valid reason"? Certainly not the worker. In the case of absence from work, a worker had to present a certificate from the doctor that he was sick and therefore unable to work. No other reason was accepted as valid. Workers absent without this "valid reason" or coming to work late were subject to arrest and imprisonment. During the same period, no laws were passed which would protect Soviet citizens from unjust accusations and arbitrary arrests.

As previously noted, by the end of the second purge, in January 1934, Belorussian nationalism was already destroyed. The dictatorship of the Party, not to speak of the dictatorship of the proletariat, was replaced by the dictatorship of one person, Stalin. The Russian chauvinists, whom Stalin was supporting, originated the "doctrine of the older brother"—Russia—whom the younger brothers—the other nationalities—had to obey. A period of hypocrisy and flattery began. Such Belorussian writers and journalists as had escaped the purges began to praise virtually all of the undertakings of the Soviet government. "Tyrants love to be flattered," Aristotle anciently observed,[62] and the Belorussian writers, following the direction and example of the "older brother," soon were busily applying the maxim. A resolution adopted at the general meeting of Belorussian writers on December 15, 1933, concerning the reform of Belorussian grammar and orthography, stated, "The guidance of Comrade Stalin, ingenious theorist and practitioner concerning the problem of nationalities, serves us as a guiding star in the struggle

---

[61] *Rabochii*, no. 254 (18 November 1932): 1.
[62] *Politics of Aristotle*, p. 288.

for the construction of a culture 'national in form, Socialist in content.' "[63]

Exaltation of Stalin by Belorussian writers and poets reached its height in the so-called "Letter of the Belorussian People to Great Stalin," written in poetic form and published on July 11, 1936, in the newspaper *Rabochii* (Worker), official organ of the Central Committee of the Belorussian Communist Party.

> Now we will tell you true stories of old,
> How we lived for ages without happy days,
> How our backs, bent with troubles, we straightened
>   up bold
> Warmed clear through with your loving care.
> . . . .
> You—the wise teacher, the genius of geniuses,
> Sun of the workers, sun of the peasants,
> Your constitution—banner of generations,
> The hope and the light of all down-trodden countries.
> . . . .
> Your image stands over the earth like a summons,
> It calls the whole world to the Bolshevik fight.
> In our hearts we are all in the Kremlin with you,
> And the best of the songs that we sing are of you.
>
> For us you're the sun that illumines the world
> You—the glory and pride of the working-class homes,
> You are the great power of full, rushing rivers,
> Of their source, the clearness, our leader beloved.
> . . . .
> Raising on high the banner of battle,
> Our gratitude, love, and unbounded esteem
> As a gift from our hearts, as a song of the millions
> We, the Belorussian people, bring unto you.[64]

This poem was supposed to follow a literary method known as "Socialist realism," which was proclaimed at the First All-Union Congress of Soviet Writers held in Moscow in August 1934. Stalin said that Soviet writers should be "engineers of the human soul," and the Soviet press immediately followed, advising writers to

[63] *Pis'menniki Belaruskai SSR ab reforme pravapisa Belaruskai movy* (Minsk, 1934), p. 93.
[64] *Rabochii*, no. 153 (11 July 1936): 1. The poem occupies the entire front page.

"portray the image of the man of Stalin's epoch."[65] The writers indeed produced this image, and it appeared to be that of Stalin himself. Thus, from 1934 to 1953, Stalin as a "great hero" in the epoch of the building of Socialism, "ingenious teacher" and "philosopher," dominated the mythology of the Soviet press and literature.

Long ago Machiavelli commented that the prince must be able to play the role of the humanitarian as well as that of the beast.[66] Stalin in his practice adroitly followed Machiavelli's advice. Thus, after the purges of 1929–1934, which eliminated the political opposition within the Communist Party and liquidated the national and cultural movements in the Union republics, Stalin wanted to "pretend to be concerned with human welfare." In 1936, a draft constitution was worked out for the Soviet Union and the public was informed that Stalin himself was its architect. Stalin, in turn, spoke about it as the greatest document ever written. At the Eighth Congress of Soviets, on November 25, 1936, he said:

> The bourgeois constitutions usually are limited by fixation of the formal rights of the citizens and do not care about the conditions necessary to guarantee these rights. The project of the new constitution does not limit itself to defining the formal rights of the citizens, but transfers the center of gravity to the problem of guaranteeing these rights. This project does not merely proclaim equality of rights for citizens, but insures it by giving legislative embodiment to the fact that the regime of exploitation has been abolished, to the fact that all the citizens have been emancipated from all exploitation.[67]

The congress approved the document, which became known as the "Stalin Constitution."

The new constitution provided for nominally free elections, but limited freedom of choice by two "joker" articles. Article 141 specified: "The right to nominate candidates is secured to public organizations and societies of toilers: Communist Party organizations, trade unions, cooperatives, youth organizations, cultural societies." To make the meaning clear, Article 126 proclaimed the Communist Party to be the "directing kernel" within all of these

---

[65] Ibid., no. 33 (10 February 1936): 3.
[66] Niccolo Machiavelli, *The Prince* (New York, 1947), p. 50.
[67] *Istoricheskii zhurnal*, no. 12 (1936): 11.

organizations. Thus, the Soviet Union became the first state in human history ruled by one highly centralized party to pretend to hold free elections. Even more curious, the Soviet Union wanted to demonstrate this after Stalin had established his personal dictatorship.

The explanation for these elections may well have resided not in the Soviet Union but abroad. The Communist Party, nervously eyeing the rise of Hitler and German military might, was trying hard to project in Western Europe an image of the Soviet Union as a "fellow democracy" which also hated "fascism." In terms of international Communist strategy, this was the period of the "united front." Thus, the Soviet Constitution with its provision for elections attracted attention not only in the Soviet Union but in the outside world. Roy Howard, of the Scripps-Howard newspaper chain, arranged an interview with Stalin in 1936, seeking to ascertain Stalin's views concerning these elections. Stalin gave the following explanation:

> Yes, under the 1936 constitution, elections will be lively. They will be conducted around numerous very acute problems, principally of a practical nature, of first-class importance for the people. Our new electoral system will tighten up all institutions and organizations and compel them to improve their work. Universal, equal, direct, and secret suffrage in the USSR will be a whip in the hands of the population against the organs of government which work badly. In my opinion, the new Soviet constitution will be the most democratic constitution in the world.[68]

It was, in fact, mostly window-dressing. There have been no free elections since the "Stalin Constitution" was adopted in 1936. On the electoral ballot appears only one candidate, selected by the Communist Party; his name, in most cases, is unfamiliar to the voters, since he does not necessarily reside in their district. In the elections for the Supreme Soviet in December 1937, for example, the Belorussian SSR elected nineteen deputies to the Soviet of the Union, of whom eight were military men, including Marshal Klimenti Voroshilov, the commissar of defense of the USSR. None of the well-known Belorussian party or government officials was elected at all.[69] There was no need to count the votes because all of the

[68] *Bol'shevik*, no. 6 (1936): 8.
[69] *Sovetskaia Belorussia*, no. 64 (17 December 1937): 1–2.

"Party candidates," as it was announced, were elected by very close to 100 percent of the votes in the electoral districts.

Stalin, even while talking about the constitution, elections, democracy, and freedom, was also planning to undertake a third purge, later known as the Great Purge of 1936–1938. He needed this further purge to complete the destruction of his old political opponents, the leaders of the Left- and Right-Wing Oppositions, the most important of whom were out of power but still alive. For the most part, these were men of independence, dignity, and high political ideals—qualities a tyrant cannot tolerate. Labeling his opponents "enemies of the people," Stalin launched his Great Purge with the aim of destroying everyone who could challenge his absolute authority. Soon after this purge began, he became suspicious that Genrikh Yagoda, the head of the People's Commissariat of Internal Affairs (NKVD), was tiring of fulfilling his orders for prosecutions.[70] In a telegram from Sochi dated September 25, 1936, addressed to the members of the Politburo, Stalin complained that "the NKVD was four years behind in this matter."[71] A few months later, Yagoda was replaced by Nikolai Yezhov, whose work in the security police Stalin had watched for several years. Stalin "inculcated in him his own methods,"[72] very cruel methods, indeed. The Soviet press greeted Yezhov as "a friend and closest pupil" of the "beloved leader and teacher," Stalin. Under Yezhov, the NKVD intensified its activities in fulfilling "with an accelerated rhythm the sinister task prescribed by the 'great humanitarian,' Stalin."[73]

All leaders of the Left- and Right-Wing Oppositions were brought to trial during 1936–1938. They were accused as "enemies of the people," condemned to death, and executed. Many of Stalin's opponents of the second rank were executed without trial. "It was determined that, of the 139 members and candidates of the Party's Central Committee who were elected at the Seventeenth Party Congress, 98 persons, i.e., 70 percent, were arrested and shot (mostly in 1937–1938)."[74] Most of them were also members of the Supreme Soviet.

[70] In 1934 the GPU was renamed the NKVD.
[71] Nikita S. Khrushchev, *The Crimes of the Stalin Era: Special Report to the 20th Congress of the Communist Party of the Soviet Union* (New York, 1962), p. 23.
[72] Boris Souvarine, *Stalin: A Critical Survey of Bolshevism* (New York, 1939), pp. 606–07.
[73] Ibid., p. 629.
[74] Khrushchev, *Crimes of the Stalin Era*, p. 20.

During the first half of this period, the Belorussian writers were purged. "Altogether about 90 percent of the Belorussian writers and poets were arrested, and most of them were shot or tortured to death in prisons."[75] The continuation of the purge in 1937 affected the top officials of the Belorussian soviet apparatus and the military.[76] Mikola Haladzed, chairman of the Council of People's Commissars, was accused of Rightist deviation.[77] In June 1937, he was arrested and shot without trial.[78] General Ieronim Uborevich, commander of the Belorussian military district, was arrested together with Marshal Mikhail Tukhachevskii. They were brought before a military tribunal, condemned to death, and executed on June 12, 1937, "for espionage and treason to the Fatherland."[79] Aleksandr Charviakou, president of the Belorussian Republic, one of the oldest Belorussian Communists and really the founder of Soviet Belorussia, was accused in June 1937 as "the inspirer and the leader of the Belorussian nationalist deviation in the KP(b) of Belorussia."[80] He committed suicide on June 16, 1937, to escape torture and humiliation.[81] His death left the door wide open for Stalin's servants in the government of the Belorussian SSR.

After the deaths of Haladzed and Charviakou, many thousands of high-ranking government officials died during long confinement in prison or in the concentration camps of the USSR.[82] Finally in 1938, the Central Committee of the Belorussian Communist Party was purged. Vasil' Sharanhovich, who, as one of the secretaries of the Party during the period of collectivization, had "carried out Moscow's orders according to the brutal rules of Stalinist terror," was arrested and brought to trial, together with the leaders of the Right-Wing Opposition, in March 1938.[83] In the summer of 1937 for a short time, he had been made First Secretary of the Belorussian

---

[75] Ostrowski, *Spotlight on Byelorussia*, p. 19.

[76] During the two previous purges, the Soviet apparatus remained almost untouched.

[77] *Rabochii*, no. 127 (4 June 1937): 2.

[78] Alexander Orlov, *The Secret History of Stalin's Crimes* (New York, 1953), p. 242. See also *Rabochii*, no. 124 (1 June 1937): 1.

[79] Merle Fainsod, *Smolensk under Soviet Rule* (Cambridge, Mass., 1958), p. 59.

[80] *Rabochii*, no. 141 (21 June 1937): 2.

[81] Ibid., no. 139 (18 June 1937): 4.

[82] U.S., Congress, House, Select Committee on Communist Aggression, *Communist Takeover and Occupation of Byelorussia* (Washington, D.C., 1955), p. 15.

[83] Orlov, *Secret History of Stalin's Crimes*, p. 295.

Communist Party by order of Stalin, and he was used at the Sixteenth Congress of the Belorussian Communist Party in the summer of 1937 as an accuser of previously arrested Party members. Now at the Moscow trial of the Right-Wing Opposition leaders, he was accused himself of being the leader of the Belorussian underground movement and of having been a "Polish spy since 1921."[84] Sharanhovich, physically and mentally broken, agreed to the accusations forced upon him by the NKVD.[85] Nikolai Bukharin, however, who was supposed to have had a contact with Poland through Sharanhovich and with Germany through Trotsky, denied at the trial all of Vyshinskii's accusations of espionage.[86] The leaders of the Right Wing were accused of spying and of wanting to "bring about the dismemberment of the USSR, to hand over the Soviet Maritime Region to the Japanese, Soviet Belorussia to the Poles, and the Soviet Ukraine to the Germans."[87] Answering these accusations, Bukharin said: "There was talk not of detaching the Ukraine or Belorussia, not giving them to the Germans, but of national independence."[88]

The execution of the last leaders of the opposition reduced Soviet citizens to fear and despair. Those men remaining in power were, by their very nature, prepared to serve their cruel and ambitious master. More than this Stalin did not wish or demand. In the case of Belorussia and the Ukraine, the picture was much darker than in the other Union republics. In the Russian Republic, Stalin liquidated mainly his political enemies but left those "Russian chauvinists, scoundrels, and violators" against whom Lenin had warned the Party in his letter of December 30–31, 1922.[89] In the Belorussian and Ukrainian republics, he liquidated not only his political enemies but the nationalists as well. "Not a single man who had labored for

---

[84] Andrei Vyshinskii, *Sudebnye rechi* (Moscow, 1948), p. 475. Sharanhovich was the only Belorussian ever to serve as First Secretary of the Central Committee of the Belorussian KP(b). There is evidence that he was promoted to this position by Moscow for strategic reasons. The leaders of the Right Opposition were accused of spying for Germany and Poland. Hence, a man from Belorussia was needed through whom they supposedly had contact with the Polish intelligence department. Sharanhovich was simply Moscow's choice for this role.

[85] Ibid., p. 500.

[86] *Sovetskaia Belorussia*, no. 50 (3 March 1938): 3. While the Nazis were murdering the Jews in Germany, Trotsky, a Jew, was accused at the Moscow trial of conducting secret negotiations with the Germans against the Soviet Union!

[87] *Istoriia VKP(b)*, pp. 331–32.

[88] Grigori A. Tokaev, *Comrade X* (London, 1956), pp. 96–97.

[89] Lenin, *Sochineniia*, 4th ed. (Moscow, 1946–1958), 36:553–59.

the establishment of the Belorussian home under the Soviets in the 1920s was alive or free in 1939."[90] Purged Belorussian national leaders usually were replaced by Russians.[91] At the Sixteenth Congress of the Belorussian Communist Party, which assembled in July 1937, were 629 delegates, among them 245 Belorussians, 225 Russians, 140 Jews, and 19 Poles.[92] Thus the Belorussians, who composed more than 80 percent of the population of the republic, composed only 38.9 percent of the delegates. The Russians, on the other hand, who made up less than 8 percent of the population, were represented by 35.7 percent of the delegates.[93]

When the Eighteenth Congress of the All-Union Communist Party assembled in March 1939, there was no more need to mention the Union republics. The delegates were selected from the regions throughout the USSR without regard for the division into republics.[94] Of the seventy-one members elected to the Party's Central Committee, not one was from Belorussia.[95]

The situation was the same in the soviets. In the elections to the Supreme Soviet of the BSSR, held on June 26, 1938, 273 deputies were chosen. Among them were Stalin and all the members of the Politburo, high officers of the Red Army, and those Russians sent to Belorussia to replace the purged Belorussians.[96] In July of the same year, a new Belorussian government was formed. Again, the Council of People's Commissars and the key commissariats in the council were headed by Russians, including V. K. Kiselev, chairman of the Council of People's Commissars; E. I. Uralova, commissar of education; A. A. Nasedkin, commissar of internal affairs (NKVD); and S. I. Lodysev, commissar of justice.[97]

The new "governors" sent to Belorussia from Moscow were even more ruthless than those once sent by the tsars from Petersburg. The tsarist governors neither knew the needs of the people nor cared about their opinions. The new governors, in contrast, claimed to know popular needs better than the people themselves. They were

[90] Vakar, *Belorussia*, p. 150.
[91] *Sovetskaia Belorussiia*, no. 174 (29 July 1938): 1.
[92] *Rabochii*, no. 138 (17 June 1937): 1.
[93] *Prakticheskoe razreshenie natsional'nogo voprosa v BSSR* (Minsk, 1927), 2:12.
[94] *Vosemnadtsatyi s"ezd Vsesoiuznoi Kommunisticheskoi Partii (bol'shevikov) 10–21 marta 1939 goda: stenograficheskii otchet* (Moscow, 1939), pp. 693–724.
[95] Ibid., p. 688.
[96] *Sovetskaia Belorussiia*, no. 149 (29 June 1938): 1–2.
[97] Ibid., no. 174 (29 July 1938): 1.

confident in their undertakings and, like their master, liked to be flattered for the "good" they were doing for the people. During the Great Purge and afterwards, it was very common to read in the Belorussian press letters of thanks, not only to Stalin, but also to the republican leaders. The farmers from the collective farm "GPU" of Minsk district, for example, in a letter published in the newspaper *Sovetskaiia Belorussiia* (Soviet Belorussia) at the beginning of 1938, wrote: "Our life has become prosperous and happy."[98] Their collective farm bore the name of an institution which, in Stalin's time, symbolized terror. Their alleged prosperity and happiness are open to considerable doubt. Truth had to be expressed in a more veiled fashion. A Belorussian man, for example, in 1938 wrote to his son in Leningrad, "My dear son, you were asking me how I'm living? I'm living wonderfully—exactly like old Mikola in our village. I hope you can remember him." But old Mikola had been a beggar. Such was life in East Belorussia at the end of Stalin's third purge.

[98] Quoted in *Istoriia BSSR*, 2:322.

9.

West Belorussia under Poland

Turning aside from the grievous impact of the Stalinist purges in Soviet Belorussia, let us review briefly the hardly less unfortunate plight of the part of Belorussia under Polish control. It will be recalled that Poland, through the Treaty of Riga in 1921, received a large part of the Ukrainian territory and more than one-third of Belorussia. This was much less land than the Polish leaders wanted. They were aware, however, of their weak strategic position and therefore were prepared to be "generous" to Soviet Russia at Riga by abandoning their claims to the so-called Polish "historical boundaries."[1]

The Polish eastern frontier, according to the treaty, was drawn more or less along the Russian-Polish boundary that existed after the Second Partition of Poland in 1793. The Poles accepted it as a compromise solution between what they wanted in accordance with their concept of "historical boundaries" in the east and what was ethnographically theirs. However, this so-called "compromise eastern boundary" included within the Polish state a large number of non-Polish people. Indeed, in Eastern Poland the Belorussians and the Ukrainians constituted a majority of the population.[2] There were also large Jewish and German minorities. Thus, in the Polish state which came into existence after World War I, the population was nearly 40 percent non-Polish.[3] The size of this non-Polish component, or the minority nationalities, as they were called, greatly complicated the administration of the state and especially weakened the possibility of equal justice for all.

At first it seemed that the Polish leaders, realizing these difficulties, intended to seek an equitable solution. The government proclaimed that peoples' rights, freedom of religion, and freedom of speech would be protected by law.[4] The rights of the national minorities also were conferred and protected by the international obligations of Poland. According to the Minority Nationalities Treaty of Versailles, signed by the Entente powers and Poland on June 28, 1919, the Belorussians, Ukrainians, and other minority nationalities in Poland were guaranteed protection of their life, freedom, religious convictions, instruction in their native language, property, use of their language in the courts, and organization of their educational, social, and charitable institutions.[5]

The Treaty of Riga, too, guaranteed the rights of the national minorities in Poland. Paragraph seven of this treaty obligated Poland, in accordance with the principle of the equality of nationalities, to guarantee to the people of Belorussian, Ukrainian, and Russian nationalities freedom in the development of their culture, freedom of religion, and freedom to use their native language.[6]

The first years of the Polish-Belorussian-Ukrainian relation were, indeed, very encouraging. The Polish government, in accordance with its international agreements, immediately granted the Belorussians and the other minority nationalities in Poland the same rights as were granted the Poles. They were assured freedom in developing their social, cultural, and religious life.[7] These rights were also specified in the Polish constitution of March 17, 1921. In the case of the Belorussians, despite the disbandment of the Lutskevich "government-in-exile," which cooperated with the Poles during the war, their national activities were permitted in the Vilna and Grodno provinces.[8] The Belorussians, Ukrainians, and other minority nationalities also took an active part in political activities.

These early tokens of freedom, however, soon proved illusory. The Polish nationalists, by no means in accord with the international agreements their government had signed, resorted to demographic

[1] Bernard Neuman, *Russia's Neighbor—The New Poland* (London, 1946), p. 86.
[2] V. Minaev, *Zapadnaia Belorussiia i Zapadnaia Ukraina pod igom panskoi Pol'shi* (Moscow, 1939), p. 14.
[3] Ibid., p. 13.
[4] Nicholas P. Vakar, *Belorussia: The Making of a Nation* (Cambridge, Mass., 1956), p. 120.
[5] U.S., Congress, House, Select Committee on Communist Aggression, *Communist Takeover and Occupation of Byelorussia* (Washington, D.C., 1955), p. 19.
[6] *Bor'ba trudiashchikhsia Zapadnoi Belorussii za sotsial'noe i natsional'noe osvobozhdenie i vossoedinenie s BSSR: dokumenty i materialy* (Minsk, 1962), vol. 1, document no. 6, p. 34.
[7] T. Gorbunov, *Vossoedinenie Belorusskogo naroda v edinom Sovetskom Sotsialisticheskom gosudarstve* (Moscow, 1948), p. 76.
[8] Vakar, *Belorussia*, p. 121.

TABLE SEVENTEEN

ETHNOGRAPHIC COMPOSITION OF WEST BELORUSSIA, 1931

Nationality	Number	Percent of Total Population
Belorussians	3,460,900	77.9
Jews	450,000	10.2
Poles	260,000	5.9
Russians	101,400	2.3
Lithuanians	70,400	1.6
Ukrainians	60,200	1.3
Germans	25,500	0.6
Others	9,800	0.2
TOTAL	4,438,200	100.0

Source: Mikola Volacic, "The Population of Western Belorussia and Its Resettlement in Poland and the USSR," *Belorussian Review*, no. 3 (1956): 12. See also Wiktor Ostrowski, *Spotlight on Byelorussia and Her Neighbours* (London, 1959), p. 76; Nicholas P. Vakar, *Belorussia: The Making of a Nation* (Cambridge, Mass., 1956), p. 121.

metamorphosis. In the general census of 1921, "the Roman Catholic Belorussians, who formed 20 percent of the entire Belorussian minority of the former north-eastern Poland, were considered as Poles."[9] More than 700,000 Belorussians from the Polesie region were simply designated as "local Slavs."[10] A large number of Belorussians were intimidated and many were afraid to say what their real nationality was. Some were forced to register themselves as Poles; others were not asked their nationality but were automatically counted as Poles.[11] Many of them could not even speak Polish, but the purpose of the Polish nationalists was achieved. In the general census of 1921 the total number of Belorussians was reduced to 1,041,700.[12] The second Polish census of 1931 showed only 989,900.[13]

These results, though perhaps impressive as a feat of thaumaturgy, are statistically unreliable. In reality the ethnographic composition of the population of the whole of West Belorussia at the time of the second census was as shown in Table Seventeen.

[9] Walter Kolarz, *Russia and Her Colonies* (New York, 1952), p. 160.
[10] Ibid., p. 160.
[11] Wiktor Ostrowski, *Spotlight on Byelorussia and Her Neighbours* (London, 1959), p. 76.
[12] Vakar, *Belorussia*, p. 121.
[13] Stephan Horak, *Poland and Her National Minorities, 1919–1939* (New York, 1961), p. 88.

The first elections in Poland, which took place in 1922, were not quite free. The candidates campaigning for the seats in the Polish Parliament from the Belorussian and Ukrainian territories were harassed by the Polish police and the results in many instances were falsified.[14] In spite of all this, the Belorussians were able to elect seven deputies to the Polish Sejm (lower chamber) and three senators.[15]

The elections and census caused disappointment but the Belorussian leaders in West Belorussia were prepared to cooperate with the Polish government. To do this more effectively, they organized their own social and political organizations within the rights granted by the constitution. Their aim was to present the interests of the Belorussian people in an organized manner and thus work for the common good of the country. The Belorussian deputies to the Sejm formed a political club called *Belaruskaia Sialianska-Rabotnitskaia Hramada* (Belorussian Peasants' and Workers' Association). It began its activities in social and cultural work among the natives and soon developed into the largest political party in West Belorussia with anti-Soviet views. In 1927 its membership grew to 150,000.[16] Thus it represented the mass of the people.

The second Belorussian political party was the Belorussian Christian Democratic Party (BCD). In the beginning, the adherents of this party were almost exclusively Roman Catholics. But in time its ranks were reinforced by Belorussians of the Greek Orthodox faith. The official program of the party was based upon the principle of the unification of the Belorussian lands and the independence of the country.[17] It attracted predominantly the Belorussian intelligentsia.

A major strain in the Polish-Belorussian-Ukrainian relationship began to develop in 1923, when the deputies of the National Democratic Party, who formed a strong Right Wing in the lower chamber, proposed the establishment of a purely Polish majority in Parliament. This proposal soon found support among other Polish parties.[18] The result was an all-Polish coalition government which left

[14] Ostrowski, *Spotlight on Byelorussia*, p. 77.
[15] Horak, *Poland and Her National Minorities*, p. 172. In 1922, 444 deputies were elected to the Sejm. See William John Rose, *Poland, Old and New* (London, 1948), pp. 117–18.
[16] *Bor'ba trudiashchikhsia Zapadnoi Belorussii*, vol. 1, document no. 402, p. 554.
[17] S. J. Paprocki, ed., *Minority Affairs and Poland: An Informatory Outline* (Warsaw, 1935), p. 104.

the minorities politically powerless. Henceforth, lacking a significant parliamentary voice, Belorussian complaints could be dismissed as mere "troublemaking" or even as evidence of dangerous disaffection.[19]

The "colonels group" of Pilsudski's legionnaires, who at that time constituted the real locus of power in Poland, were highly unsympathetic toward Poland's international obligations with regard to the rights of the minority nationalities. They regarded these commitments as infringements, imposed from abroad, upon the national sovereignty of Poland.[20] Eventually, to avoid blame for violations of the Minority Nationalities Treaty, the Polish government officially renounced it in 1934.[21]

Poland's constitutional obligations toward decent treatment of national minorities were eased by the promulgation of a new constitution on April 23, 1935. Article five made plain that freedom of religion, of speech, and of public assembly would henceforth be subjected to the consideration of "common good," and the executive authority was made the judge.[22] Indeed, the Polish constitution of 1935 opened the door to official suppression of the minority nationalities. After that time no more Belorussian representatives were elected to the Sejm.[23] In the last four years before World War II, Poland was ruled by a military group and its bureaucrats were Polish by nationality.

In Poland, as earlier in tsarist Russia, there was a great need for land reform. On July 15, 1920, while the Red Army was marching toward Warsaw, the Sejm passed a Law of Land Reform which provided for the dispensation of land to farmers who had none or needed more. As soon as the danger of a Bolshevik conquest was removed, land reform became principally a means for discriminatory economic manipulation.[24] After the conclusion of the Treaty of Riga, the Polish government used the Law of Land Reform to sell land belonging to farmers who had emigrated to Russia during the war

---

[18] Robert Machray, *Poland of Pilsudski* (New York, 1937), p. 171; Rose, *Poland, Old and New*, pp. 117–18.
[19] Machray, *Poland of Pilsudski*, p. 172.
[20] Paprocki, *Minority Affairs*, p. 17.
[21] Stanislaw Mackiewicz, *Colonel Beck and His Policy* (London, 1944), p. 57.
[22] Vakar, *Belorussia*, p. 130; Paprocki, *Minority Affairs*, p. 30.
[23] Ostrowski, *Spotlight on Byelorussia*, p. 77.
[24] *Istoriia BSSR*, 2d ed. (Minsk, 1961), 2:352.

and the Revolution and did not afterwards return.[25] In addition, the lands of many big Orthodox landowners were confiscated. One of these, Count Butenev, lost all his land.[26] Such land was sold not to the Belorussian poor peasants, who needed it, but to Poles who were sent there from the Polish provinces.[27] Many of them were the Polish military colonists called *osadnicy*.[28]

The Polish policy of colonization of West Belorussia and West Ukraine was clearly formulated by Vincent Witos, a leader of the Polish Peasant Party, who once said, "Because of Poland's dispute with Russia over the eastern lands, we have had fifteen wars and three uprisings and this dispute is not yet solved. It could be solved only through colonization of this land by the Poles and through assimilation."[29] Another aspect of the Polish policy of colonization found its expression in a law passed on December 28, 1925, which provided for the partition of the large estates annually to about five million acres over a period of ten years.[30] The Belorussian and Ukrainian small farmers were, however, highly dissatisfied with this law because it fixed the maximum area of private property at about 1,000 acres in the eastern provinces but only 450 acres in Poland proper.[31] To the peasants, estates of 1,000 acres seemed too large. (In reality, there were much larger estates left than this figure indicates.) Furthermore, the Polish colonists in West Belorussia and West Ukraine received the land free of charge.[32] They also received long-term loans for building houses, buying farm equipment, and developing farming.[33]

Thus, the Polish land reform of the 1920s, so far as it affected the Belorussian peasants, proved little more than a device to deprive

[25] Vasil' Rahulia, *Uspaminy* (New York, 1957), p. 57. Rahulia was a teacher and a deputy to the Polish Sejm from West Belorussia from 1922 to 1928. In 1928 he was elected a senator, but soon was accused, along with the other Belorussian senators and deputies, of "disloyalty" to the Polish state and was sentenced to jail for two years.

[26] Ibid., p. 36.

[27] *Istoriia BSSR*, 2:352.

[28] On 17 December 1920, the Sejm passed a special law pertaining to the colonization of the eastern provinces (West Belorussia and West Ukraine) by Polish settlers, "The Union of the Farmer Defenders of the Eastern Borderlands" was formed and its members were called *osadnicy*. See: *Istoriia BSSR*, 2:353; Rahulia, *Uspaminy*, p. 37.

[29] Gorbunov, *Vossoedinenie Belorusskogo naroda*, p. 75.

[30] Machray, *Poland of Pilsudski*, p. 206.

[31] Oscar Halecki, *A History of Poland* (London, 1955), p. 292.

[32] Gorbunov, *Vossoedinenie Belorusskogo naroda*, p. 88.

[33] Ostrowski, *Spotlight on Byelorussia*, pp. 77–78; Gorbunov, *Vossoedinenie Belorusskogo naroda*, p. 88.

them of their lands. The result of the reform was that 37 percent of all arable land and about 90 percent of the forest area of West Belorussia fell into the hands of Polish landlords.[34]

In 1939 in West Belorussia there were 37,000 farms of the Polish civil colonists.[35] In addition, there were from 35,000 to 40,000 farms belonging to Polish military colonists in West Belorussia and West Ukraine.[36] The average size of their farms was about 100 acres, at a time when the average size of the Belorussian peasant's farm was only 5 to 7 acres.[37] The Belorussian peasants could not legally enlarge their farms without permission of the district administrator and there is no evidence that an Orthodox Belorussian peasant ever succeeded in obtaining such permission.[38] Consequently, the Belorussian peasants, having little or no land, were forced to work for the Polish landlords or go to neighboring countries as seasonal workers in order to support their families.[39]

The Polish government did nothing to develop the Belorussian regional economy. Many small industrial enterprises in West Belorussia which were built before the Revolution were put out of commission in the 1920s and 1930s. Between 1929 and 1939, for example, the number of such enterprises in West Belorussia was reduced from 1,463 to 1,242.[40] Generally, the policy of the Polish government was to keep the region backward and to make it an agrarian appendage of Poland proper. This was fundamentally a colonial policy.

In the early 1920s there were some grounds for optimism in the field of education in West Belorussia. Over 400 elementary schools, 7 gymnasiums (secondary schools), and 3 teachers' colleges were opened, all with instruction in Belorussian.[41] The private schools were also supported. According to Article 1 of the law concerning national minority schools in Poland, passed on July 31, 1924, private

[34] Gorbunov, *Vossoedinenie Belorusskogo naroda*, p. 87; Vakar, *Belorussia*, p. 132.
[35] Gorbunov, *Vossoedinenie Belorusskogo naroda*, p. 90.
[36] Minaev, *Zapadnaia Belorussiia*, p. 25.
[37] Gorbunov, *Vossoedinenie Belorusskogo naroda*, p. 90; Vakar, *Belorussia*, p. 132.
[38] Rahulia, *Uspaminy*, p. 37.
[39] Ostrowski, *Spotlight on Byelorussia*, pp. 77–78.
[40] Gorbunov, *Vossoedinenie Belorusskogo naroda*, p. 77.
[41] Vakar, *Belorussia*, p. 121. During World War I and the German occupation of West Belorussia there were 514 elementary and 5 high schools. See Ostrowski, *Spotlight on Byelorussia*, p. 81.

schools in the mother tongue for the children of all the nationalities living in Poland could be opened under the same conditions as those offering Polish language instruction.[42] During the early 1920s the Polish government also supported a Belorussian Teachers' Association, a Belorussian National Museum, and other nationalist institutions. It also subsidized, for reasons probably not altogether cultural, the Belorussian press.[43]

Thus, with respect to education and cultural affairs, the West Belorussians initially had few grounds for complaint, though the situation was less than perfect. Higher education could be obtained only at the Polish university in Vilna, to which only a few students of Belorussian nationality were admitted.[44] Furthermore, Vilna University did not recognize diplomas received at the Belorussian gymnasiums, although they were recognized by the Czech, Estonian, and Latvian universities, and those of other countries.[45]

Any optimism as to the future of Belorussian education, however, did not long survive. In the latter part of 1924 the Polish government began to suppress the national schools. In December most of the Belorussian elementary schools were turned into Polish schools or closed down.[46] The teachers were dismissed and many of them were taken to concentration camps.[47] In 1937, the last of the Belorussian gymnasiums was closed and the Union of Belorussian Teachers dissolved.[48] Thus, the Belorussian youth was given a choice of going to the Polish schools or remaining illiterate. Those who went to the Polish schools were forbidden to use their native language, even in private conversations.[49] In fact, the Belorussian language was outlawed. It could not be spoken in the state institutions, in the courts, at the post offices, or at the railroad stations. Even singing in Belorussian was prohibited.[50] Possession of Belorussian books was considered a "sign of disloyalty."[51] In 1924 many Belorussian newspapers were suspended and their editors sent to

---

[42] *Bor'ba trudiashchikhsia Zapadnoi Belorussii*, vol. 1, document no. 32, p. 67.
[43] Vakar, *Belorussia*, p. 121.
[44] *Bor'ba trudiashchikhsia Zapadnoi Belorussii*, vol. 1, document no. 22, p. 57.
[45] Ibid.
[46] Vakar, *Belorussia*, p. 123.
[47] Ostrowski, *Spotlight on Byelorussia*, p. 81.
[48] Vakar, *Belorussia*, p. 131; *Istoriia BSSR*, 2:356.
[49] Vakar, *Belorussia*, p. 131.
[50] G. Egorov, *Zapadnaia Belorussia* (Moscow, 1939), p. 29.
[51] Vakar, *Belorussia*, p. 131.

jail. The Belorussian libraries and clubs were closed. By 1939 there was not a single publication left in the Belorussian language.[52]

The Polish government sought a complete denationalization and Polonization of the national minorities. The objective was acknowledged very frankly in 1925 by Skulski, a member of the Polish cabinet. Referring to complaints about the closing of the Belorussian schools, he said, "I assure you that in ten years you will not find, even with a candle, a single Belorussian in Poland."[53]

The new educational policy did nothing to improve the quality of education in Poland, which between 1920 and 1939 was educationally one of the most backward countries in Europe. When World War II broke out, many of the Polish young people were illiterate. In the Polish provinces where national minorities were numerically predominant, illiteracy was even higher than in Poland proper. In the Polesie provinces of West Belorussia, for example, in 1938 the illiteracy rate was about 70 percent.[54]

There was no freedom of religion for the minority nationalities in Poland. In a belt about sixty-two miles wide along the Soviet border, the Orthodox were forced to accept the Roman Catholic faith, and those who refused were taken away from their homes under the provisions of martial law. In the area outside of this belt, most of the Orthodox churches were closed and those that remained open were forced to use the Polish liturgical texts, even in regions where people could neither speak nor read Polish.[55]

In the face of such discriminatory practices, the Belorussian parliamentary deputies and senators vigorously protested. They openly accused the government of violating the constitution and Poland's international obligations. Boldly and tirelessly, they protested brutal mistreatment of the Belorussian people, closure of the Belorussian schools and churches, and the agricultural "reforms" which were swiftly depriving the Belorussian peasants of their land and handing it over to the Polish colonists.

Vasil' Rahulia, a Belorussian deputy in the Sejm, in a speech delivered June 25, 1925, portrayed a menacing situation: "The land should be given to the Belorussian peasants. If this is not done, they will take the land themselves. The Belorussian peasants in Po-

[52] *Istoriia BSSR*, 2:357; Vakar, *Belorussia*, p. 123.
[53] Quoted in *Istoriia BSSR*, 2:357.
[54] Ibid., p. 357.
[55] Vakar, *Belorussia*, pp. 130–31.

land know that their relatives in East Belorussia received land. No barrier between Poland and her eastern neighbor would prevent the peasants in Poland from using the same methods as were used in Russia in order to get the land."[56] The speech verged, of course, upon subversion, yet the patience of the Belorussians had been sorely tried. The Belorussian deputies in the Sejm—Branislau Tarashkevich, Symon Rak-Mikhailouski, Pavel Valoshyn, Piatrok Miatla, Iury Sabaleuski, Ihnat Dvarchanin, and others—protested 52 times against forcible seizures of private land, 82 times against economic exploitation, and 218 times against personal offenses by Polish officials.[57] But the protests of the Belorussian deputies from the floor of the Sejm had no effect. As a last resort they turned to the League of Nations for help. Here is a part of their memorandum addressed to the fifth session of the League:

> The Belorussian people are suffering unbelievable terror from the Poles. . . . Corporal punishment is administered to Belorussian peasants, individually and in mass. Sometimes all the inhabitants of a village are flogged. The police and the landlords beat up Belorussian peasants wherever they happen to lay hands upon them, in the fields, in the woods, in their homes, at police stations, even in churches. . . . At the beginning of this year Deputy Tarashkevich visited Polesie province; he could not find a single village where there was even one man who had escaped merciless Polish beating. . . . The Polish police do not stop at simple beating with gun butts, knuckle dusters, or fists. . . . They have developed a system of refined torture.[58]

Such cruel treatment of a subject people was hardly to be expected in a free democracy, and indeed the Poland of that period, for all its democratic trappings, retained many of the characteristics of a feudal state.[59] Poland as a state had not existed on the map of Europe from the time of the third partition in 1795. Thus, Pilsudski started in 1918 where the last Polish king, Stanislaus Augustus Poniatowski, had left off. In Poland at the end of the eighteenth century, feudalism still existed, and in the Poland of Pilsudski and his successors, feudalism continued.

[56] Rahulia, *Uspaminy*, p. 101.
[57] Vakar, *Belorussia*, p. 123.
[58] Ibid., pp. 123–24.
[59] In the memorandum were described methods of torture from which even the GPU and Gestapo could have learned. For details of the cases enumerated in the memorandum, see Vakar, *Belorussia*, p. 124.

The Belorussian leaders of the Hramada, the deputies to the Sejm, and the senators did not escape the tortures of the Polish police. Because of their protests, they were accused of disloyalty in 1928. By order of the Polish government, the Hramada was declared dissolved, that is, illegal. Fifty-six leaders of the Hramada were taken to the courts and tried behind closed doors; the press made no mention of these trials. "Deputy Tarashkevich had been brought into the courtroom in shackles, the Deputies Dvarchanin and Hauryliuk were beaten to death, and others were treated in a like manner."[60] Those who survived the beatings were sent to jail. The local Belorussian leaders who were accused of un-Polish activities were sent to a concentration camp at Bereza Kartuska.

Political terror in Poland, directed against the minority nationalities, led to internal disturbances. In several parts of West Belorussia and West Ukraine there were strikes and continuous unrest.[61] Communist agitators wasted no time in taking advantage of the situation. Consequently, the number of Communists in West Belorussia grew fast. "While in 1924 the total number of members in the Communist Party in West Belorussia (KPZB) was barely fifteen hundred, a year later there were eighteen hundred Communists in the local jails alone."[62] In their accusations of disloyalty among the West Belorussians, the Polish police were not altogether wrong. The ultimate reason for the disloyalty, however, lay in the short-sighted policies of the Polish government, which had served to alienate rather than assimilate the minority nationalities. Now, victimized and oppressed, they waited hopefully for the collapse of the Polish state. The bitter disillusionment of the Belorussian peoples in West Belorussia was well expressed by Aleksandr Tsvikevich, a former member of the BNR government:

> Yesterday we and the Poles were two nations on the same side of the fence. Poland, "a nation crucified," was our elder brother in the momentous struggle against tsarism, and her example gave us strength and courage. We lived in the hope that freedom would come at the same time for both our people—and what happened? Revolution came, and with it, freedom for all. But as soon as Poland had risen from the dead, her scourge began to play over the white body of Belorussia. Behind the big-worded manifestoes of Pilsudski, gendarmes came to our land, and with the gendarmes, Polish-

[60] Ibid., p. 126; Rahulia, *Uspaminy*, p. 75.
[61] Minaev, *Zapadnaia Belorussiia*, p. 40.
[62] Vakar, *Belorussia*, p. 125.

Austrian (Galician) officials and Catholic priests. . . . We mistook the Polish people, or to be more accurate, the Polish revolutionary idealists, for the Polish state. Life has pitilessly crushed our illusion.[63]

The Polish government officials continued to ignore the complaints and protests of the Belorussians, who in the course of time lost any hope for improvement of their position in Poland. Their prevailing attitude is well apprehended by Nicholas Vakar: "World War II found West Belorussian loyalties divided between Communism and nationalism—but none whatsoever for Poland."

[63] Quoted in ibid.

10.

The Reunion of West & East Belorussia

Just a week before the German attack upon Poland, the Non-aggression Pact of August 23, 1939, was concluded between the Soviet Union and Germany. By Article 1 of this pact, both countries agreed to refrain from any act of violence, any aggressive action, or any attack against each other, whether individually or jointly with other powers.

Simultaneously, the governments of the Soviet Union and Germany secretly agreed to a forthcoming partition of Poland.[1] Accordingly, just as the German army was about to complete the occupation of Poland proper, on September 17, 1939, the Soviet Red Army marched into Poland from the east. The Soviet government on this day made the following declaration:

> In Poland a situation has been created which requires special consideration on the part of the Soviet Government concerning the security of the state. Poland has become a convenient ground for all sorts of accidents and surprises which could menace the safety of the USSR. Therefore, the Soviet Government considers it her sacred duty to render help to the brothers of the Russians who live in Poland. For this reason the Soviet Government has directed the Supreme Command of the Red Army to order the army to cross the Soviet-Polish border and to take over the protection of the life and property of the people in West Ukraine and West Belorussia.[2]

As the Red Army rolled into West Belorussia, the people greeted it with great enthusiasm. Here, they thought, was liberation from the Polish oppression. Now, thought the peasants, they would receive the lands of the Polish landlords. Henceforth, thought the

THE PARTITION OF POLAND, SEPTEMBER 1939

townspeople, they would have work and freedom. The people in West Belorussia were happy because now they were to be reunited with their brothers of East Belorussia. Their old dream had come true. Therefore, "the liberators, in accordance with an old custom, were offered bread and salt in the streets."[3]

The German campaign against Poland, which began on Sep-

[1] Whitney R. Harris, *Tyranny on Trial: The Evidence at Nuremberg* (Dallas, 1954), pp. 151–52.
[2] *Istoriia BSSR* (Minsk, 1961), 2:387.
[3] Nicholas P. Vakar, *Belorussia: The Making of a Nation* (Cambridge, Mass., 1956), p. 156.

tember 1, 1939, and the Soviet campaign, which began on September 17 of the same year, brought to an end the Polish state. The entire territory of Poland was divided between the USSR and the German Reich on the basis of the Soviet-German agreement concluded on September 28 in Moscow. The demarcation line established between these two countries, often called the Molotov-Ribbentrop Line after the authors of the treaty, in general "followed the Curzon Line corrected in the Belorussian sector in favor of Belorussia in accordance with the ethnographic western frontiers."[4] In reality, however, it was the old ethnographic boundary between the Polish population on one side and the Belorussian and Ukrainian populations on the other. As far as the Soviet Union was concerned the fourth partition of Poland restored to Russia its northwest boundary of 1795.[5]

Though the Soviet government wanted an immediate incorporation of West Belorussia and West Ukraine into the USSR, it wished this assimilation to appear voluntary. For that purpose, elections were ordered in West Belorussia and West Ukraine for national assemblies, which in turn would decide the state adherence of these two regions. Since the major object of the elections was to show that the people approved the incorporation, the preparation of the elections was entrusted to provisional administrations which had been organized in the occupied territories.[6]

In West Belorussia the members of the provisional administration were assisted by Communist Party officials sent from East Belorussia. As Party officials admit, "along with the first units of the Red Army the Bolshevik Party sent to West Belorussia its best people to help their blood brothers in creating Soviet conditions of life."[7] Many of these "best people," in fact, directed the provisional administration in West Belorussia[8] and the Committee of Supervision formed at Bialystok to manage the election campaign. Among the

---

[4] Wiktor Ostrowski, *Spotlight on Byelorussia and Her Neighbours* (London, 1959), p. 57.

[5] The Soviet-German demarcation line went from the San River in the south up to Iaroslav, followed the Iaroslav–Rava–Ruska–Sokal railway and the Bug River north to the Bialystok–Warsaw railroad intersection, then turned northwest, encircling the cities of Bialystok and Lomzha, touched the East Prussian border, and went northeast to the southern boundary of Lithuania.

[6] John A. Armstrong, *The Politics of Totalitarianism: The Communist Party of the Soviet Union from 1934 to the Present* (New York, 1961), p. 123.

[7] Quoted in U.S., Congress, House, Select Committee on Communist Aggression, *Communist Takeover and Occupation of Byelorussia* (Washington, D.C., 1955), p. 20.

[8] Armstrong, *Politics of Totalitarianism*, p. 123.

members of this committee, for example, were such high-ranking officials as Mikola Natalevich, chairman of the Central Executive Committee of the BSSR, three Red Army commanders (Gaisin, Makeev, and Spasin), and many other high-ranking Party officials, most of whom were not native Belorussians.[9]

During the election campaign the people were told that they were free to decide their own future and that the elections would be held in accordance with a democratic electoral law published by the Central Preelection Committee of West Belorussia.[10] The elections were held quickly. On October 6, the Soviet Military Command announced that the "general elections to a National Assembly of West Belorussia would take place on October 22, based on the universal, equal, direct, and secret ballot."[11] On that day, 2,672,000 people, or 96.7 percent of the eligible voters, took part in the election of the "national candidates," and 90.7 percent voted for them.[12] But, as in all elections in Communist countries, a single ticket of Communist-picked candidates was offered.

On October 28, six days after the elections and after only six weeks of Soviet occupation of West Belorussia, the National Assembly convened in Bialystok and unanimously decided to demand the reunion of West Belorussia with the Belorussian SSR. A delegation of sixty-six members was sent to Moscow to take part in the Fifth Extraordinary Session of the Supreme Soviet of the USSR.[13] In response to the "demand" of the West Belorussian delegation, the Supreme Soviet on November 2, 1939, adopted a law by which West Belorussia was included in the USSR and reunited with the Belorussian SSR.[14] Thus, East and West Belorussia became a single state, and the Belorussian constitution was amended to guarantee its territorial integrity, national status, and sovereignty within the USSR.[15] On February 24, 1940, the first elections for representatives to the Supreme Soviet of the BSSR and that of the USSR were held in Belorussia. The process of reunion and incorporation was thus officially confirmed.

[9] Vakar, *Belorussia*, p. 158.
[10] *Istoriia BSSR*, 2:385.
[11] Vakar, *Belorussia*, p. 157.
[12] *Istoriia BSSR*, 2:385; Vakar, *Belorussia*, p. 158.
[13] *Istoriia BSSR*, 2:387.
[14] *Belorussiia: informatsionnye materialy pravitel'stva Belorusskoi SSR* (Minsk, 1945), p. 9; *Istoriia BSSR*, 2:387.
[15] I. Trainin, *Natsional'noe i sotsial'noe osvobozhdenie Zapadnoi Ukrainy i Zapadnoi Belorussii* (Moscow, 1939), p. 78; Vakar, *Belorussia*, p. 158.

Several months before West Belorussia was formally incorporated into the USSR, the Soviet government, taking full advantage of its deal with Hitler, turned its attention to Lithuania, Latvia, and Estonia. A series of ultimatums, backed by military and NKVD pressure, speedily inflicted upon these small nations Communist-controlled governments which soon thereafter petitioned for incorporation of their countries into the Soviet Union. As usual in Communist policy, the stick was accompanied by some small offering of carrots—gestures of brotherly friendship and offers of concessions. To Lithuania, for example, the concession was a slice of Belorussian territory. On the basis of a Soviet-Lithuanian agreement of October 10, 1939, the western part of the BSSR was reduced by 2,750 square miles and a population of 457,500. This territory, with the city of Vilna and part of the Vilna region, was transferred to the Lithuanian state,[16] despite the fact that the Lithuanian population there was in the minority. The official explanation for this action was given by Viacheslav Molotov, commissar of foreign affairs, at the Fifth Extraordinary Session of the Supreme Soviet: "The Vilna territory belongs to Lithuania not by reason of population. No, we know that the majority of population in this region is not Lithuanian. But the historical past and the aspirations of the Lithuanian people have been intimately connected with the city of Vilna, and the government of the Soviet Union considered it necessary to honor these moral factors."[17]

For several months the Soviet economic policy in West Belorussia was not very restraining. In the beginning the Soviet government limited its actions to nationalization of the banks, industry, and trade. Such confiscations, however, did not greatly distress the Belorussians for these institutions had been almost exclusively in the hands of Poles.[18]

In agriculture, too, the initial policy was lenient. The Bolsheviks did not force the peasants to join the collective farms. Consequently, the peasantry divided the land and livestock of the large estates, formerly owned by Poles, and in most instances individual farms increased in size. Of course, the Communist agitators immediately started their propaganda presenting the advantages of collective

[16] Mikola Volacic, "The Population of Western Belorussia and Its Resettlement in Poland and the USSR," *Belorussian Review*, no. 3 (1956): 5.
[17] *Izvestiia*, 1 November 1939, p. 1.
[18] Vakar, *Belorussia*, p. 162.

farming. But the peasants tended to ignore it and continued to consolidate their private farms. Many assumed that they would be permitted to retain this land and had no desire for further change. In the face of such an attitude, agricultural collectivization in West Belorussia progressed very slowly. In fact, "only forty collective farms had been formed by the spring of 1940."[19]

The forced collectivization took place in the latter half of 1940, when peasants were given a choice between joining the collective farms and exile in Siberia. Not surprisingly, by the end of 1940 there were 1,115 collective farms in West Belorussia.[20] By the spring of 1941, the individual farms were almost completely eliminated.[21]

By early 1940 the army-controlled provisional administration of West Belorussia had been dissolved and the Communist Party and the Soviet governmental administration were firmly in charge.[22] Only a few local people were given important jobs.[23] Even the members of the Communist Party of West Belorussia (KPZB) were ignored; not one of them was given a responsible Party post.[24] Instead, thousands of Party officials, administrators, journalists, teachers, and others were sent from the outside to direct the Party, the Soviet organizations and, in fact, every aspect of public life.[25] Some of these outsiders were from East Belorussia and were indeed Belorussians, but a significant number of them were Russians who resided in East Belorussia or were sent from Russia. These "imported" officials continued to predominate until the Soviet Union's entry into World War II.[26]

A more ominous import of Soviet officialdom was the NKVD, the Soviet security police, which had accompanied the Red Army into West Belorussia. They brought with them prepared lists of undesirables, mostly former Polish officials, whom they proceeded to arrest immediately.[27] Their presence and their networks of secret informants, moreover, soon became uncomfortably evident in other ways. In 1940, a further purge of the Belorussian nationalists was

[19] Ibid.   [20] *Istoriia BSSR*, 2:403.
[21] *Belorussia: informatsionnye materialy pravitel'stva BSSR*, p. 166.
[22] Armstrong, *Politics of Totalitarianism*, p. 123.
[23] Robert S. Sullivant, *Soviet Politics in the Ukraine, 1917–1957* (New York, 1962), p. 237.
[24] Jan Zaprudnik, "The Communist Party of Belorussia: An Outline of Its History," *Belorussian Review*, no. 7 (1957): 39.
[25] Sullivant, *Soviet Politics in the Ukraine*, p. 237.
[26] Armstrong, *Politics of Totalitarianism*, p. 123.
[27] Volacic, "Population of Western Belorussia," p. 13.

ordered. Such well-known Belorussians as Aleksandr Ulasau, founder of *Nasha niva* (Our Land), Anton Lutskevich, former head of the BNR, and Ianka Pazniak, editor of *Krynitsa* (Fountain), were arrested. Many other nationalist leaders were arrested, including the writers Makar Kostsevich, Anton Trepka, S. Busel, and U. Samoila. All were taken away from West Belorussia. "Some of them, including Lutskevich, were shot; others, including Ulasau, died in prisons; and still others were sent to labor camps or to jails. No one has heard of them since."[28]

In the last months of 1940 and the first half of 1941, the purge spread from the cities to the villages. There was no security for anyone who had been politically active in or taken part in the national movement in the past. Those Belorussian national leaders who were popular among the people under the Polish administration were a special target of the NKVD. The more popular they were, the worse it was for them.[29]

The members of the Communist Party of West Belorussia did not escape the purge, either. Until the coming of the Red Army, most of them were hardly aware of the scope of forced collectivization and Stalin's political purges. They knew of life in the Soviet Union mainly from Soviet propaganda literature. They knew of Soviet Communism in theory; now they viewed it in practice. The Communists sent to West Belorussia from the USSR realized the extent of this disillusionment and were too suspicious to risk its consequences. The West Belorussian Communists became the victims of their own Party.

An even worse time was to come. When the German-Soviet war began on June 22, 1941, the NKVD redoubled its efforts to eliminate remaining "enemies of the Soviet state." In a few days thousands of people were killed by the Communist security police during the evacuation disorders, many perished under bombardment, and at least 50,000 were deported to the Soviet Union. Altogether, between September 1939 and June 1941, about 300,000 people of West Belorussia were deported to the eastern and northern parts of the USSR.[30]

The Communist administration and the terror of the NKVD in West Belorussia had a shocking effect. The very people who had greeted the Red Army so enthusiastically in September 1939 were glad when, under the pressure of the German army, it departed in June 1941.

[28] Vakar, *Belorussia*, p. 165.   [29] Ibid.
[30] Volacic, "Population of Western Belorussia," p. 14.

II.

Belorussia under German Occupation

> State boundaries are made by man and changed by man.... We stop the endless German movement to the south and west, and turn our gaze toward the land in the east.... Here Fate itself seems desirous of giving us a sign.
>
> Hitler[1]

Geographically, Belorussia occupies a passageway between the East and the West. For this reason, in every European war in which Russia has participated, Belorussia has been an important theater of military action. Historically, in the face of two great invasions—those of Charles XII of Sweden and Napoleon—the Belorussian peasants remained loyal to their country. In June 1941, however, many of them welcomed the advancing German troops as liberators. The contrast deserves notice: the serfs of the Polish kings and the Russian tsars in Belorussia did not welcome the foreign invaders, but the serfs of Stalin's Communist Party did.

In Soviet Belorussia, anti-Communist feeling was strong among the collectivized farmers and the intellectuals.[2] The former could neither forget the terror during the collectivization nor accept their fate in the collective farms. The latter had equally bitter memories of the political purges of the 1930s. Thus, the people of Belorussia were, like the people of the Ukraine, weary of long-continued misery and terror. They had, it seemed, nothing to lose except their chains.

Many people, as yet unaware of Nazi aims and methods, believed that Hitler was going to liberate them from Bolshevik slavery. This delusion was unwittingly fostered by Bolshevik propagandists, who up to the time of the Soviet-German nonaggression pact had ceaselessly portrayed Hitler as the worst enemy of the Communist Party. Among those Belorussians who had learned to hate the Party —and there were now many of them—Hitler came to be viewed as a champion.

In the beginning of the invasion, the German army marched through Belorussia almost without resistance. Its average daily advance was twenty to twenty-five miles, and it moved forward as much as thirty-five to forty miles on some days. On July 9, the Germans captured Minsk.[3] In about three weeks the entire BSSR was overrun.[4]

Soviet apologists have attributed the Red Army's initial failures to the superior battle experience of the German troops and to German accomplishment of full mobilization at a time when the Soviet forces were only partially deployed. On the eve of invasion, for instance, Germany had concentrated along the western frontier of the USSR "a huge invasion army totaling 190 divisions, including 153 German divisions that had almost two years' experience in modern warfare."[5] This was the greatest invasion army in human history up to that time. It seems most unlikely that the Soviet government was unaware of this military concentration. However, the Stalin purges had liquidated many of the best officers of the Soviet high command, and in this emergency Soviet strategy floundered.[6]

Perhaps as important, the soldiers of the Red Army showed singularly little will to fight. At the very beginning of the war many of them surrendered to the Germans. Evidently "the Soviet soldiers did not wish to fight for the USSR and looked upon the war situation as a possible opportunity to throw off the Communist oppressors."[7]

[1] Adolf Hitler, *Mein Kampf* (New York, 1943), pp. 653–54.
[2] Alexander Dallin, *German Rule in Russia, 1941–1945* (London, 1957), p. 199.
[3] Grigorii Deborin, *The Second World War: A Politico-Military Survey* (Moscow, [1950s]), p. 155.
[4] Nicholas P. Vakar, *Belorussia: The Making of a Nation* (Cambridge, Mass., 1956), p. 171.
[5] *Istoriia Kommunisticheskoi Partii Sovetskogo Soiuza*, 2d ed. (Moscow, 1962), p. 539.
[6] Ibid.
[7] U.S., Congress, House, Select Committee on Communist Aggression, *Communist Takeover and Occupation of Byelorussia* (Washington, D.C., 1955), p. 20.

For a time it looked as though the Red Army was on the verge of total collapse.

Menaced by the German advance, the Soviet civil administration in Belorussia yielded to panic. Government officials, Communist Party leaders, NKVD officials, and militiamen fled to the East long before the appearance of the Germans and left the civilian population to their fate.[8] Indeed, the confusion was so great that "large stocks of provisions were abandoned; bags full of Soviet currency were moved from the state banks as far as the stadium and dropped there."[9] Seeing this, the Belorussian people were more impressed by the sudden collapse of the Communist authority than by the superiority of the German military might.

Even in their retreat the Communists continued those actions which had won for them the bitterness of the Belorussians. They burned down both public buildings and private residences. Along the highways in the rural areas, agricultural machinery and livestock were destroyed or moved away. Wherever the Communists succeeded in enforcing their plan of destruction, the population was left without livestock and without any means of production.[10] Panic was vented in atrocity. Seldom did the NKVD abandon its political prisoners. "In some cases they drove the prisoners on foot to the East and, when pressed by the Germans, the NKVD guards killed them. In many cases the NKVD killed all the prisoners in the prisons, as in Berezvech."[11] In Vitebsk the city jail was burned, together with two hundred prisoners.[12] In other parts of Belorussia "in the first days of the war all prisoners with a prison term of more than ten years and all the political prisoners, including those who were not yet tried, were shot."[13] It seemed that Stalin's security police wished to leave behind no living witnesses to their crimes in Belorussia.

The first Germans who came into contact with the Belorussian people found them to be friendly and awaiting protection and order. On many occasions people greeted the Germans, according to their

---

[8] Wiktor Ostrowski, *Spotlight on Byelorussia and Her Neighbours* (London, 1959), p. 34; and U.S., Congress, House, *Communist Takeover and Occupation of Byelorussia*, p. 20.

[9] *Sotsialisticheskii vestnik*, no. 10 (1950): 197.

[10] Vakar, *Belorussia*, p. 171.

[11] U.S., Congress, House, *Communist Takeover and Occupation of Byelorussia*, pp. 20–21.

[12] Vakar, *Belorussia*, p. 171.

[13] *Sotsialisticheskii vestnik*, no. 5 (1949): 87.

traditional custom, with bread and salt.¹⁴ But their first contact with the Germans left an impression of shock and despair.

> In the villages occupied by German authorities the peaceful peasant population was subjected to unrestrained depredation and robbery. . . . In many cases, the Germans drew the rural population, including the old people, women and children, out of their dwellings as soon as the village was occupied and they were compelled to seek shelter in mud huts, dugouts, forests or even under the open sky. In broad daylight the invaders stripped the clothing and footgear from anyone they met on the road, including children, savagely ill-treating those who tried to protest against, or offer any kind of resistance to such highway robbery.¹⁵

Behind the German army came the administrators of the newly captured territory, and their aims were unequivocal conquest and dispossession—to acquire a German *Lebensraum* in the East. These desires were frankly expressed by the top Nazi Party leaders long before they came to power. The most notorious of them, Adolf Hitler, had written in *Mein Kampf*:

> The right to possess soil can become a duty if without extension of its soil a great nation seems doomed to destruction. . . . Germany will either be a world power or there will be no Germany. And for world power she needs that magnitude which will give her the position she needs in the present period, and life to her citizens. . . . If we speak of soil in Europe today, we can primarily have in mind only Russia and her vassal border states. . . . The end of Jewish rule in Russia will also be the end of Russia as a state. We have been chosen by Fate as witnesses to a catastrophe which will be the mightiest confirmation of the soundness of the folkish theory.¹⁶

Thus, the new German Reich under Hitler's leadership was to follow in the steps of the Teutonic Knights to obtain soil for the German peasantry. As Himmler stated:

> For us, the end of this war will mean an open road to the East, the creation of the Germanic Reich in this way or that. . . . The

---

¹⁴ Heinz Guderian, *Panzer Leader* (New York, 1952), pp. 193–94. General Guderian recalls that when his tank army appeared on the central front the women would come from their villages onto the very battlefield, bringing them wooden platters of bread, butter, and eggs.

¹⁵ *Trial of the Major War Criminals before the International Military Tribunal, November 14, 1945–October 1, 1946* (Nuremberg, 1947), 3:28.

¹⁶ Hitler, *Mein Kampf*, pp. 654–55.

fetching home of 30 million human beings of our blood so that still during our life time we shall be the people of 120 million Germanic souls. That means that we shall be the sole and decisive power in Europe. That means that we shall then be able to tackle the peace, during which we shall be willing for the first 20 years to rebuild and spread out our villages and towns and that we shall push the borders of our German race 500 kilometers farther to the East.[17]

In the spring of 1940, Hitler appointed Alfred Rosenberg as Reichminister for the entire eastern area, from the Baltic to the Black Sea. His aim was to eliminate the Russian state. Two days before the German attack against the Soviet Union, at a secret meeting on June 20, 1941, Rosenberg said that the German government was initiating the war in the East in order to "carry out the German world politics."[18] Confident of German victory, Rosenberg planned to divide the huge territory of the Soviet Union into four blocs: Great Finland, Ostland, the Ukraine, and the Caucasus. Ostland, or the Reichskommissariat Ostland, was to be composed of Estonia, Latvia, Lithuania, and Belorussia. Each of the four ethnic parts of the Ostland formed a *Generalbezirk*, each of which was under its own general commissar. Belorussia was designated the Weissruthenische Generalbezirk.[19]

The object of the Reichskommissariat for Estonia, Latvia, Lithuania, and Belorussia was to form a German protectorate, and then, by the Germanization of racially suitable elements, by colonization of Germanic races, and by expulsion of racially undesirable elements, to transform this region into a part of the Greater German Reich.[20] In Belorussia the Nazis planned to oust and exterminate 75 percent of the population. The remaining 25 percent, considered racially suitable for Germanization, was to be assimilated.[21]

In the meantime the boundaries of the Weissruthenische Generalbezirk were revised in the following manner: The Bialystok and Grodno regions were incorporated into East Prussia; Vilna and the territory around it were left under the Lithuanian Generalbezirk; and Brest, Pinsk, and Gomel provinces were included in the Reichskommissariat of the Ukraine. Thus, the territory of the Belorussian

[17] *Trial of the Major War Criminals*, 3:585.
[18] *Istoriia Velikoi Otechestvennoi Voiny Sovetskogo Soiuza, 1941–1945*, 1st ed. (Moscow, 1960), 1:358.
[19] Vakar, *Belorussia*, p. 176.
[20] *Trial of the Major War Criminals*, 3:583–84.
[21] *Prestupleniia nemetsko-fashistskikh okkupantov v Belorussii, 1941–1944* (Minsk, 1963), p. 14.

BELORUSSIA UNDER GERMAN OCCUPATION DURING WORLD WAR II

Generalbezirk was greatly reduced. However, the Germans planned to expand this area eastward. "The Smolensk province and perhaps parts of Briansk province still under German occupation, were to be incorporated into the Belorussian Generalbezirk."[22]

This Belorussia, the boundaries of which were drawn by the Germans, was divided into two zones—the civilian and the military. The border between them was traced along the Berezina River.[23] Minsk was chosen as the seat of the general commissar of Belorussia, Wilhelm Kube, who was appointed in July 1941. Kube had certain sympathies towards the Belorussians. He condescendingly declared his liking for the "blondies and blue-eyed Aryans who came under his rule." Emphasizing that they never had been ruled by the Mongols, he was willing to admit that to some extent they also belonged to the Aryan race. "He compared their history to that of the Irish people." In his conversations "he spoke of rearing them to maturity

[22] Vakar, *Belorussia*, p. 176.
[23] Ibid.

out of the 'tutelage' of the Bolshevik Muscovites and the feudal Polish landlords."[24]

Such flatteries and promises meant nothing, for Nazi policy in the occupied eastern European countries was based on a theory of "super race" which almost inevitably consigned lesser races to the role of slaves or undesirable animals. More than two and a half months before the Nazi invasion of the Soviet Union, at a meeting on March 30, 1941, Hitler said that in the coming war with the Soviet Union "chivalry and military honor will not be necessary."[25] Erich Koch, the general commissar of the Ukraine, was willing to prove this. "I will draw the very last out of this country. I did not come here to spread bliss. I have come to help the Fuehrer. The population must work, work and work again.... We have come here to create the basis for victory. We are a master race."[26] Martin Bormann, Hitler's deputy, said much the same thing. "The Slavs are to work for us. In so far as we don't need them, they may die. They should not receive the benefits of the German health system.... As to food, they will not get any more than is possibly necessary. We are the masters, we come first."[27]

As might be expected from such basic attitudes, the Germans displayed unmitigated arrogance in their treatment of the native population. In this respect the SS troops were especially notorious. "The uniformed Nazis walked around with their sticks hitting people in the face, showing no respect for either age or sex."[28] In the villages and towns occupied by the Germans, the populace was subjected to unrestrained depredation and robbery. According to an order issued by Hitler, German soldiers could not be brought to trial by court martial for acts committed against Soviet citizens. The same order granted even more extensive rights to all German officers. "They could destroy the Russian population according to their own discretion."[29]

Field Marshal Wilhelm Keitel, chief of the Combined German

---

[24] Dallin, *German Rule in Russia*, p. 204. Kube for many years had been a Nazi member of the Reichstag. After Hitler's accession to power, he occupied high administrative posts, such as the gauleiter of Kurmark and the oberpräsident of Brandenburg in West Prussia.
[25] *Istoriia Velikoi Otechestvennoi Voiny*, 1:358.
[26] *Trial of the Major War Criminals*, 3:406.
[27] Ibid., 5:333.
[28] Vakar, *Belorussia*, p. 186.
[29] *Trial of the Major War Criminals*, 8:488.

General Staff, issued a whole series of military orders which speak for themselves. His order of May 13, 1941, issued more than a month before the attack on the Soviet Union, concerned "certain military measures" which were to be taken in the area "Barbarossa." According to this order, the partisans and the civilian population who rendered even the smallest resistance to the occupiers were to be ruthlessly eliminated. "All suspected were to be shot without a court hearing."[30] On July 23, 1941, Keitel issued an amplification of this order, saying that security in the eastern occupied areas could not be maintained by legal prosecutions but only by spreading such terror as to crush any will of the population to resist.[31]

The overbearing principles of Hitlerism dominated the thoughts and actions of the Nazis in the occupied lands. Hitler's racial concept required that segments of the native population, such as Jews, Gypsies, and most of the Slavic people, be exterminated.[32] Hitler's directive to the German armed forces and the authorities in the occupied eastern lands stated, "We must exterminate the population, for this is a part of our mission of safeguarding the German population. We shall have to develop techniques for annihilation."[33]

At the very beginning of the German occupation of Belorussia, the Nazis isolated and confined the Jews in ghettos and the Belorussians were forbidden contact with them. In the autumn of 1941 the Nazis began exterminating the Jews. The sadism of the Nazi executioners can be judged from a report of October 30, 1941, written by Carl, the German commissioner of Slutsk region, to the commissar general of Belorussia, describing the actions and manners of the Einsatzkommando (special task force) sent to Slutsk:

> As regards the execution of Jews, I must point out to my deepest regret that the latter almost bordered on sadism. The town itself during action offered a picture of horror, with indescribable brutality on the part of both the German police officers and particularly of the Lithuanian partisans. The Jewish people, also with them White Ruthenians, were taken out of their dwellings and herded together. Everywhere in the town shots were to be heard, and in different streets the corpses of Jews who had been shot, accumulated. The White Ruthenians were in the greatest anguish to free themselves from encirclement. . . . The White Ruthenians them-

---

[30] *Istoriia Velikoi Otechestvennoi Voiny*, 1:358–59.
[31] *Trial of the Major War Criminals*, 4:458–59.
[32] Deborin, *Second World War*, p. 135.
[33] Quoted in ibid.

selves were also beaten with clubs and rifle butts. It was no longer a question of action against the Jews. It looked much more like a revolution. . . .

In conclusion I find myself obliged to point out that the police battalion looted in an unheard-of manner during the action . . . not only in Jewish houses, but equally in those of the White Ruthenians. Anything of use, such as boots, leather, cloth, gold, and other valuables, was taken away. According to the statements of the troops, watches were torn off the arms of Jews openly in the streets and rings pulled off their fingers in the most brutal manner.[34]

Other Nazi practices particularly antagonized the Belorussians. Frequently the Nazis would surround public markets and seize the younger people, including young women, to be shipped back to Germany for forced labor. For this purpose, the Nazis sometimes even raided churches during religious services. In Germany these captives were housed in separate camps, had to wear a degrading badge, *Ostarbeiter*, and "were exposed to many other humiliations."[35] Another German practice which inflicted much anguish was taking Belorussian children from their parents so that they might be sent to Germany for intensive "Germanization." In his speech to the SS generals at Posen on October 4, 1943, Himmler said, "What the natives can offer in the way of good blood of our type we will take, if necessary, by kidnapping their children and raising them here with us. Whether other natives live in prosperity or starve to death interests me only insofar as we need them as slaves for our culture; otherwise, it is of no interest to me."[36] In short, the adults and the children racially unfit for assimilation were to be treated as slaves or killed. "On the territory of the Latvian SSR the German usurpers killed thousands of children, which they had brought there with their parents from the Belorussian SSR."[37]

In desperation, the Belorussians began to fight back, hiding in the forests and from there waging guerrilla war. A German general, Heinz Guderian, has since admitted, "The so-called 'Reich Commissars' soon managed to alienate all sympathy from the Germans

---

[34] *Trial of the Major War Criminals*, 4:248. The word partisans here refers to pro-Nazi Lithuanians who went underground against the Red Army during the Soviet occupation of Lithuania in 1940–1941. See Victor H. Bernstein, *Final Judgement: The Story of Nuremberg* (New York, 1947), p. 198.
[35] Georg von Rauch, *A History of Soviet Russia* (New York, 1958), p. 333.
[36] *Trial of the Major War Criminals*, 3:406.
[37] Ibid., 2:64.

and thus to prepare the ground for all the horrors of partisan warfare."[38]

In retrospect, one can see that in country after country the German occupation created a similar situation. The "underground resistance" was not, however, a completely spontaneous phenomenon. Stalin, in a radio speech of July 3, 1941, called on the people in the areas of Nazi occupation to organize "diversion groups" and "partisan units" to fight against the Nazis behind the front line.[39] Those Communists who had been unable to flee to the East when the Germans marched through Belorussia were instructed to start organizing this underground movement and to provide its initial leadership.

On July 18, 1941, the Central Committee of the All-Union Communist Party decided upon an "organization of partisan warfare behind the front line."[40] Shortly afterward, Panteleimon Ponomarenko, First Secretary of the Central Committee of the Belorussian Communist Party, was made chief of the general staff of the Belorussian guerrilla movement, with headquarters in Moscow. General Masul'ski was appointed as his chief assistant.[41] Thereafter, from time to time, I. P. Hanenko and N. E. Aukhimovich, the Secretaries of the Central Committee, were sent from Moscow to occupied Belorussia to maintain contact with the Communists in the underground and to help them in their organization.[42] By the summer of 1941, an underground regional committee of the Communist Party at Minsk, headed by V. I. Kozlov, I. D. Varashenia, I. A. Bel'ski, V. I. Bonder, and others, was already organized.[43]

In the spring of 1942, schools were organized in the East to prepare the underground fighters. Members of the Communist Youth (Komsomol) of Belorussian and Ukrainian nationalities, both men and women, were released from the institutes, the universities, and the army, and were given two months of intensive training before being sent to the areas occupied by the Germans. In six months, more than 26,000 guerrilla fighters were trained and sent across the front line.[44] People and military supplies were infiltrated into Belo-

[38] Guderian, *Panzer Leader*, p. 194.
[39] "Vystuplenie po radio Predsedatelia Gosudarstvennogo Komiteta Oborony I. V. Stalina" [Radio Speech of the Chairman of the State Committee of Defense I. V. Stalin], *Pravda*, 3 July 1941, p. 1.
[40] *Istoriia Velikoi Otechestvennoi Voiny*, 2:121.
[41] Vakar, *Belorussia*, p. 192.
[42] *Istoriia Velikoi Otechestvennoi Voiny*, 2:124.
[43] I. S. Kravchenko and I. E. Marchenko, *Belorusskaia SSR* (Moscow, 1959), p. 42.
[44] *Istoriia BSSR*, 2d ed. (Minsk, 1961), 2:446.

russia mainly through the so-called "Surazh" or "Vitebsk" gate. This forested area constituted, in effect, a breach in the German front line. It was protected by the first Belorussian partisan brigade.[45]

Agents of the NKVD also were sent to Belorussia.[46] Their duty was to organize the secret service of the underground movement and to direct actions of sabotage and terrorism. According to some reports, 4,650 spies and saboteurs trained in Russia were sent to German-occupied Belorussia as early as the fall of 1941.[47] These agents were instructed to pose as the most devoted German collaborators and at the same time "to do all which was possible in order to prevent the enemy from gaining any support from the population of Belorussia."[48] Their favorite method was to use terrorism against German soldiers and officers in order to provoke drastic German retaliations upon the peaceful civil population and thus to stir their hatred for the Germans.[49]

To such tactics the German authorities reacted with predictable severity. On September 16, 1941, Field Marshal Keitel ordered that for each German soldier killed by the partisans, from fifty to a hundred civilians were to be executed. The order pointed out that the "way in which the sentence is carried out should still further increase the deterrent effect."[50] A further order, dated October 1, 1941, also dealt with the taking and killing of hostages. Keitel directed his military commanders always to have at their disposal a number of hostages of varied political categories—Communists, Nationalists, and Democratic-bourgeois.[51] The prospect of mass executions seems to have had a strong appeal to the German high command. Hitler had said on July 16, 1941, "Partisan warfare has an advantage for us. It gives us an opportunity to exterminate more people."[52]

Faced with such a policy, many of the Belorussian people saw no alternative but to fight, if only for survival, and the warfare became increasingly ferocious. Under a pretense of fighting against the partisans, the Germans burned whole villages and towns and

---

[45] Ibid., pp. 446–47.
[46] Ivan Novikau, "Darohi skryzhyvalisia u Minsku," *Polymia*, no. 4 (1964): 76–77.
[47] Vakar, *Belorussia*, p. 193.
[48] *Sotsialisticheskii vestnik*, nos. 11–12 (1950): 122.
[49] Vakar, *Belorussia*, p. 193.
[50] *Trial of the Major War Criminals*, 4:459.
[51] Ibid., 10:193.
[52] *Prestupleniia nemetsko-fashistskikh okkupantov*, p. 14.

massacred their populations, sometimes by shooting, sometimes by hanging, sometimes with public torture of the victims.[53]

Thus, in most areas of Belorussia the people began to join the guerrilla units. In the meantime, in order to win the sympathy of the population for the Communist side, the partisans spread reports of great changes in the Soviet Union. They told about the granting of freedom of religion, freedom of speech, and other freedoms. From airplanes leaflets in the Belorussian language were dropped, which said that "our struggle against Fascism is a struggle for life and freedom."[54] These strengthened the hope of the Belorussian people that the Soviet Union after a victorious war might become a freer country, perhaps through the influence of the United States and Great Britain. On the other hand, the people realized that in the event of a German victory, they had nothing to gain and everything to lose.

In 1942, the situation behind the German front line in Belorussia began to change. As the NKVD agents multiplied their acts of sabotage, the Germans blamed the local population and inflicted drastic punishments. "In Gomel the Germans rounded up the population, tortured and tormented them, and then took them to the center of the city and shot them in public."[55] In September 1943, NKVD agents dynamited the Gestapo dining hall in Minsk, killing one German officer. On the order of Wilhelm Kube, "The residents of two streets were summarily arrested and shot."[56] Two weeks later, on September 22, Kube himself was killed by a bomb put in his bed by a servant girl.[57]

Kube was replaced by SS General Von Gottberg, who was even more cruel than his predecessor. A new wave of terror spread over Belorussia. The Germans continued their arrests and executions, often of Belorussians who had no connection with the Communists. Most of those arrested at that time were Belorussian nationalists.[58] The Germans disliked them because they wanted freedom and independence for their country, while the Germans planned other-

[53] *Trial of the Major War Criminals*, 1:52.
[54] *Zbornik listovak usenarodnai partyzanskai barats'by u Belorusi u hady Vialikai Aichynnai Vainy* (Minsk, 1952), p. 16.
[55] *Trial of the Major War Criminals*, 1:49.
[56] Dallin, *German Rule in Russia*, p. 219.
[57] Vakar, *Belorussia*, p. 193.
[58] "Belaruski vyzvoleny rukh u chase niametskai akupatsyi, 1941–1945" [The Belorussian Liberation Movement during the Time of German Occupation, 1941–1945], *Belaruskae slova*, 25 March, 1950, p. 4.

wise. Rosenberg said in September 1942 that "arbitrary rule and tyranny will be an extremely suitable form of government in Eastern Europe."[59]

The extension of German terror in Belorussia was paralleled by the growth of the partisan movement. In 1943 the partisans controlled nearly 60 percent of the territory of Belorussia.[60] Their total number at the end of that year was about 300,000.[61]

For reasons already described, the Belorussian national movement was greatly weakened at the start of World War II. Nevertheless, immediately after the retreat of the Red Army and the flight of the Soviet administration, the Belorussians, to maintain such semblance of public order as they could, began to organize their own administration and police forces.[62] The civil administrators in the German area of occupation, though hardly sympathetic toward any Belorussian independence movement, were willing to use the movement for their own purposes. Thus, in Belorussia, at least, the activities of the nationalists were tolerated to some extent. The anticommunist political refugees who had fled to Germany were permitted to return, and they were greatly helpful in reorganizing local administrative institutions. They were initially far more hopeful than the actual circumstances justified.[63]

The German administrators, very willing to play both ends against the middle, also brought to Belorussia many Russian political exiles who had resided in various European countries now under German occupation. Most of these Russian emigrants were members of the N.T.S. (*Natsional'no-Trudovoi Soiuz*), otherwise known as "solidarists."[64] Their aspirations for the future of Belorussia differed radically from those of the nationalists. The "solidarists" wanted a united Russia; the Belorussian nationalists were separatists.[65] Consequently, a struggle between them for domination of the local administration in Belorussia was impending.

Also complicating this struggle for power were the Poles. Many of them, it will be recalled, had settled in Belorussia during the period

[59] *Niurnbergskii protsess: sbornik materialov*, 2d ed. (Moscow, 1954), 1:273.
[60] Kravchenko and Marchenko, *Belorusskaia SSR*, p. 44.
[61] *Istoriia BSSR*, 2:466.
[62] U.S., Congress, House, *Communist Takeover and Occupation of Byelorussia*, p. 22.
[63] Ostrowski, *Spotlight on Byelorussia*, p. 35.
[64] Vakar, *Belorussia*, p. 187.
[65] Ibid.

of Polish control. Now, in a fluid political situation, a struggle developed between the Belorussian nationalists and the Polish intruders, which the Nazis exploited "for their own ends."[66]

For the time, however, it seemed that the Belorussian nationalists were winning. Dr. Ivan Ermachenko was selected as chief adviser to General Commissar Kube. Dr. Vitaut Tumash was appointed mayor of Minsk. Radaslau Astrouski, a former director of the Belorussian gymnasium at Vilna and BNR minister of education in 1918, was selected to head the Mogilev and Smolensk regional *Uprava* (Municipal Council). In most Belorussian towns the *upravas* were headed by the Belorussian nationalists.[67] Furthermore, "various local committees that had sprung up under military occupation were unquestionably native in composition."[68]

The Germans did not intervene in the religious affairs of the Slavic people. Martin Borman wrote, "Religion we leave to them as a means of diversion."[69] The Belorussians took advantage of this and from the very beginning of the German occupation began to organize their religious life. In the eastern part of Belorussia all churches had been closed by the Communists, and the priests executed or exiled. The believers there at once began to repair the churches and renew the services. The priests came from West Belorussia, where many churches still remained open because of the brevity of the Communists' control of that area. Thus, within a short time, the churches were open throughout the country. The German authorities even allowed the organization of a Belorussian Autocephalous Orthodox Church, with Metropolitan Panteleimon as its head.[70] During the difficult years under German occupation, the church remained a source of spiritual comfort and tried to give the people what little protection it could.

Most of the schools were closed in 1941–1942 because of the great destruction of the war. However, in the first year of German occupation, school sections were organized in every administrative division, beginning with the counties and ending with the General Commissariat. The next year more elementary schools were opened. The German authorities refused, however, to grant permission for

[66] U.S., Congress, House, *Communist Takeover and Occupation of Byelorussia*, p. 23.
[67] Vakar, *Belorussia*, p. 178.
[68] Ibid., p. 189.
[69] Bernstein, *Final Judgement*, p. 138.
[70] U.S., Congress, House, *Communist Takeover and Occupation of Byelorussia*, p. 23.

reopening the secondary schools. According to their plans of colonial policy, Belorussia had to be an agrarian country and the Belorussians had to be farmers and cattle raisers; for such, elementary schools were sufficient.[71] As Martin Borman wrote about the Slavs, "We don't want them educated; it is enough if they can count up to 100. Such stooges will be more useful for us."[72] The Nazis considered every educated person as a potential future enemy. However, defeats of the German armies on the eastern front and the alarming growth of the anti-German partisan movement in Belorussia led the Germans to modify their policies in all spheres, including education. As a result, permission was given to open some secondary schools and middle professional schools in the major towns of Belorussia. In Mogilev a medical institute was opened. As the front moved closer to this town, the institute was moved to Novaia Vileika.[73]

The Belorussian nationalist leaders wanted to set up some organization or organizations which would give them an opportunity simply to contribute to the welfare of their people and to promote their feeling of national unity. To this end, in the fall of 1941, on the initiative of Dr. Apanas Antanovich, a Belorussian Red Cross was organized in Minsk to help the local population. The Germans, however, liked neither the name nor the idea of this organization. "The idea of a Red Cross as an institution of an international character connected with the International Red Cross did not suit Nazi plans for the full control of Belorussia. Soon after the arrival of the German civil administration, the Belorussian Red Cross was liquidated."[74] The Germans did, however, grant permission to organize a "self-help" organization, known as *Samapomach*, or by its official initials as the BNS.[75]

The original authority of the *Samapomach* was limited, but it supplied the Belorussian nationalists with a legal institution of their own. With Dr. Ermachenko at its head, the *Samapomach* gradually grew into a political organization which played a great role in the life of the Belorussian population. It was hoped that it would create the basic foundation for future self-government.[76] The Germans, on

---

[71] Ibid., p. 24.
[72] *Trial of the Major War Criminals*, 5:333.
[73] U.S., Congress, House, *Communist Takeover and Occupation of Byelorussia*, p. 24.
[74] Ibid., p. 23.
[75] Dallin, *German Rule in Russia*, p. 217.
[76] "Belaruski vyzvoleny rukh," p. 4.

the contrary, viewed the *Samapomach* as an instrument to control Belorussia created by the natives.[77] But the Belorussian nationalists were not willing to cooperate with the Germans unconditionally. They protested the cruel German treatment of the civil population and prisoners of war. They also protested the administrative removal of western and southern territories from Belorussia. The Germans ignored these protests. The Belorussian nationalists then resentfully undertook more radical measures. An underground *Belaruskaia Nazalezhnitskaia Partyia* (Party of Belorussian Independence) was formed on July 7, 1942, in Minsk.[78] The Christian Democrats formed *Belaruski Narodny Front* (Belorussian People's Front) under the leadership of Father Hadleuski. Both of these parties conducted underground attacks against Belorussians who collaborated with the Germans. Their slogan, "Neither the Russians nor the Germans," attracted more and more people as the discontent with the occupying forces grew.[79]

The Germans reacted quickly. In the summer of 1942, many Belorussian leaders were arrested. Some were sent to Germany, some were shot. Father Hadleuski was executed. In Slutsk several nationalists were arrested and hanged on a Sunday in the public square.[80] So it was in the other villages and towns.

In the spring of 1943, the *Samapomach* sharply criticized the German policy of burning villages and killing the innocent population, and demanded the creation of Belorussian armed forces under Belorussian command. In their view, the Belorussians themselves should fight against the partisans. Soon afterward, Dr. Ermachenko was ousted and arrested.[81]

In the meantime, the situation was becoming worse. The Communist underground saboteurs intensified their terror against both the Germans and the Belorussian nationalist leaders. In 1943 many German officials were assassinated, ranging from the general commissar of Belorussia to the city commandant of Baranavichy. Also assassinated were several prominent Belorussian nationalists, among them Frantsishak Aliakhnovich, a dramatist and publicist; Fabian Akinshyts, an organizer and propagandist; Uladyslau Kazlouski, the editor of *Belaruskaia hazeta* (Belorussian Gazette); Professor

[77] Dallin, *German Rule in Russia*, p. 217.
[78] *Bats'kaushchyna*, 15 October 1951; Vakar, *Belorussia*, p. 189.
[79] Vakar, *Belorussia*, p. 190.
[80] Ibid.
[81] U.S., Congress, House, *Communist Takeover and Occupation of Byelorussia*, p. 26; "Belaruski vyzvoleny rukh," p. 4.

Vatslau Ivanouski, the mayor of Minsk; and many priests, teachers, and workers of the *Samapomach*.⁸²

And yet, as previously noted, military reverses were causing the Germans to grant concessions in order to win the support of the Belorussian nationalists. Even Commissar Kube came to realize the necessity for changes, and only a few months before his assassination he admitted, "The problems of the East cannot be solved by military means alone."⁸³ On June 27, 1943, Kube announced the formation of a *Rada Muzhou Daveru* (Council of Men of Confidence), which was to act as an advisory body to Kube himself in matters of local government and education. Shortly afterward, the formation of a Union of Belorussian Youth, *Saiuz Belaruskai Moladzi*, was proclaimed. "Both were to help bolster the furious but futile fight against the guerrillas and especially to counter the growing support they received from the rank and file."⁸⁴

The limited authority of the *Rada Muzhou Daveru*, however, did not satisfy its members, who tried to persuade the general commissar to widen the scope of the Council's authority beyond local affairs and education, arguing that this would enable them to count on the support of the Belorussian people.⁸⁵ The Germans grudgingly granted a few concessions, but only after the assassination of Kube on September 22, 1943, did the new general commissar, General Von Gottberg, "after long hesitation and apparently without orders from Berlin," decide "to play the carols of Belorussian patriotism in anti-guerrilla warfare." He called the *Rada Muzhou Daveru* into its first formal session on December 2, 1943, and asked for advice.⁸⁶ On December 21 he approved the status of the *Belaruskaia Tsentral'-naia Rada* (Belorussian Central Council, or B.Ts.R.). On January 22, 1944, the B.Ts.R. was formed, with Radaslau Astrouski as its president. In accepting the position, Astrouski demanded several drastic changes: 1) a convocation of the Second All-Belorussian Congress to decide all matters of the Belorussian people's future administration; 2) formation of Belorussian forces of defense; and 3) use of these forces only against the Bolsheviks in the territory of Belorussia.⁸⁷

⁸² *O partiinom podpol'e v Minske v gody Velikoi Otechestvennoi Voiny, Iiun' 1941–iiul' 1944* (Minsk, 1961), p. 74.
⁸³ Dallin, *German Rule in Russia*, p. 220.
⁸⁴ Ibid., p. 219.
⁸⁵ "Belaruski vyzvoleny rukh," p. 4.
⁸⁶ Vakar, *Belorussia*, p. 202.
⁸⁷ "Belaruski vyzvoleny rukh," p. 5.

After a prolonged discussion, these conditions were accepted by the German authorities. It was a considerable triumph for the Belorussian nationalist leaders, for the B.Ts.R. was supposed not only to replace the *Samapomach* in the fields of local government, education, and cultural affairs, but also to have some authority in handling civil affairs in general. The B.Ts.R. immediately accredited the consultants to various German commissars in the provinces and began to issue decrees in its own name. "It looked as though the country was going to have a national government."[88]

Indeed, from further developments it seemed that the B.Ts.R. was acquiring more and more power. At its demand, for example, a corps of *Kraevaia Aborona* (Country's Defense) was set up, wearing the Belorussian white-red-white emblem on their caps. Early in March 1944, a Belorussian Defense Committee was formed. An officers' school was opened in Minsk, and on March 6, Astrouski declared a mobilization "for Belorussian National Defense."[89] About 100,000 men were drafted. The Germans delayed, however, in handing over arms to them, presumably because they were not sure of their loyalty. Thus, only about 36,000 soldiers were armed and organized into battalions.[90] Some of them were sent to fight the partisans. Later, as the Red Army advanced and occupied all Belorussia, the Belorussian battalions loyal to the B.Ts.R. were withdrawn to Germany and reorganized into a combat division.[91]

One of the next German concessions was a decision to separate the Generalbezirk of Belorussia from Ostland. This was done by a decree signed by Hitler on April 1, 1944, by which Belorussia was established as a separate entity, the General Commissariat, subordinate directly to Berlin.[92]

The final stage of German concessions to the Belorussians was concluded on June 27, 1944, when the Second All-Belorussian Congress was called to reaffirm the principles of Belorussian independence and democracy announced twenty-six years before and to appoint a government responsible to the B.Ts.R. There were 1,039 delegates at the Congress who supposedly represented all classes of people irrespective of race and creed.[93] The basic decisions of the

[88] Vakar, *Belorussia*, p. 202.
[89] U.S., Congress, House, *Communist Takeover and Occupation of Byelorussia*, p. 27.
[90] Ostrowski, *Spotlight on Byelorussia*, p. 36.
[91] Dallin, *German Rule in Russia*, p. 223.
[92] Ibid.
[93] Ostrowski, *Spotlight on Byelorussia*, p. 36.

congress as the supreme representative body of the Belorussian nation were as follows:

1) Confirmation of the Declaration of Belorussian Independence of March 25, 1918.

2) Repudiation of the Belorussian SSR.

3) Denunciation of all the treaties and agreements concluded between the government of the USSR and the former government of Poland as well as all those which the government of the USSR and the Polish governments-in-exile might conclude among themselves or with a third power in regard to Belorussia.

4) Declaration of the B.Ts.R. as the only legitimate body to represent the Belorussian people at that time.[94]

It was an empty triumph. The Red Army, advancing westward, was already not far from Minsk. The delegates were compelled to conclude their work hurriedly and, together with the members of the B.Ts.R., to flee their country.

[94] *Za dziarzhaunuiu nezalezhnasts' Belarusi* (London, 1960), pp. 116–17.

12.

Belorussia after World War II

Because of its geographic situation Belorussia suffered from the Nazis more than any other country in Eastern Europe. One American who traveled through it in 1946 wrote, "During six months I traveled from one end of this republic to the other, and I can only think of it as the most devastated territory in the world."[1] During the three years of occupation, the Germans had destroyed and burned 209 towns and 9,200 villages in Belorussia.[2] Eighty percent of Minsk, the capital of the Belorussian SSR, was destroyed. Ninety percent of Vitebsk, the second largest city, was destroyed. All other cities of the republic were at least as badly wrecked.[3] In many districts, the people of all the towns and villages were homeless and without bread.[4] All in all, in the towns and villages about 3,000,000 people were left homeless and with no means of subsistence.[5] Between 80 and 90 percent of the industrial enterprises in the cities and towns, such as Minsk, Vitebsk, Gomel, Mogilev, Polotsk, Molodechno, Orsha, Borisov, and Zhlobin, were destroyed.[6] The size of Belorussian industry in 1945 was only about 20 percent of that of 1940.[7]

There was cultural ruin, also. With mingled vandalism and rapacity, the Germans had destroyed or looted the finest monuments of the material and spiritual culture of Belorussia—its educational, cultural, and scientific institutions. They took away or destroyed the most valuable historical documents and books of the Belorussian Academy of Sciences, burned the Lenin State Library, and devastated the palace of Prince Paskevich-Erivanski in Gomel, which had been considered "one of the loveliest buildings in the republic."[8] They also looted or destroyed the finest exhibits of the state art galleries. On order of Himmler, a large and very valuable collection of art treasures and paintings was packed by the SS and shipped to Germany.[9] Altogether, the Germans destroyed more than 6,000 school buildings and nearly all institutions of higher learning, theaters, and museums.[10]

During the three years of German occupation, Belorussia lost 61 percent of its horses, 69 percent of its cattle, 89 percent of its pigs, and 78 percent of its sheep.[11] In general, according to official sources, the direct losses alone under German occupation were estimated at 75 billion rubles.[12] Belorussia lost more than half of its national wealth.[13]

Because of such great material losses, rehabilitation required an effort far beyond the republic's own capability. To avert a major famine, the United Nations Relief and Rehabilitation Administration (UNRRA) delivered to Belorussia a considerable quantity of supplies.[14] The Soviet Union, now in its turn a looter from the Germans, contributed much money, technical equipment, and machinery.[15] "The manpower problem was solved by establishing slave labor camps, either moved westward from other parts of the Union or filled on the spot with the repatriated 'ostarbeiters' from Germany."[16] With such aid, Belorussia's villages were rebuilt and its industry gradually restored.

After the war, the Soviet government changed its policy toward the industrialization of the Belorussian Republic. Before the war, the Soviet leaders had not wanted to build heavy industry in Belorussia because it neighbored on the capitalist Western world so that

[1] Quoted in Nicholas Vakar, *Belorussia: The Making of a Nation* (Cambridge, Mass., 1956), p. 209.
[2] *Istoriia BSSR*, 2d ed. (Minsk, 1961), 2:501.
[3] *Bol'shaia sovetskaia entsiklopediia*, 2d ed. (Moscow, 1950–1958), 4:491.
[4] *Istoriia BSSR*, 2:501.
[5] N. N. Akimov, ed., *Nekotorye voprosy istorii KPB v poslevoennyi period* (Minsk, 1961), p. 5.
[6] Ibid., p. 4.
[7] P. F. Hlebka, ed., *Farmiravan'ne i razvits'tsio Belaruskai satsyialistychnai natsyi* (Minsk, 1958), p. 163.
[8] Vakar, *Belorussia*, p. 210.
[9] Victor H. Bernstein, *Final Judgement: The Story of Nuremberg* (New York, 1947), p. 229.
[10] I. S. Kravchenko and I. E. Marchenko, *Belorusskaia SSR* (Moscow, 1959), p. 51.
[11] I. E. Makarenko, ed., *Khrestomatiia po istorii BSSR* (Minsk, 1962), 2:117.
[12] *Niurnbergskii protsess: sbornik materialov*, 2d ed. (Moscow, 1954), 1:739.
[13] K. V. Kiselev, ed., *Belorusskaia SSR na mezhdunarodnoi arene* (Moscow, 1964), p. 20.
[14] John A. Armstrong, *The Politics of Totalitarianism: The Communist Party of the Soviet Union from 1934 to the Present* (New York, 1961), p. 204.
[15] Akimov, *Nekotorye voprosy istorii KPB*, p. 42.
[16] Vakar, *Belorussia*, p. 210.

any industry there could be easily destroyed in case of war. Now, however, Belorussia's neighbors in the West became the Latvian and Lithuanian Soviet republics and the People's Republic of Poland. With such improved protection, the Belorussian Republic was permitted to build heavy industry, and railroad, locomotive, tractor, and automobile plants were constructed in Minsk, Vitebsk, Gomel, and other cities. By 1950 the value of the industrial production of Belorussia was 15 percent higher than in 1940.[17]

During the German occupation, Belorussia suffered great losses of human life, perhaps as many as 1,400,000 civilians.[18] About 380,000 predominantly young people of both sexes were taken to Germany as slave laborers, many of whom died there of hard work and mistreatment.[19]

The tragedy of the Belorussian people did not end, however, in the summer of 1944 when Belorussia was "liberated" from the Germans. They soon learned that Stalin and the Soviet regime under his leadership remained unchanged. Moreover, his "cult of personality" was reaching a climax as the victory over the Nazis neared completion. Inflicting terror had long been a source of Stalin's power, and he was now determined to use it to the fullest extent in the territories reoccupied by the Red Army. "On Stalin's order whole nations totally or in a considerable part were taken by the NKVD men from their homes and sent thousands of miles away from their native lands where hard labor, hunger, and death were waiting for them." All Crimean Tartars and all natives of the Chechen-Ingush Autonomous Soviet Republic were sent behind the Urals. These two "Soviet autonomous republics "were liquidated.[20] As officially depicted, these mass deportations were punishments for collaboration with the Germans against Soviet interests, and nonresistance to the Germans during the years of occupation. To Stalin, an adequate reason for the deportations was "disloyalty to the father of the people."[21]

In Belorussia, too, after the expulsion of the Nazis by the Red Army, a "bloody reprisal" on the people immediately began. "Every-

[17] Kravchenko and Marchenko, *Belorusskaia SSR*, p. 56.
[18] *Prestupleniia nemetsko-fashistskikh okkupantov v Belorussii, 1941–1944* (Minsk, 1963), p. 353. In 1939 in Belorussia there were 737,240 Jews. Almost all of them were exterminated by the Germans in 1941–1944.
[19] *Istoriia BSSR*, 2:501.
[20] B. Dvinov, "Velikoe pereselenie narodov SSSR," *Sotsialisticheskii vestnik*, no. 3 (12 March 1947): 38.
[21] Ibid.

thing which had a national character was wiped from the face of the Belorussian land as a manifestation of Belorussian bourgeois nationalism."[22] Many thousands of Belorussians were accused of being bourgeois nationalists, collaborators with the Germans, or simply disloyal to the Soviet regime, and were sent to the concentration camps in Siberia.[23] Even those Belorussians who had survived in the slave labor and prison camps in Germany did not escape persecution after their return home.[24] From Stalin's paranoid point of view, these were ideologically contaminated people, to be viewed with great suspicion.

How many Belorussians were imprisoned or sent to Siberian concentration camps is not yet known and perhaps never will be. Even an estimate is difficult. In the early postwar years there was a considerable exchange of population between the Belorussian SSR and Poland, and figures have not been disclosed as to how many Poles left Belorussia and how many Belorussians returned from Poland. In addition, Belorussia experienced many territorial changes between 1939 and 1951, as a result of which part of its territory went to Lithuania and Poland. However, available data support the view that the Belorussian SSR lost a larger percentage of population during World War II and the postwar years of Stalin's political terror and mass deportations than any other republic of the Soviet Union. In September 1939, the population of BSSR was approximately 10.5 million.[25] Twenty years later, in 1959, the population was only 8,054,600.[26] The fact that many Russians were sent to Belorussia after World War II also has to be taken into consideration.[27]

With the ending of the war, the Communist Party of Belorussia was faced with the grand task of providing the backbone for the returning Soviet administration. The first task was to establish Soviet law and order. All elements disruptive of totalitarian unity had to be removed, including the now suspect *ostarbeiters* and former prisoners of war. But of primary importance to the Communists was liquidating the Belorussian national liberation movement. The

[22] U.S., Congress, House, Select Committee on Communist Aggression, *Communist Takeover and Occupation of Byelorussia* (Washington, D. C., 1955), p. 28.
[23] Dvinov, "Velikoe pereselenie narodov SSSR," p. 40.
[24] Vakar, *Belorussia*, p. 208.
[25] *Bol'shaia sovetskaia entsiklopediia*, 2d ed., 4:468.
[26] *Belorusskaia SSR: itogi vsesoiuznoi perepisi naseleniia, 1959* (Moscow, 1963), p. 6.
[27] *Sotsialisticheskii vestnik*, no. 4 (April 1960): 62.

Communists could hardly ignore the fact that on June 27, 1944, despite difficult circumstances, a Second All-Belorussian Congress, assembled in Minsk, had decided to repudiate the Belorussian SSR and had confirmed the declaration of Belorussian independence proclaimed in 1918. There could hardly be more solid evidence of the influence of the national liberation movement at the end of the war on the Belorussian intelligentsia, farmers, and working class. All of them opposed Stalin's brand of Communism.

But the range of Communist suspicion was limitless. There were, for example, millions of Soviet people who, having served in the Red Army during the war, had seen life in the West and thus "became a potential source for new ideas and a basis for demands for greater freedom."[28] Greatly alarmed, the Communist leadership inaugurated throughout the country a campaign to tighten Party control at all levels.[29] The Communist propaganda changed its target. If in prewar propaganda and literature the writers had generally shown the struggle between the Soviet people and the enemies of the Soviet system, in postwar literary works the center of attention shifted to the rooting out of survivals of capitalism in the life and mode of life of "backward citizens." In the Communist vocabulary, citizens who were nationally conscious and dissatisfied with the totalitarian methods of Communist administration became "bourgeois nationalists." These were accused of being servants of "international reaction" and of being supported by the capitalist countries, most of all by the American "imperialists."[30] They were to be exposed and liquidated as "enemies of the people." The following warning statement, expressed by Stalin in 1939, was popularized in the Communist press in the postwar years: "Our task is to maintain the utmost vigilance and to be on guard. And if we are vigilant, comrades, we will surely beat our enemies in the future just as we are beating them at present and have beaten them in the past."[31]

The Communist leaders had some reason to worry. The Germans had blundered grievously in their occupation policies; nevertheless, considerable numbers of Ukrainians and Belorussians had chosen to fight on the German side. The war, moreover, had brought about vast dislocations of the Soviet population, with a consequent

---

[28] U. Hlybinny, "Belorussian Culture after World War II," *Belorussian Review*, no. 6 (1958):45.
[29] Robert S. Sullivant, *Soviet Politics in the Ukraine, 1917–1957* (New York, 1962), p. 272.
[30] *Izvestiia Akademii Nauk BSSR*, 1949, p. 8.
[31] Iosif Stalin, *Sochineniia*, 1st ed. (Moscow, 1946–1952), 11:64.

weakening of the patterns of Party discipline. Moscow decided to proceed immediately with ideological education and reeducation of Party members and at the same time to instigate a purge of the Party cadres.

The Central Committee of the All-Union Communist Party adopted a decision on "education and reeducation of the Communist and Soviet leaders" in 1946. In accordance with this decision, the whole system of Party schools in Belorussia was reorganized. A higher Party school with three years of study and 177 Party schools with two years of study were founded.[32] For the Communists and Communist youth who were not sufficiently prepared politically, elementary political schools were organized. In 1948, there were about 2,500 such schools at which more than 24,000 Communists and 21,000 non-Party persons studied. By 1952, the number of political schools in Belorussia had increased to 2,800. In addition, there were evening Party schools.[33]

Stalin's general tendency, however, was to emphasize coercive rather than persuasive methods to achieve conformity. "It is much safer to be feared than to be loved," Machiavelli had advised rulers.[34] Stalin hardly needed the advice. Consequently, "the wholesale purge of collaborators, nationalists, and even neutrals (*kosmopolity*) suspected of divided loyalties, was ordered after the liberation of Belorussia."[35]

From the very beginning the purge in Belorussia was directed against the influence of the "rotten West" in general.[36] Soon it affected all Party members on the local level. By the middle of 1946, 90 percent of all district Party secretaries, 96 percent of all district and city administrative officials, and 82 percent of all the collective farm chairmen had been purged.[37]

The political terror in Belorussia became especially intensive in 1947–1948. During this period great emphasis was put on cleansing the Party of "cosmopolitanism" and Western ideas.[38] Stalin's old slogan that "from time to time, the master without fail must go through the ranks of the Party with a broom in his hand," was

---

[32] Akimov, *Nekotorye voprosy istorii KPB*, p. 45.
[33] Ibid., p. 52.
[34] Niccolo Machiavelli, *The Prince* (New York, 1947), p. 48.
[35] Vakar, *Belorussia*, p. 212.
[36] I. Volkov, "Na Belorussii," *Sotsialisticheskii vestnik*, no. 7 (30 July 1948): 142.
[37] *Partiinaia zhizn'*, no. 2 (January 1947): 39.
[38] *Pravda*, 8 November 1946, p. 1.

Belorussia after World War II

again raised. Such action, according to Kremlin leaders, was particularly necessary in the western republics—Belorussia and the Ukraine. In Belorussia, both the top Party leader and lower Party officials were accused of bourgeois nationalism, cosmopolitanism, and being influenced by Western ideas.[39]

Who had brought all these influences to Belorussia? Certainly not the Germans, who only in the gravest extremity had yielded few concessions to the Belorussian "bourgeois nationalists." Nothing in their policy toward Belorussia could be related to "cosmopolitanism" or to any "Western idea" except the doctrine of their own racial supremacy. In reality, the Communist accusations of the Belorussians were altogether specious. The Belorussians had been guilty of nothing more than wanting more freedom in their national affairs. This Stalin could not permit.

Consistent with Stalin's actions and, indeed, his public statements, was a conviction that the primacy of the Party was—and had to be—synonymous with the primacy of Moscow. Through the years of his personal dictatorship, Stalin had found that Great Russian chauvinism served as a good foundation for the Communist system of dictatorship. The struggle against Hitler convinced him that he was right. He openly acknowledged this in a speech delivered at a reception of Red Army commanders at the Kremlin on May 24, 1945, in which he said:

> Comrades, permit me to propose still one last toast.
> I would like to propose a toast to the health of our Soviet people and above all of the Russian people.
> I drink above all to the health of the Russian people because it is the most outstanding nation of all the nations of the Soviet Union.
> I propose a toast to the health of the Russian people because it has merited in this war a general recognition as the guiding force of the Soviet Union among all the peoples of our country.
> I propose a toast to the health of the Russian people not only because it is the leading people but because it possesses a clear mind, a staunch character, and patience.
> Our government made not a few mistakes and there were moments in 1941–1942 when our situation was desperate, when our army had retreated, had abandoned our own villages and towns of the Ukraine, Belorussia, Moldavia, Leningrad region, the Baltic area, the Karelo-Finnish republic, had abandoned them because

[39] "Kryvavy diktatar Belarusi," *Bats'kaushchyna*, 1 June 1952, p. 2.

there was no other possibility. Another people might have said to its government: you have not fulfilled our expectations, away with you, we shall establish another government which will conclude peace with Germany and bring us rest. However, the Russian people did not do so, because it believed in the correctness of the policy of its government, and it sacrificed itself in order to ensure the defeat of Germany. And this faith of the Russian people in its government became the decisive force which guaranteed our historic victory over the enemy of mankind, over Fascism.

Thanks to it, the Russian people, for its faith!

To the health of the Russian people![40]

This sentiment was reflected in the Kremlin's postwar policy toward the Union republics' Party leadership. This policy was simply to purge the leaders of non-Russian nationalities and replace them with Russians. In Belorussia, the purge which affected the Communists on both regional and republican levels started in the first half of 1948. Formally, it was preceded by a decision of the plenum of the Party's Central Committee for Belorussia on March 7, 1947, to divide the positions of First Secretary of the Central Committee and Chairman of the Council of Ministers.[41] Nikolai Gusarov, a Russian, was appointed first secretary.[42] His duty was to bring about the complete centralization of the Communist Party apparatus, which he now controlled, and to tighten up the Soviet apparatus. This was ordered from Moscow and was an official Moscow policy. Andrei Zhdanov, Leningrad's Party Secretary and a member of the politburo, seems to have played the first role after Stalin himself.

Under Gusarov's leadership, secretariats for industry, agriculture, and propaganda were organized, and the secretaries who headed them were made members of the Belorussian Politburo.[43] This gave them authority higher than that of a governmental minister.[44] The top Belorussian Communists who occupied governmental positions now became subjects for purges. On March 18, 1948,

[40] *Bol'shevik*, no. 10 (May 1945): 1–2.
[41] These two positions were fused during wartime and were occupied by P. Ponomarenko, a Ukrainian. Stalin himself occupied both positions on the all-union level from 1939 until his death in March 1953.
[42] *Pravda*, 8 March 1947.
[43] Vakar, *Belorussia*, p. 213.
[44] The Soviet system is a dual system. Constitutionally, the Presidium of the Supreme Soviet and the Council of Ministers are the highest authorities. The Central Committee of the Communist Party and its Presidium (Politburo) are not mentioned in the constitution at all; but, in practice, their authorities are higher than that of the government.

Mikola Natalevich, the long-time president of the Supreme Soviet of the Belorussian SSR and vice-president of the USSR Soviet of Nationalities, was deposed and stripped of the Order of Lenin and the title "Hero of the Soviet Union." No reason was given for his removal, but significantly he was succeeded by a Russian, B. N. Kozlov.[45] On September 22, 1948, A. Kleshchev, another Russian, who had been one of the partisan leaders in Belorussia during World War II, was appointed chairman of the Council of Ministers of Belorussia.[46] By the end of 1948 all top Belorussian Communists had been purged and replaced by Russians. This signified completion of the centralization of the Communist Party apparatus in Belorussia and made it directly subordinate to Moscow, like other Russian provincial Party organizations.

The death of Zhdanov on August 31, 1948, greatly affected the All-Union Communist Party organization as a whole. Many of the Kremlin leaders closely associated with him disappeared. The best-known case is probably that of Nikolai A. Voznesenskii, the most important Party economist and theorist, who was accused of developing a "heretical theory" contrary to the teachings of Stalin.[47] The purge of Zhdanov's followers was related to the growing prominence of Georgi Malenkov, who seemed to be playing a leading role in the Kremlin power struggle.

The Belorussian Communist Party organization was not affected greatly by Zhdanov's death, though there were a few changes of personnel. Gusarov, for instance, was replaced as First Secretary of the Central Committee by another Russian, Nikolai Patolichev.[48] It can be assumed that Gusarov was a supporter of Zhdanov.

Between 1948 and 1953, the replacement of Belorussian Communist officials by Russians continued, in both Party and government organizations. Thus, by the time of Stalin's death, almost all responsible Party and governmental positions in the BSSR were occupied by Russians. In 1951, for instance, of the thirty-three members of the Belorussian government, twenty-two were Russians, one was a Jew, one was a Georgian, and nine were Belorussians.[49]

The Belorussian intelligentsia during the last years of Stalin's

[45] *Pravda*, 18 March 1948. Natalevich and all other Belorussians who occupied high positions in the Party and government organizations were liquidated.
[46] *New York Times*, 23 September 1948, p. 3.
[47] *Pravda*, 24 December 1952, p. 2.
[48] Vakar, *Belorussia*, p. 215.
[49] Ibid.

life was constantly accused of "nationalism," "attempts to separate the Belorussian national culture from the culture of the Russian people," and other "crimes."[50] Therefore, it was systematically destroyed and replaced by the new Stalinist breed of intelligentsia. So thoroughly was this accomplished that the Party has never since been obliged to repeat the process.

Stalin ruled the Soviet Union in the postwar years as a dictator-despot. He left little to chance, including, ironically enough, his own position in Soviet history. He promoted what the Party later called his "cult of personality" mainly through the Soviet press, which portrayed him as "a great leader of the Soviet people and the Red Army" who had led the Soviet Union to victory in World War II.[51] The Soviet press wrote that "the genius of Stalin as a military leader was in his ability to combine the strategical and political factors in planning big military operations."[52] He was described as "the only leader who correctly defined the methods of Socialist realism."[53] Soviet poets wrote innumerable panegyrics in his praise.

But Stalin was, according to the Soviet press, a genius in many fields, including linguistics. He was praised for his work "Marxism and the Problems of Linguistics," in which he criticized the leading Soviet linguists because of their concept of the "class language" and their belief that "language is a superstructure of the economic basis." Stalin pointed out that these men "were unable to master the method of dialectical materialism and to apply it to linguistics."[54] He propounded instead "the concept of language as a social phenomenon." He also pointed out that the existence of dialects and jargons does not deny, but on the contrary confirms, the existence of the general national language of which they are branches and to which they are subordinate.[55]

In truth, Stalin's "works of linguistics" were intended to show that the Russian language was the language of all people of the Soviet Union and that the languages of non-Russian people were only dialects or jargons which were destined to "dwindle to nothing, to disappear."[56]

[50] *Izvestiia Akademii Nauk BSSR*, no. 2 (1949): 8.
[51] *Bol'shevik*, no. 13 (June 1945): 1.
[52] Ibid., p. 2.
[53] Ibid., no. 24 (December 1951): 21.
[54] *Pravda*, 20 June 1952, pp. 2–3.
[55] *Bol'shevik*, no. 12 (June 1951): 31.
[56] Ibid., p. 36.

Stalin's speech at the Kremlin on May 24, 1945, and his works in linguistics gave the Russian chauvinists an excuse for their campaign of Russification after World War II. The Communist Party, dominated by the Russians, openly identified itself with this campaign. The journal *Bol'shevik*, an official organ of the Central Committee of the All-Union Communist Party, immediately began to quote and interpret Stalin's speech and his works in linguistics and to fit them into the policy of Russification. In the November 1946 issue, for example, this journal stated "The Russian culture is the leading culture in the development of the socialist culture because the Russian people are the most outstanding people among all the people of the Soviet Union."[57]

The Russian chauvinists, supported by Stalin, began intensive and complete Russification in the republics. Belorussian history was rewritten. The Institute of Linguistics of the Belorussian Academy of Sciences was ordered to study further reforms of Belorussian grammar and orthography in order to bring them closer to the Russian language. In the meantime, "most of the textbooks were simply sent to Belorussia from the Russian Republic in the Russian language."[58] Toward the end of Stalin's life, the Russian language definitely occupied a privileged position in the Soviet Union. "Sixty-seven percent of all newspapers, 80 percent of the books, and nearly 90 percent of all magazines were published during these years in Russian."[59] In Belorussia the percentage of publications in Russian was much higher than these figures indicate. The Belorussian press was kept alive only for the sake of propaganda, because during these years it hailed Stalin as "a creator of the Belorussian Republic."[60]

The death of Stalin brought considerable change to Belorussia. The mass political purges of the Communist Party stopped. The new leaders in Moscow, locked in a dog-eat-dog struggle for the succession, seemed little inclined to pursue the course of mass violence which had been Stalin's favorite weapon.

Important changes in Belorussian leadership were made after the Twentieth Congress of the Communist Party of the Soviet Union, which took place in February 1956. At this congress Nikita

[57] Ibid., no. 22 (November 1946): 1.
[58] Vakar, *Belorussia*, p. 215.
[59] John A. Armstrong, *Ideology, Politics, and Government in the Soviet Union* (New York, 1962), p. 116.
[60] A. Denisov, *Sovetskoe gosudarstvo i pravo* (Moscow, 1947), p. 211.

Khrushchev denounced Stalin. Shortly after, Patolichev, a long-time Party boss in Belorussia, was replaced by a Belorussian member of the Central Committee, Kiryl Mazurau. At the same time, N. Aukhimovich, another Belorussian member of the Central Committee, was elected chairman of the Council of Ministers.[61] Since that time both of these important Party and government positions in the Belorussian SSR have usually been occupied by Belorussians.

[61] *Bats'kaushchyna*, 19 August 1956.

13.

Belorussia & War Diplomacy

So far we have examined modern Belorussian history from a somewhat parochial viewpoint, as a sequence of frequently painful events within the country itself. Simultaneously, however, Belorussia served as a pawn in the maneuverings of wartime diplomacy. Among the results of this maneuvering were two historical developments: a drastic shifting of Belorussia's western boundary and the amazing appearance of the Belorussian SSR as an original member of the United Nations.

The Soviet Union and its Western allies had trouble, both during and after World War II, in planning and defining the western frontier of Belorussia. The government of the Soviet Union at that time supported the concept of the Curzon Line, which defined the western boundaries of both Belorussia and the Ukraine. This line, it will be recalled, was a creation of the victorious Entente powers of World War I, and was designed to limit Poland's policy of expansion to the east. From 1921 to 1939, however, the Curzon Line remained only a historical concept. Poland ignored it and during the Soviet-Polish War of 1919–1920 was able to conquer large parts of West Belorussia and West Ukraine. According to the Soviet-Polish peace treaty concluded at Riga in 1921, more than ten and one-half million Belorussians and Ukrainians were left in Poland.[1]

After the partition of Poland by Germany and the Soviet Union in September 1939, the western boundary of the Belorussian SSR was shifted westward to add the Bialystok and Augustov districts. These districts historically and ethnically belonged to Belorussia.[2] This new version of the Curzon Line was an important subject of international discussions during World War II. On July 30, 1941, the Soviet government and the Polish government-in-exile signed an agreement providing for a renewal of diplomatic relations and the

THE BELORUSSIAN S.S.R. AFTER WORLD WAR II

nullification of all treaties concluded between the Soviet Union and Germany, including the agreements of 1939 for the division of Poland.[3]

The officials of the Polish government-in-exile, as it turned out, interpreted this Soviet-Polish agreement in their own way: that the Soviet government after the victory over Nazi Germany would restore the Polish-Soviet frontier existing before World War II. In this they were mistaken. At the Tehran Conference, which took place from November 27 through December 2, 1943, Stalin stated clearly that it was "not just for the Poles to try to get back the Ukraine and White Russia; that the frontiers of 1939 had returned

[1] Wiktor Ostrowski, *Spotlight on Byelorussia and Her Neighbours* (London, 1959), p. 57.
[2] Ibid.
[3] Mikola Volacic, "The Population of Western Belorussia and Its Resettlement in Poland and the USSR," *Belorussian Review*, no. 3 (1956): 17.

the Ukrainian soil to the Ukraine, and White Russian soil to White Russia. The Soviet Government adheres to the 1939 line and considers it just and right."[4]

During the period between the Tehran and Yalta conferences there were discussions of the frontiers of Poland among top government officials of the Soviet Union, the United States, Great Britain, and Poland. In the Moscow Conference of October 9–22, 1944, Stalin, Churchill, W. Averell Harriman, and a Polish delegation headed by Boleslaw Bierut and Stanislaw Mikolajczyk took part in the deliberations. The Soviet leaders apparently were prepared to make "certain concessions" to Poland in order to win the sympathies of the Polish government which, they hoped, would soon be a Communist government. They expressed their readiness to retreat from the defense of the Soviet-Polish boundary of September 1939 and to accept the Curzon Line without "modifications." "The Polish delegation officially agreed on the Curzon Line as the Eastern frontier of Poland."[5]

Aside from ulterior designs for Communist expansion, Stalin apparently viewed the Curzon Line as a territorial solution which would appeal to the Western Allies because it had been their own idea in the first place. He expressed this point in the "Debate on World Security and a Settlement for Poland" at the Yalta Conference:

> In regard to the Curzon Line, concessions in regard to Lwow and the Lwow province, and Mr. Churchill's reference to a magnanimous act on our part, it is necessary to remind you that not Russians but Curzon and Clemenceau fixed this line. The Russians had not been invited and the line was established against their will. Lenin had opposed giving Bialystok province to the Poles, but the Curzon Line gives it to Poland. We have already retreated from Lenin's position in regard to this province.[6]

The Western representatives did not oppose Stalin on this matter, being of the opinion that Polish claims to the eastern frontiers be-

[4] U.S., Dept. of State, *The Conferences at Cairo and Tehran, 1943: Diplomatic Papers of the Foreign Relations of the United States* (Washington, D.C., 1961), p. 599.
[5] Mikola Volacic, "The Curzon Line and Territorial Changes in Eastern Europe," *Belorussian Review*, no. 2 (1956): 70.
[6] *New York Times*, 17 March 1955, p. S53. The official record of the Yalta Conference was disclosed by the United States Department of State on 16 March 1955.

yond the Bug River were groundless. Churchill expressed the view that the claim of the Soviet Union to the area east of the Bug was "one not founded on force but upon right."[7]

The extent to which Soviet officialdom was already contemplating a postwar *cordon sanitaire* of Communist-ruled satellites can only be guessed, but it is clear that Stalin and Molotov were, at the time of the Yalta Conference, confident that Poland would become a Communist state. To please the Poles, they proposed a modification of the Curzon Line in some regions from five to eight kilometers in favor of Poland. This Soviet proposal was accepted by Roosevelt and Churchill.[8]

The decision was confirmed by the Potsdam Conference and the Polish-Soviet agreement of September 19, 1945. Although both the Soviet and Polish governments had declared the Belorussian-Polish boundary to be final, it was somewhat modified again on March 22, 1951—this time in favor of Belorussia.[9] This was the last of the "modifications" of the Curzon Line. At the present time, the territory of the Belorussian SSR encompasses 80,150 square miles.[10] Its political boundaries are confirmed and guaranteed by the constitutions of both the Belorussian SSR (Article 14) and the Soviet Union (Article 29).

In almost every important respect, the Yalta Conference proved a triumph of Kremlin diplomacy. Included in that triumph was a successful arrangement for the inclusion of two of the Soviet republics, in addition to the Soviet Union itself, within the forthcoming United Nations. This was, of course, somewhat the equivalent of giving votes in the UN General Assembly to the states of New York and California. The basis of this Soviet achievement was partly legalistic and reveals once again the frequent contradiction that exists between Communist claims and Communist reality.

The first constitution of the Soviet Union was approved by the Second Congress of Soviets of the USSR on January 31, 1924.[11] In

---

[7] James F. Byrnes, *Speaking Frankly* (New York, 1947), p. 29.

[8] U.S., Dept. of State, *The Conferences of Malta and Yalta, 1945: Diplomatic Papers of the Foreign Relations of the United States* (Washington, D.C., 1955), p. 938.

[9] Nicholas P. Vakar, *Belorussia: The Making of a Nation* (Cambridge, Mass., 1956), p. 207.

[10] M. L. Polonskii and M. I. Rostovtsev, *Belorusskaia SSR* (Moscow, 1964), p. 157.

[11] *Outline History of the USSR* (Moscow, 1960), p. 285.

this constitution the USSR was described as a voluntary union of equal peoples, each retaining the right of free withdrawal from the Union, provided that the remaining republics approve.[12] In practice, however, the withdrawal of any republic was rendered impossible, since it would not receive the approval of the other republics and most of all that of the Russian Republic, which had the interest and the means to prevent withdrawal or approval of withdrawal. The Union republics were not in a position to count on their own strength; they had neither independent military organizations nor their own foreign ministries.

The second constitution of the USSR, the so-called Stalin Constitution, which was approved in 1936, did not change the position of the Union republics. It simply repeated the article of the constitution of 1924 which designated the USSR as "a federal state, formed on the basis of a voluntary union of equal Soviet Socialist Republics."[13] The Stalin Constitution also repeated the articles of 1924 which stated that "the right freely to secede from the USSR is reserved to every Union republic."[14] However, this right continued to have only theoretical meaning.

After World War II, in order to win back the loyalties of the Belorussian and Ukrainian peoples, the Soviet government decided to make constitutional changes giving the Union republics a somewhat greater feeling and appearance of freedom. Thus, at the tenth session of the Supreme Soviet on February 1, 1944, Article 18 of the USSR Constitution was revised to give each Union republic "the right to enter into direct relations with foreign states and to conclude agreements and exchange diplomatic and consular representatives with them."[15] The republics were also authorized to form "their own Republican military formations."[16] Furthermore, the Supreme Soviet of each republic was authorized to "decide questions of representation of the Union Republic in its international relations" and to "determine the manner of organizing the Republic's military formations."[17] In accordance with these changes, Articles 77 and 78 were

---

[12] *The Constitution of the Union of Soviet Socialist Republics* (Washington, D.C., 1924), sect. 1, p. 7.

[13] *The Constitution (Fundamental Law) of the Union of Soviet Socialist Republics* (Moscow, 1952), Art. 13, p. 19. This constitution was later amended and added to.

[14] Ibid., Art. 17, p. 24.

[15] Ibid., Amendment A to Art. 18, pp. 24–25.

[16] Ibid., Amendment B to Art. 18, p. 25.

[17] Ibid., Art. 60, sections E and F, p. 50.

revised with the aim of converting the ministries of defense and foreign affairs from All-Union to Union-republican ministries.[18] These constitutional changes were made almost exactly a year before the Yalta Conference.

Molotov, addressing the Supreme Soviet on February 1, 1944, stressed that recognition by the Supreme Soviet of the increased requirements of the republics in their activities, including foreign affairs, would only serve to strengthen the fraternal relations among the peoples of the Soviet Union and reveal still more fully to the peoples of the world the historic meaning of the existence of the Soviet Union.[19] Stalin undoubtedly had other ideas. But he now had the badly needed propaganda to convince the outside world of the purity of Soviet intentions. At that time the Red Army was advancing into several East European countries which were soon to be transformed into obedient "people's republics," each with a pattern of "free" institutions curiously similar to those now conferred upon the Soviet republics. In addition, Stalin now had a convenient showcase to impress President Roosevelt and Prime Minister Churchill that the Soviet republics were constitutionally free countries and legally suitable for admission to the United Nations.

At the Yalta Conference (February 1–11, 1945), the Soviet representatives proposed this very thing.[20] On February 7, Soviet Foreign Minister Molotov first requested the admission to the United Nations of three Union republics: Belorussia, Lithuania, and the Ukraine. He emphasized that "these three republics had borne the greatest sacrifices in the war and were the first to be invaded by the enemy; it was only fair, therefore, that these three, or at any rate, two, be original members of the United Nations." He also said that "the Soviet views were based on the constitutional changes which had occurred in February of last year and he did not think that this conference should ignore this request."[21] In concluding his presentation, Molotov conveyed a subtle hint to Churchill, saying that the Dominions of the British Commonwealth had achieved independence gradually and patiently and had reached an important position in international affairs. "This was an example for Russia," he said.[22] Great Britain certainly could not agree to any international

---

[18] Ibid., Art. 77 and 78, pp. 61–64.
[19] *Pravda*, 2 February 1944.
[20] The extent to which Stalin was informed beforehand of U.S. planning remains undetermined.
[21] *New York Times*, 17 March 1955, p. C55.
[22] Winston S. Churchill, *Triumph and Tragedy* (Boston, 1953), p. 357.

organization which would exclude its dominions from full participation, and Prime Minister Churchill reacted accordingly. He declared that he had great sympathy with the Soviet request, stating, "My heart goes out to White Russia, bleeding from her wounds while beating down the tyrants."[23]

President Roosevelt by no means rejected the Soviet proposal, though it was considerably less than ideal from the American standpoint. Great Britain anticipated having "four or five members, six if India was included,"[24] and the Soviet Union was now requesting at least two additional members, whereas the United States would have only one vote in the UN General Assembly. Neither Roosevelt nor Churchill was so naive as to accept the Soviet proposal without misgivings. They were inclined to believe that the real aim of the Soviet leader was to get more votes in the United Nations, and were also skeptical of the validity of the constitutional changes on which the proposal was based. Molotov reassured them. "The amendments had been made to the Soviet Constitution which gave the Soviet Republics the right to have contact with foreign states. The Soviet Union was a union of states. The constitution had now been revised to increase the rights of the republics. The development of relations between the republics and foreign states which had already begun was in this direction and was developing according to democratic principles."[25]

Roosevelt and Churchill, apparently mollified by this assurance and desirous of believing in the good intentions of the Soviet Union's postwar leadership, agreed to recommend to the first session of the United Nations at San Francisco the admission of Belorussia and the Ukraine as original members of the United Nations.[26]

At the San Francisco Conference in April 1945, final steps were taken toward Belorussia's admission to the United Nations. On April 27, Molotov addressed the conference on behalf of the Belorussian and Ukrainian republics, proposing that the delegates support the decision of the Yalta Conference that these two republics be admitted to original membership.[27] Molotov took the occasion to remind the delegates about the constitutional rights of the Soviet republics. "The Soviet Union Republics are sovereign states. The

---

[23] James F. Byrnes, *Speaking Frankly*, p. 39.
[24] Churchill, *Triumph and Tragedy*, p. 359.
[25] *New York Times*, 17 March 1955, p. C57.
[26] Ibid., p. C59.
[27] United Nations, *Documents of the United Nations Conference on International Organization* (San Francisco, 1945), 5:90.

constitution of the Soviet Union, as well as the constitutions of the individual Soviet Union Republics, insure them the right even to leave the Soviet Union whenever they desire to do so. The Union Republics have rights, also, to take part in international conferences and to establish diplomatic relations with foreign countries."[28] President Harry S Truman, also in support of the decision of the Yalta Conference, sent the following letter to Secretary of State Edward R. Stettinius, chief of the American delegation:

> My dear Mr. Secretary:
>
> As you are aware, at the Yalta Conference President Roosevelt on behalf of the government of the United States supported a Soviet proposal to admit the Ukrainian Soviet Socialist Republic and the Belorussian Soviet Socialist Republic to initial membership in the proposed international organization. President Roosevelt felt that the importance of the Ukraine and Belorussia among the Soviet Republics and their contributions to the prosecution of the war and the untold devastations and sacrifices which their peoples have undergone in the cause of the United Nations entitled them to special consideration.[29]

Molotov's speech and Truman's letter exerted a strong influence upon the delegates, and on April 27 the steering committee of the conference voted unanimously for the admission of Belorussia and the Ukraine.[30] A further proposal that the Belorussian and Ukrainian representatives immediately take their seats at the conference was unanimously approved on April 30.[31] Thus, Belorussia and the Ukraine were made original members of the United Nations, to the exclusion of all other republics of the USSR.

At the Yalta Conference, Stalin and Molotov had sought admission of Belorussia and the Ukraine to the United Nations mainly for three reasons. The first of these was of a purely practical character—to obtain two additional votes in the international organization. The second was to convince the Belorussians and Ukrainians that Moscow indeed wished to satisfy their national aspirations.[32] The third was to convince the outside world of Soviet goodwill and

[28] Ibid., pp. 90–91.
[29] *New York Times*, 28 April 1945, p. 10.
[30] Ibid.
[31] U.N., *Documents of the U. N. Conference*, 5:155.
[32] *Bats'kaushchyna*, 1 November 1953, p. 1.

ability to understand and solve the national problems within the Soviet Union.[33] In the first aim, the Soviet representatives achieved without much difficulty a minor diplomatic coup. The further aims, however, were never greatly fulfilled. On the contrary, during the entire history of the United Nations so far, the Soviet leaders have not been able to demonstrate that the Soviet republics have freedom of action in their domestic and foreign affairs.

Despite the constitutional changes of February 1944, the Soviet Union's republics have fewer rights than do the states in the United States. The White House, for instance, could not send a candidate for election to a state in which this candidate had not been born and had never resided. Yet this is a common practice in the Soviet Union, and it serves to continue the primacy of Moscow in the republics. As we have seen, during Stalin's lifetime the top executive position in each Union republic was occupied by a Communist sent from Moscow, usually a Great Russian. The same situation existed in the so-called "ministries" of foreign affairs which were formed in the Belorussian and Ukrainian republics after the constitutional changes of 1944. Therefore, it is not surprising that throughout the existence of the United Nations the Belorussian and Ukrainian delegates have not once voted independently of the delegation of the Soviet Union. On the contrary, their functions in the United Nations consist only of unconditional support of the Soviet Union's delegation and of making "these or other tactical steps when the Soviet delegation prefers to be in the shadow."[34]

Molotov's promise at the Yalta and San Francisco conferences that the Belorussian and Ukrainian republics were to establish diplomatic relations with other foreign countries has remained unfulfilled. In March 1950, the British government proposed the establishment of diplomatic relations with the Ukraine. The Soviet government, however, completely ignored this proposal,[35] though no denial was given, because legally there had to be a positive answer. Certainly, Belorussia and the Ukraine, as original members of the United Nations, have the right granted by the UN Charter to develop friendly relations with other members.[36] The Soviet government could not publicly deny this right because in doing so it would

[33] Vladimir Lenin, *Sochineniia*, 4th ed. (Moscow, 1946–1958), 36:553–59.
[34] *Bats'kaushchyna*, 7 November 1954, p. 1.
[35] *New York Times*, 16 March 1950, p. 30.
[36] United Nations, *Charter of the United Nations and Statute of the International Court of Justice* (New York, 1945), Chapt. 1, Art. 1.

have contradicted not only the UN Charter but also the Constitution of the Soviet Union.

At the Yalta Conference, Stalin seemed to be critical of those future members of the United Nations who did not have diplomatic relations with the Soviet Union. There he said that "among the states which would be represented at the San Francisco Conference there were ten who had no diplomatic relations with the Soviet Union. He said that it was somewhat strange for the Soviet Government to attempt to build future world security with states which did not desire to have diplomatic relations with it."[37] To this day the Belorussian and Ukrainian republics do not have diplomatic relations with countries not in the Communist sphere. It does, indeed, seem "somewhat strange."

[37] *New York Times*, 17 March 1955, p. C59.

14.

Conclusion

The Belorussian national movement originated and grew up in the second half of the nineteenth century and the beginning of the twentieth, as the renaissance of a distinctive regional culture and as a protest against Russian social, political, and national suppression. World War I brought such destruction and suffering to Belorussia that the February Revolution was greeted with great enthusiasm and hope. The leaders of the Belorussian national movement were eager to cooperate with the Provisional Government in Petrograd, in the belief that the new Russia would be a democratic country with no place for social and political injustice. The Belorussians hoped also that the new Russia would not be a centralized state as old Russia had been, but a federation of national autonomous republics, one of which would be the Belorussian autonomous republic.

The Provisional Government was too slow in dealing with the problem of nationalities, even though it tolerated the national movements of various minority nationalities and was prepared to discuss a possible federalization of Russia. It was also too slow in dealing with agricultural reform, but it promised to solve this matter in a legal way after the election of the Constituent Assembly. As long as possible, the Belorussian national leaders and an overwhelming majority of the people stood behind the Provisional Government.

The overthrow of the Provisional Government by the Bolseviks in the October Revolution was a setback to the Belorussian national movement because the Bolsheviks, despite their theoretically attractive policy toward the nationalities, in practice neither recognized nor tolerated views and desires other than their own. The political and individual freedoms granted by the Provisional Government were immediately suppressed by the Bolsheviks. The Belorussian national leaders reacted by convening an All-Belorussian National

Congress at the end of December 1917, which was to decide the attitude of Belorussia toward the Bolshevik government in Russia. The congress, by majority vote, expressed itself for the independence of Belorussia. Thus, between the February Revolution and the October Revolution, the Belorussians turned from a demand for autonomy to a demand for complete separation from Russia. They made this radical decision because they opposed the Bolsheviks' antidemocratic concept of state.

During the three years of Civil War and foreign intervention (1917–1920), Belorussia was an arena for the contest between Polish and German imperialist desires on the one hand, and Communist aspirations on the other. Bolshevik policy was dominated by propaganda recognition of Belorussian "sovereignty" accompanied by forcible attempts to create a Russian-controlled Communist Belorussia. The Bolsheviks became convinced, however, that the Belorussians really were prepared to fight for the independence of their country, and at the end of the Civil War granted independence to the Belorussian Soviet Socialist Republic. Thus, during 1920–1922 the Belorussian SSR formally occupied the position of an independent state. In December 1922, the BSSR, together with the other three Soviet republics—Russian, Ukrainian, and Transcaucasian—formed the Union of Soviet Socialist Republics, each with the right to secede from the Union at will. There were, however, two factors in the arrangement of the Union which later proved fatal to the concept of a union of equals, to the rights of the Union republics, and to the preservation of decentralized authority. These factors were domination of the Union by the Russian Soviet Federated Socialist Republic, and domination of the Soviet government by the highly centralized Russian Communist Party, which refused to recognize the autonomy of the Communist parties of the Union republics.

These factors, however, did not have an immediate effect on the administration of the USSR. During the period of the New Economic Policy, the Communist Party could not intervene much in the administration of the state, because these were the years when Stalin was still struggling for control of the Party. The Russian Republic, for its part, showed a good deal of consideration for the wishes of the smaller Union republics. The credit for this should go especially to Nikolai Bukharin and Aleksei Rykov, the leaders of the Right-Wing Opposition, who popularized the ideas of Socialist democracy in practice. The results achieved during this period in Belorussia's industry, agriculture, and education, and, most important, in establishing a new state, were impressive. This convinced many people in the Union republics that they could make great progress if the initiative in the administration of the state was left in their hands.

Under the NEP, the central government did not suppress the national-cultural movements in the Union republics, but, on the contrary, supported them. In Belorussia this movement was called Belorussification. Its basis was the belief that the Belorussian people, like many other minority nationalities, had suffered national and cultural oppression before the Revolution. Now, therefore, they should be given an opportunity to develop their own culture, including language, literature, theater, and arts. Behind all this was the thought that the people of such a multinational state as the Soviet Union could not be equal unless their cultures were on a par with one another. It was decided, therefore, that the national minorities should not copy the Russian culture but should develop their own, already deeply rooted in their traditions.

Many visionary Communists thought that the Union of Soviet Socialist Republics, in solving the problem of nationalities in such a way, could set a good example for the unification of all countries in the world. The Belorussian nationalists, on their side, were ready to forget the bitter memories of their country's fate under old Russia. They idealized the new state, too, believing that in the Soviet Union the class of workers and the class of peasants represented a united power which stood above that of the state, and that every nation of the Soviet Union identified itself with this power of the people as a whole. Therefore, there could be no weak or strong nations and there was no need to fear the possible revival of Great Russian chauvinism, which could affect the Soviet policy of nationalities to the disadvantage of the small nations of the Soviet Union.

The tragic mistake of these visionaries, both nationalists and Communists, was their failure to realize that it was not the working class or the peasant class, but the Communist Party which stood above the power of the state. They failed also to realize that the Party, as a highly centralized organization, could easily be subordinated to the will of an ambitious leader who wished to establish himself as a dictator. Stalin was the man who demonstrated this. He transformed Lenin's doctrine of the dictatorship of the Communist Party into the dictatorship of one person. The Russian bureaucrats, of whom Lenin was so critical, became useful servants of Stalin, once again seeking a "united indivisible" Russia. Stalin exploited this sentiment during his struggle for power, claiming that local nationalism was endangering the unity of the Soviet Union. Armed with Party power and supported by the security police, Stalin used both against the non-Russian peoples.

Stalin succeeded in becoming a dictator largely because of the support of the Great Russian chauvinists. He terminated the New Economic Policy and began a ruthless collectivization of agriculture and industrialization—"voluntary" in theory, "forced" in practice, in direct contradiction of Lenin's principles. The Belorussian and Ukrainian republics, bordering on the capitalist world, suffered particularly. Many peasants who refused to join the collective farms were sentenced to imprisonment or death without any legal proceedings. From 12 to 15 percent of the Belorussian peasants were sent to Siberia. Those who were forced to join the collective farms were subjugated to the position of serfs.

The workers, in whose name the Communist Party ruled, were not much better off than the peasants. They were persecuted for absence from work, "sabotage," and political considerations. The workers, like the peasants, could not change their place of residence at will. To prevent movement from place to place, the internal passport was introduced in December 1932.

During the period of the political purges, from 1929 to 1938, Stalin's attack on the Union republics was directed not only against his political opponents, as was the case in Russia, but also against the local nationalists. When the great purge of 1936–1938 ended, most of the Belorussian national leaders, who in the 1920s were hopeful of building a socialist democracy, were dead or in Stalin's concentration camps, and their posts were appropriated by Party bureaucrats sent from Russia. The BSSR remained formally an "equal among equals" in the Union, but de facto became again a nationally and politically oppressed province of Russia, just as it had been before the Revolution.

The Communist administration of Belorussia under Stalin's dictatorship convinced the people that one-party rule was responsible for the fact that the Soviet Union had become not a state of free and equal nations, as the Union republics had hoped, but a centralized state under a combination of traditional Russian and modern totalitarianism. Through the security police, Stalin committed horrible crimes in the name of Socialism, and thus discredited the Socialist movement in the eyes of the peoples of the Soviet Union and the outside world.

Although the Belorussian national leadership was destroyed

during Stalin's political purges in the 1930s, the people's national feeling became more intense than it had ever been. They realized that the Soviet government under Stalin offered them nothing but hunger, political terror, and exile to Siberia. In these circumstances, there started to grow a silent protest against social and political injustice and national persecution.

The Belorussian people's protest against Stalin's tyranny was openly expressed when the Germans invaded the Soviet Union in June 1941. But the German occupiers were not the liberators of Belorussia. On the contrary, they sought in East Europe a living space for the Germans, the "master race," and the death or enslavement of the Slavs. The Germans failed in their plans of conquest and barbarism only because they were defeated in war, but they helped Stalin to save his regime of terror. Because of Hitler's policy, the Slavs had no choice but to fight for their homeland. This Stalin used to his own advantage.

Conditions in the Soviet Union greatly improved after Stalin's death. The Soviet leaders in the post-Stalin period began to concentrate on improving the living conditions and lessening the political terror in the Union republics. They have sought, though insisting on strict Party primacy, to narrow the "credibility gap" between Communist theory and practice which they inherited from Stalin. There are also indications that since Khrushchev's fall two different factions have come into existence within the Communist Party of the Soviet Union. If so, this is a promising development.

seLecteb bibLioqRaphy

Only works referred to and of direct relevance to the study are included. Most items are available at the New York Public Library. Others are to be found in the Library of Congress, Indiana University Library, and Ohio State University Library.

DOCUMENTS AND OFFICIAL PUBLICATIONS

Belorussiia: informatsionnye materialy pravitel'stva Belorusskoi SSR [Belorussia: Informational Materials of the Government of the Belorussian SSR]. Minsk, 1945.

Belorusskaia SSR: itogi vsesoiuznoi perepisi naseleniia, 1959 [Belorussian SSR: Results of the All-Union Census of 1959]. Moscow: Tsentral'noe Statisticheskoe Upravlenie pri Sovete Ministrov SSSR, 1963.

Bor'ba trudiashchikhsia Zapadnoi Belorussii za sotsial'noe i natsional'noe osvobozhdenie i vossoedinenie s BSSR: dokumenty i materialy [Struggle of the Working People of West Belorussia for Social and National Liberation and Reunion with the Belorussian SSR: Documents and Materials]. Edited by V. I. Gurskii et al. Vol. 1 (1921–1929). Minsk, 1962.

Byelorussia's Independence Day, March 25, 1918: Documents, Facts, Proclamations, Statements and Comments. New York: Byelorussian-American Association, 1958.

Chetvertyi vsebelorusskii chrezvychainyi s"ezd Sovetov rabochikh, krest'ianskikh, i krasnoarmeiskikh deputatov: stenograficheskii otchet [Fourth All-Belorussian Extraordinary Congress of Soviets of Workers', Peasants' and Soldiers' Deputies: A Stenographic Report]. Minsk, March 1924.

The Constitution (Fundamental Law) of the Union of Soviet Socialist Republics. Moscow, 1952.

[This is the Second Constitution of the USSR. It was approved and published in 1936. Later it was amended and added to by the Supreme Soviet of the USSR.]

The Constitution of the Union of Soviet Socialist Republics. Washington, D.C.: Russian Information Bureau, 1924.

Correspondence between the Chairman of the Council of Ministers of the USSR and the Presidents of the USA and the Prime Ministers of

Great Britain during the Great Patriotic War of 1941-1945. 2 vols. Moscow, 1957.
Dekrety Sovetskoi vlasti [Decrees of the Soviet Government]. 2 vols. Moscow: Gospolitizdat, 1957-1959.
Direktivy VKP(b) i postanovleniia Sovetskogo pravitel'stva o narodnom obrazovanii: sbornik dokumentov za 1917-1947 gg. [Directives of the All-Union Communist Party (Bolsheviks) and Decrees of the Soviet Government on Education: A Collection of Documents, 1917-1947]. Edited by N. I. Boldyrev. 2 vols. Moscow, 1947.
Doklad Soveta Narodnykh Komissarov BSSR Sovetu Narodnykh Komissarov SSR: materialy k dokladu Adamovicha [Report of the Council of People's Commissars of the Belorussian SSR to the Council of People's Commissars of the USSR: Materials Prepared for the Report of Adamovich]. Minsk: Upravlenie Delami Soveta Narodnykh Komissarov BSSR, 1926.
Dokumenty i materialy po istorii Belorussii, 1900-1917 gg. [Documents and Materials on the History of Belorussia, 1900-1917]. Edited by V. N. Pertsev et al. Vol. 3. Minsk, 1953.
Dokumenty po istorii grazhdanskoi voiny v SSSR [Documents on the History of the Civil War in the USSR]. Edited by I. Minets and E. Gorodetskii. Vol. 1. Moscow, 1940.
Dzeviaty z'ezd Savetau: stsenagrafichnaia spravazdacha [Ninth Congress of the Soviets: A Stenographic Report]. Minsk, May 1928.
Interpeliatsyi Belaruskikh Paslou u Pol'ski Sejm, 1922-1926: zbornik dakumentau ab panskikh hvaltakh, katavan'niakh i zdzekakh nad sialianami i rabochymi u Zakhodniai Belarusi [Interpellations of the Belorussian Representatives to the Polish Diet: A Collection of Documents on the Overlords' Violence, Mockery, and Persecution of the Peasants and Workers in Western Belorussia]. Minsk: Belaruskae Dziarzhaunae Vydavetstva, 1927.
Istoriia Sovetskoi Konstitutsii v dokumentakh, 1917-1956 [History of the Soviet Constitution in Documents, 1917-1956]. Edited by S. S. Studenikin. Moscow, 1957.
Itogi vypolneniia pervogo piatiletnego plana razvitiia narodnogo khoziaistva BSSR [The Results of the Realization of the First Five-Year Plan of the Development of the National Economy of the Belorussian SSR]. Minsk: Izdanie Gosplana BSSR, 1933.
Iz istorii grazhdanskoi voiny v SSSR: sbornik dokumentov i materialov v trekh tomakh, 1918-1922 [From the History of the Civil War in the USSR: Collected Documents and Materials in Three Volumes, 1918-1922]. Moscow: Institut Marksizma-Leninizma, 1960-1961.
Iz istorii ustanovleniia Sovetskoi vlasti v Belorussii i obrazovaniia BSSR: dokumenty i materialy po istorii Belorussii [Documents and Materials on the History of the Establishment of the Soviet Power in Belorussia

Selected Bibliography   195

and the Formation of the Belorussian Soviet Socialist Republic]. Edited by A. I. Azarov et al. Vol. 4. Minsk, 1954.
Kalhasy BSSR: papiaredniia vyniki absledvan'niau kalhasau u 1928 i 1929 hadokh [The Collective Farms of the Belorussian SSR: Preliminary Results of the Inspection of the Collective Farms in 1928 and 1929]. Minsk: Tsentral'naia Statystychnaia Uprava BSSR, 1929.
Kanstytutsyia: asnauny zakon Belaruskae Savetskae Respubliki [Constitution: A Basic Law of the Belorussian Soviet Republic]. Minsk: Vydan'ne Ts.V.K. BSSR, 1927.
Kastrychnik na Belarusi: zbornik artykulau i dakumentau [October in Belorussia: A Collection of Articles and Documents]. Edited by S. Ahurski. Minsk, 1927.
Kommunisticheskaia Partiia Sovetskogo Soiuza v rezoliutsiiakh i resheniiakh s"ezdov, konferentsii i plenumov Ts.K., 1898–1960 [The Communist Party of the Soviet Union in the Resolutions and Decisions of Congresses, Conferences, and Plenums of the Central Committee, 1898–1960]. 7th ed. 4 vols. Moscow, 1954–1960.
Mataryialy da spravazdachy uradu X z'ezdu Savetau BSSR [Materials for the Report of the Government to the Tenth Congress of Soviets of the Belorussian SSR]. Minsk, 1931.
Narodnoe khoziaistvo BSSR v 1925–1926 khoziaistvennom godu [The National Economy of the BSSR in the Budget Year 1925–1926]. Minsk: Izdanie Gosplana BSSR, 1926.
Niurnbergskii protsess: sbornik materialov [Nuremberg Trial: Collected Materials]. 2d ed. Vol. 1. Moscow: Gosudarstvennoe Izdatel'stvo Iuridicheskoi Literatury, 1954.
"Official Record of the Yalta Conference." *New York Times*, 17 March 1955.
   [The State Department described this as a "substantially correct" record of the Yalta Conference of President Franklin D. Roosevelt, Prime Minister Winston Churchill, and Marshall Stalin in 1945.]
Perspektivy razvitiia narodnogo khoziaistva BSSR: stenogramma doklada predsedatelia gosplana BSSR Karlina o perspektivakh razvitiia narodnogo khoziaistva BSSR na piatiletie, 1927–1932 [The Prospects of the Development of the National Economy of the Belorussian SSR: The Stenographic Report of Karlin, Chairman of the State Planning Committee, on the Prospects of the Development of the National Economy of the Belorussian SSR in 1927–1932]. Minsk: Izdanie Gosplana BSSR, 1928.
Piatiletnii plan narodnogo khoziaistva i kul'turnogo stroitel'stva BSSR na 1928–1933 gg [Five-Year Plan for the Development of the National Economy and the Cultural Development of the Belorussian SSR, 1928–1933]. Minsk: Izdanie Gosplana BSSR, 1929.
Pis'menniki Belaruskai SSR ab reforme pravapisa belaruskai movy

[Writers of the Belorussian SSR about the Reform of the Orthography of the Belorussian Language]. Minsk: Akademiia Navuk BSSR, 1934.

Prakticheskoe razreshenie natsional'nogo voprosa v Belorusskoi Sovetskoi Sotsialisticheskoi Respublike [Practical Solution of the National Problem in the Belorussian Soviet Socialist Republic]. 2 parts. Minsk: Izdanie Tsentral'noi Natsional'noi Komissii Ts.I.K. BSSR, 1927.

Prestupleniia nemetsko-fashistskikh okkupantov v Belorussii, 1941–1944: dokumenty i materialy [The Crimes of the German-Fascist Occupants in Belorussia, 1941–1944: Documents and Materials]. Edited by P. P. Lipilo and V. F. Romanovskii. Minsk, 1963.

Promyshlennost' BSSR: itogi i perspektivy [Industry of the Belorussian SSR: Results and Prospects]. Minsk: Izdanie Gosplana BSSR, 1928.

Promyshlennost' BSSR v diagramakh i tablitsakh [Industry of the Belorussian SSR in Diagrams and Tables]. Minsk: Izdanie Vysshego Soveta Narodnogo Khoziaistva BSSR, 1928.

Revoliutsionnoe dvizhenie v Rossii posle sverzheniia samoderzhaviia: dokumenty i materialy [The Revolutionary Movement in Russia after the Overthrow of Autocracy: Documents and Materials]. Edited by L. S. Gaponenko et al. Moscow, 1957.

Revoliutsionnoe dvizhenie v Rossii v mae-iiune 1917 g.: dokumenty i materialy [The Revolutionary Movement in Russia in May–June 1917: Documents and Materials]. Edited by D. A. Chugaev. Moscow, 1957.

Revoliutsionnoe dvizhenie v Rossii v iiule 1917 g.: dokumenty i materialy [The Revolutionary Movement in Russia in July 1917: Documents and Materials]. Edited by D. A. Chugaev. Moscow, 1959.

Revoliutsionnoe dvizhenie v Rossii v avguste 1917 goda: dokumenty i materialy [The Revolutionary Movement in Russia in August 1917: Documents and Materials]. Edited by D. A. Chugaev et al. Moscow, 1959.

Revoliutsionnye Komitety BSSR i ikh deiatel'nost' po uprochneniiu Sovetskoi vlasti i organizatsii Sotsialisticheskogo stroitel'stva v iiule-dekabre 1920 g.: sbornik dokumentov i materialov [Revolutionary Committees in the Belorussian SSR and Their Activities on the Strengthening of the Soviet Power and the Organization of the Socialist Construction in July–December 1920: Collected Documents and Materials]. Edited by S. P. Margunskii. Minsk, 1957.

The Russian Provisional Government, 1917: Documents. Selected and edited by Robert Paul Browder and Alexander F. Kerensky. 3 vols. Stanford, California, 1961.

Sbornik dokumentov partarkhiva pri Ts.K. KP(b)B [Collected Documents of the Party Archive at the Central Committee of the Communist Party (Bolsheviks) of Belorussia]. Minsk: Gosizdat BSSR, 1947.

Semnadtsatyi s"ezd Vsesoiuznoi Kommunisticheskoi Partii (bol'shevikov)

Selected Bibliography

26 ianvaria–10 fevralia 1934 goda: stenograficheskii otchet [Seventeenth Congress of the All-Union Communist Party (Bolsheviks), 26 January–10 February 1934: Stenographic Report]. Moscow, 1934.

S"ezdy Sovetov Soiuza SSR, Soiuznykh i Avtonomnykh Sovetskikh Sotsialisticheskikh Respublik: sbornik dokumentov v trekh tomakh, 1917–1936 gg. [The Congresses of the Soviets of the USSR, of the Union and the Autonomous Soviet Socialist Republics: Collected Documents in Three Volumes, 1917–1936]. Moscow, 1959–1960.

Shestnadtsataia konferentsiia Vsesoiuznoi Kommunisticheskoi Partii (bol'shevikov): stenograficheskii otchet, 23–29 aprelia 1929 g. [Sixteenth Conference of the All-Union Communist Party (Bolsheviks): Stenographic Report, 23–29 April 1929]. Moscow, 1962.

Shestnadtsatyi s"ezd Vsesoiuznoi Kommunisticheskoi Partii (bol'shevikov), 26 iiunai–13 iiulia 1930 g.: stenograficheskii otchet [Sixteenth Congress of the All-Union Communist Party (Bolsheviks), 26 June–13 July 1930: Stenographic Report]. Moscow, 1930.

Sluzhachyia dziarzhaunaha i kaaperatyunaha apparatu BSSR [Employees of the State and the Cooperative Apparatus of the Belorussian SSR]. Minsk: Dziarzhplian BSSR, 1930.

Sobranie ukazanii BSSR [Collected Decrees of the Belorussian SSR]. Minsk, [1920s]–.

Sobranie zakonov i rasporiazhenii raboche-krest'ianskogo pravitel'stva Soiuza Sovetskikh Sotsialisticheskikh Respublik, izdavaemoe upravleniem delami Soveta Narodnykh Komissarov Soiuza SSR i STO [Collected Laws and Decrees of the Workers'-Peasants' Government of the USSR, Issued by the Managing Department of the Council of People's Commissars of the USSR and the Council of Labor and Defense]. Moscow, 1924–1949. [Part 1, microprint in Indiana University Library.]

Soviet Documents on Foreign Policy, 1917–1941. Selected and edited by Jane Degras. 3 vols. London: Royal Institute of International Affairs, 1951–1953.

Soviet-Polish Relations, 1918–1943: Official Documents. Washington, D.C.: Polish Embassy, by Authority of the Government of the Republic of Poland [1940s].

Statut Velikogo Kniazhestva Litovskogo 1529 goda [The Statute of the Grand Duchy of Lithuania of 1529]. Edited by K. I. Iablonskis [a member of the Academy of Sciences of the Lithuanian SSR]. Minsk, 1960.

Trial of the Major War Criminals before the International Military Tribunal, November 14, 1945–October 1, 1946. Official Documents in 42 vols. Nuremberg, Germany, 1947–1949.

United Nations. *Charter of the United Nations and Statue of the International Court of Justice.* New York: United Nations Department of Public Information, 1945.

United Nations. *Documents of the United Nations Conference on International Organization.* San Francisco, 1945. [Published in cooperation with the Library of Congress.]

U.S., Congress, House, Select Committee on Communist Aggression. *Communist Takeover and Occupation of Byelorussia.* Special Report No. 9. 83d Congress, 2d Session, 31 December 1954. Washington, D.C.: Government Printing Office, 1955.

U.S., Department of State. *The Conferences at Cairo and Tehran, 1943: Diplomatic Papers of the Foreign Relations of the Untied States.* Washington, D.C.: Government Printing Office, 1961.

——. *The Conferences at Malta and Yalta, 1945: Diplomatic Papers of the Foreign Relations of the United States.* Washington, D.C.: Government Printing Office, 1955.

——. *Papers Relating to the Foreign Relations of the United States, 1920.* Vol. 3. Washington, D.C., 1936.

Velikaia Oktiabr'skaia Sotsialisticheskaia Revoliutsiia: khronika sobytii v chetyrekh tomakh [Great October Socialist Revolution: A Chronicle of Events in Four Volumes]. Edited by P. N. Sobolev et al. Moscow, 1957–1961.

Vosemnadtsatyi s"ezd Vsesoiuznoi Kommunisticheskoi Partii (bol'shevikov) 10–21 marta 1939 goda: stenograficheskii otchet [Eighteenth Congress of the All-Union Communist Party (Bolsheviks), 10–21 March 1939: Stenographic Report]. Moscow, 1939.

Vseobshchaia perepis' chlenov RKP(b), 1922 g. [General Census of the Members of the Russian Communist Party (Bolsheviks), 1922]. Moscow, 1922.

Vsesoiuznaia Kommunisticheskaia Partiia (bol'shevikov) v rezoliutsiiakh i resheniiakh s"ezdov, konferentsii i plenumov Ts.K., 1898–1939 [All-Union Communist Party (Bolsheviks) in Resolutions and Decisions of the Congresses, Conferences, and Plenums of the Central Committee, 1898–1939]. 6th ed. 2 vols. Moscow, 1940–1941.

Za dziarzhaunuiu nezalezhnasts' Belarusi: dakumanty i matar'ialy [For the National Independence of Belorussia: Documents and Materials]. Edited by I. Kasiak. London: Belorussian Central Rada, 1960.

Zbornik listovak usenarodnai partyzanskai barats'by u Belorusi u hady Vialikai Aichynnai Vainy [Collection of the Leaflets of the Peoples' Struggle in Belorussia during the Great Fatherland's War]. Minsk, 1952.

Zbornik partyinykh i Savetskikh pastanou, rezaliutsyi i tsyrkuliarau u haline Savetskaha budaunitstva [Collected Party and Soviet Decisions, Resolutions, and Circulars Concerning Soviet Construction]. Minsk: Vydan'ne Ts.V.K. BSSR, 1929.

Zbornik zakonau i zahadau rabocha-sialianskaha uradu Belaruskai Savetskai Sotsyialistychnai Respubliki [Collected Laws and Orders of the Workers' and Peasants' Government of the Belorussian SSR].

Minsk: Vydan'ne Kiraunitstva Sprau Savetu Narodnykh Kamisarau i Ekanamichae Narady BSSR, 1924-1938.

Zbor zakonau i zahadau rabocha-sialianskaha uradu Belaruskai Satsyialistychnai Savetskai Respubliki [Collected Laws and Orders of the Workers' and Peasants' Government of the Belorussian Soviet Socialist Republic]. Minsk, [1920s]-.

Zemel'nyi kodeks BSSR [The Code of Land Laws of the Belorussian SSR (before collectivization)]. Minsk: Izdanie Narodnogo Komissariata Zemledeliia BSSR, 1925.

BOOKS AND ARTICLES

Adamovich, Anthony. *Opposition to Sovietization in Belorussian Literature, 1917-1957*. Munich, 1958.

Ahurski, S. *Ocherki po istorii revoliutsionnogo dvizheniia v Belorussii, 1863-1917* [Outlines on the History of the Revolutionary Movement in Belorussia, 1863-1917]. Minsk, 1928.

Akimov, N. N., ed. *Nekotorye voprosy istorii KPB v poslevoennyi period* [Some Problems in the History of the Communist Party of Belorussia in the Postwar Period]. Minsk, 1961.

Aleksandrovich, Andrei. "Kliasavaia barats'ba na movaznauchym frontse i reforma belaruskai movy" [Class Struggle in the Field of Languages and the Reform of the Belorussian Language]. In *Pis'menniki Belaruskai SSR ab reforme pravapisa belaruskai movy* [The Writers of the Belorussian SSR about the Reform of the Orthography of the Belorussian Language]. Minsk, 1934.

Antipov, Nikolai Kirillovich. "Chistka sdelala KP(b) Belorussii eshche bolee sil'nym i splochennym otriadom VKP(b)" [The Purge Has Made the Communist Party (Bolsheviks) of Belorussia a Still Stronger and More United Detachment of the All-Union Communist Party of Bolsheviks]. *Rabochii*, no. 285 (28 December 1933).

Armstrong, John A. *Ideology, Politics, and Government in the Soviet Union*. New York, 1962.

―――. *The Politics of Totalitarianism: The Communist Party of the Soviet Union from 1934 to the Present*. New York, 1961.

Balitski, A. "Instytut Belaruskai Kul'tury" [Institute of Belorussian Culture]. *As'veta*, no. 3 (1927).

―――. "Kul'turnae budaunitstva Savetskai Belarusi" [Cultural Progress in Soviet Belorussia]. *As'veta*, no. 8 (1928).

Baumgart, Winfried. *Deutsche Ostpolitik, 1918: Von Brest-Litowsk bis zum Ende des Ersten Weltkrieges* [German Eastern Policy, 1918: From Brest-Litovsk to the End of World War I]. Vienna and Munich, 1966.

Belorussia. Subcontractor's Monograph HRAF-19. New Haven, Conn.: Human Relations Area Files, 1954-1955.

Berman, Harold J. *Russia in Focus*. Boston, 1951.
Bernstein, Victor H. *Final Judgement: The Story of Nuremberg*. New York, 1947.
Budzin, S. *Natsyianal'nae pytan'ne* [National Problem]. Minsk, 1932.
Bugaev, Evgenii Iosifovich. *Voznikovenie bol'shevistskikh organizatsii i obrazovanie Kommunisticheskoi Partii Belorussii* [Appearance of the Bolshevik Organizations and the Formation of the Communist Party of Belorussia]. Moscow, 1959.
Bunyan, James, and Fisher, H. H. *The Bolshevik Revolution, 1917–1918: Documents and Materials*. Stanford, California, 1961.
Byrnes, James F. *Speaking Frankly*. New York, 1947.
Carr, Edward Hallett. *The Bolshevik Revolution, 1917–1923*. 3 vols. New York, 1951–1953.
———. *Socialism in One Country, 1924–1926*. Vol. 1. New York, 1958.
Charviakou, Aleksandr. *Za Savetskuiu Belarus'* [For a Soviet Belorussia]. Minsk, 1927.
Churchill, Winston S. *Triumph and Tragedy*. Boston, 1953.
Dallin, Alexander. *German Rule in Russia, 1941–1945*. London, 1957.
Deborin, Grigorii. *The Second World War: A Politico-Military Survey*. Moscow, [1950s].
Delbars, Yves. *The Real Stalin*. London, 1953.
Denisov, A. *Sovetskoe gosudarstvo i pravo* [Soviet State and Law]. Moscow, 1947.
Dmowski, Roman. *Germaniia, Rossiia i Pol'skii vopros* [Germany, Russia, and the Problem of Poland]. Petrograd, 1919.
Dudkov, D. "Protiv Trotskistskoi i natsionalisticheskoi fal'sifikatsii istorii Belorussii" [Against Trotskyist and Nationalist Falsification of Belorussian History]. *Rabochii*, no. 136 (15 June 1937).
Dvinov, B. "Velikoe pereselenie narodov SSSR" [Great Transmigration of the People in the USSR]. *Sotsialisticheskii vestnik*, no. 3 (12 March 1947).
Dvornik, Francis. *The Slavs in European History and Civilization*. New Brunswick, New Jersey, 1962.
Egorov, G. *Zapadnaia Belorussia* [West Belorussia]. Moscow, 1939.
Engelhardt, Eugen von. *Weissruthenien: Volk und Land* [Belorussia: People and Land]. Berlin, 1943.
Erafeiau, Iu. "Suprats' vialikadziarzhaunaha shavinizmu u kul'turnym budaunitstve" [Against the Great Russian Chauvinism in the Development of Culture]. *Kamunistychnae vykhavan'ne*, no. 5 (1931).
Erickson, John. *The Soviet High Command: A Military-Political History, 1918–1941*. New York, 1962.
Essad-Bey. *Stalin: The Career of a Fanatic*. Translated by Huntley Paterson. New York, 1932.
Ezavitau, K. *Belarus' u minulym i suchasnym* [Belorussia, Past and Present]. Riga, 1927.

———. *Belorussy i Poliaki* [The Belorussians and the Poles]. Kovno, 1919.
Fainsod, Merle. *How Russia Is Ruled*. Cambridge, Mass., 1953.
———. *Smolensk under Soviet Rule*. Cambridge, Mass., 1958.
Fedotoff White, Dimitri. *The Growth of the Red Army*. Princeton, 1944.
Fischer, Fritz. *Germany's Aims in the First World War*. New York, 1967.
Gorbunov, T. "Lenin i Stalin v bor'be za svobodu i nezavisimost' Belorusskogo naroda" [Lenin's and Stalin's Struggle for Freedom and Independence of the Belorussian People]. *Istoricheskii zhurnal*, nos. 2–3 (1944).
———. *Vossoedinenie Belorusskogo naroda v edinom Sovetskom Sotsialisticheskom gosudarstve* [Reunion of the Belorussian People with a Unified Soviet Socialist State]. Moscow, 1948.
Grabski, Stanislaw. *The Polish-Soviet Frontier*. London, 1943.
Guderian, Heinz. *Panzer Leader*. Translated by Constantine Fitzgibbon. New York, 1952.
Halecki, Oscar. *A History of Poland*. London, 1955.
Harris, Whitney R. *Tyranny on Trial: The Evidence at Nuremberg*. Dallas, 1954.
Herzen, Aleksandr I. "Rossiia i Pol'sha" [Russia and Poland]. *Kolokol* [Bell], no. 34 (Geneva, 1887).
Hill, Ninian. *Poland and the Polish Question: Impressions and Afterthoughts*. London, 1915.
History of the Civil War in the USSR. Vol. 2, Moscow, 1947.
History of the Communist Party of the Soviet Union. Moscow, 1960.
Hitler, Adolf. *Mein Kampf* [My Struggle]. Translated by Ralph Manheim. New York, 1943.
Hlebka, P. F., ed. *Farmiravan'ne i razvits'tsio Belaruskai satsyialistychnai natsyi* [Formation and Development of the Belorussian Socialist Nation]. Minsk, 1958.
Hlybinny, U. "Belorussian Culture after World War II." *Belorussian Review*, no. 6 (1958).
———. *Dolia Belaruskai kul'tury pad Savetami: dosledy i matar'ialy* [The Fate of Belorussian Culture under the Soviets: Research Studies and Materials]. Research Studies, series 2, no. 68. Munich, 1958.
Horak, Stephan. *Poland and Her National Minorities, 1919–1939*. New York, 1961.
Ignatiev, V. I. *Sovetskii stroi* [Soviet System]. Moscow, 1928.
Ihnatouski, Usevalad, and Smolich, A. *Belorussiia: territoriia, naselenie, ekonomika, vazhneishie momenty istorii: ekonomicheskii ocherk Sovetskoi Belorussii i ee okrugov* [Territory, Population, Economy and Important Moments in the History of Belorussia: An Economic Survey of the Belorussian SSR and Its Surroundings]. Minsk, 1925.
Istoriia BSSR [A History of the Belorussian Soviet Socialist Republic]. Edited by L. S. Abetsedarskii et al. 2d ed. 2 vols. Minsk, 1961.

Istoriia grazhdanskoi voiny v SSSR [History of the Civil War in the USSR]. 1st ed. 5 vols. Moscow, 1935–1960.

Istoriia Kommunisticheskoi Partii Sovetskogo Soiuza [History of Communist Party of the Soviet Union]. 2d ed. Moscow, 1962.

Istoriia Velikoi Otechestvennoi Voiny Sovetskogo Soiuza, 1941–1945 [History of the Great Fatherland War of the Soviet Union, 1941–1945]. 1st ed. 6 vols. Moscow, 1960.

Istoriia Vsesoiuznoi Kommunisticheskoi Partii (bol'shevikov): kratkii kurs [History of the All-Union Communist Party of Bolsheviks: A Short Course]. Moscow, 1938.

Iz istorii bor'by Belorusskogo naroda za Sovetskuiu vlast' i pobedu sotsializma [From the History of the Struggle of the Belorussian People for the Soviet System of Government and a Victory of Socialism]. Minsk, 1957.

Jäger, Walter, ed. *Weissruthenien: Land, Bewohner, Geschichte, Volkswirtschaft, Kultur, Dichtung* [Belorussia: Land, People, History, Economy, Culture, and Poetry]. Berlin, 1919.

Jurgela, Constantine Radyard. *History of the Lithuanian Nation*. New York, 1948.

Kancher, E. S. *Belorusskii vopros* [The Belorussian Question]. Petrograd, 1919.

Karski, Efim F. *Belorussy* [The Belorussians]. Vilna, 1904.

———. *Kurs Belorussovedeniia* [A Course of Belorussian Studies]. Moscow, 1920.

[This is composed of lectures delivered at Moscow National University in the summer of 1918.]

Khrushchev, Nikita S. *The Crimes of the Stalin Era: Special Report to the 20th Congress of the Communist Party of the Soviet Union*. New York, 1962.

Kirkien, Leszek. *Russia, Poland, and the Curzon Line*. London, 1945.

Kiselev, K. V., ed. *Belorusskaia SSR na mezhdunarodnoi arene* [The Belorussian SSR in Foreign Affairs]. Moscow, 1964.

Knorin, Vilhelm Germanovich. "Ab rashaiuchykh 'drobiaziakh' u vialikim pytan'ni" [On the Decisive "Trifles" in a Big Problem]. *As'veta*, no. 3 (1928).

———. "My khotim priznaniia" [We Want Recognition]. *Zvezda*, no. 23 (25 January 1922).

———. *1917 god v Belorussii i na zapadnom fronte* [Belorussia and the Western Front in 1917]. Minsk, 1925.

———. *A Short History of the Communist Party of the Soviet Union*. Moscow, 1935.

———. *Zametki k istorii diktaturi proletariata v Belorussii* [Notes on the History of the Dictatorship of the Proletariat in Belorussia]. Minsk, 1934.

Kolarz, Walter. *Russia and Her Colonies*. New York, 1952.

Kolas, Iakub [Konstantin Mitskevich]. *Novaia ziamlia* [The New Land]. Munich, 1952.
[A very long poem written in 1911–1923, describing the conditions of the Belorussian peasants and their desire for more land.]
Komarnicki, Titus. *Rebirth of the Polish Republic. A Study in the Diplomatic History of Europe, 1914–1920.* London, 1957.
Kostiushko, I. I. "K stoletiiu vosstaniia 1863 g. v tsarstve Pol'skom, Litve, Belorussii i na pravoberezhnoi Ukraine" [On the Hundredth Anniversary of the Revolution of 1863 in the Kingdom of Poland, Lithuania, Belorussia and the Right Bank Ukraine]. *Voprosy istorii,* no. 1 (1963).
Kravchenko, I. S., and Marchenko, I. E. *Belorusskaia SSR* [The Belorussian SSR]. Moscow, 1959.
Kuznetsov, P. S. *Russkaia dialektologiia* [Russian Dialectology]. Moscow, 1951.
Lamtsiou, T. P. *Belaruskaia hramatyka* [Belorussian Grammar]. Minsk, 1935.
[This book contains the text of the "Decree of the Council of People's Commissars on Changes and Simplification of the Belorussian Grammar and Orthography," passed on 26 August 1933.]
Lenin, Vladimir Il'ich. *Polnoe sobranie sochinenii* [Complete Collection of Works]. 5th ed. 56 vols. Moscow, 1958–1966.
———. *Sobranie sochinenii* [Collected Works]. 1st ed. Edited by L. B. Kamenev. 19 vols. Moscow, 1920–1923.
———. *Sochineniia* [Works]. Edited by V. V. Adoratskii et al. 3d ed. 30 vols. Moscow, 1929–1939.
———. *Sochineniia* [Works]. 4th ed. 38 vols. Moscow, 1946–1958.
[Bibliographical references are included at the end of each volume.]
Lenin i Stalin u belaruskai narodnai tvorchastsi [Lenin and Stalin in Belorussian Folklore]. Minsk, 1937.
Levine, Isaac Don. *Stalin.* New York, 1931.
Liubavskii, M. K. *Ocherki istorii Litovsko-Russkogo gosudarstva do Liublinskoi Unii vkliuchitel'no* [Outlines on the History of the Lithuanian-Russian State up to the Lublin Union]. 2d ed. Moscow, 1915.
Lloyd George, David. *The Truth about the Peace Treaties.* Vol. 1. London, 1938.
Lochmel', I. F. *Ocherki istorii bor'by Belorusskogo naroda protiv Pol'skikh panov* [Outlines on the History of the Struggle of the Belorussian People against the Polish Landlords]. Moscow, 1940.
Machray, Robert. *Poland of Pilsudski.* New York, 1937.
Mackiewicz, Stanislaw. *Colonel Beck and His Policy.* London, 1944.
Magnes, Judah L. *Russia and Germany at Brest-Litovsk: A Documentary History of the Peace Negotiations.* New York, 1919.
Makarenko, I. E., ed. *Khrestomatiia po istorii BSSR* [A Reader on the History of the Belorussian SSR]. Part 2. Minsk, 1962.

Margunskii, S. P. *Sozdanie i uprochnenie belorusskoi gosudarstvennosti, 1917–1922* [Foundation and Strengthening of the Belorussian State, 1917–1922]. Minsk, 1958.

Markiianov, Boris Kirillovich. *Bor'ba Kommunisticheskoi Partii Belorussii za ukreplenie edinstva svoikh riadov v 1921–1925 gg.* [Struggle of the Communist Party of Belorussia for Strengthening of the Unity of its Ranks in 1921–1925]. Minsk, 1961.

Medynskii, Evgenii Nikolaevich. *Prosveshchenie v SSSR* [Education in the USSR]. Moscow, 1955.

Mienski, J. "Chamu dy iak byla utvorana Belaruskaia SSR" [How and Why the Belorussian SSR Was Established]. *Belaruski zbornik*, no. 1 (1955).

———. "The Establishment of the Belorussian SSR." *Belorussian Review*, no. 1 (1955).

Minaev, V. *Zapadnaia Belorussiia i Zapadnaia Ukraina pod igom panskoi Pol'shi* [West Belorussia and West Ukraine under the Yoke of Feudal Poland]. Moscow, 1939.

Nedasek, N. *Bol'shevizm v revoliutsionnom dvizhenii Belorussii: issledovaniia i materialy* [Bolshevism in the Revolutionary Movement of Belorussia: A Study and the Materials]. Munich, 1956.

———. *Ocherki istorii bol'shevizma v Belorussii: bol'shevizm na putiakh k ustanovleniiu kontrolia nad Belorussiei* [Historical Outlines on Bolshevism in Belorussia: The Development of Bolshevik Control over Belorussia]. Research Studies, no. 1. Munich, 1954.

Neuman, Bernard. *Russia's Neighbor—The New Poland*. London, 1946.

Niamiha, H. "Education in Belorussia before the Rout of 'National Democracy,' 1917–1930." *Belorussian Review*, no. 1 (1955).

———. "Education in the Belorussian SSR and Communist Doctrine." *Belorussian Review*, no. 3 (1956).

Nicolson, Harold. *Curzon: The Last Phase, 1919–1925*. Boston and New York, 1934.

Novikau, Ivan. "Darohi skryzhyvalisia u Minsku" [The Roads Crossed at Minsk]. *Polymia*, 1964.

Ocherki po istorii gosudarstva i prava Belorusskoi Sovetskoi Sotsialisticheskoi Respubliki [Outlines of the History of the State and Law of the Belorussian Soviet Socialist Republic]. Edited by B. E. Babitskii and V. A. Dorogin. Minsk, 1958.

O partiinom podpol'e v Minske v gody Velikoi Otechestvennoi Voiny, Iiun' 1941–Iiul' 1944 [About the Party Underground Work in Minsk during the Years of the Great Fatherland's War, June 1941–July 1944]. Minsk, 1961.

Orlov, Alexander. *The Secret History of Stalin's Crimes*. New York, 1953.

Ostrowski, Wiktor. *Spotlight on Byelorussia and Her Neighbours*. London, 1959.

Outline History of the USSR. Translated by George H. Hanna. Moscow, 1960.
Paprocki, S. J., ed. *Minority Affairs and Poland: An Informatory Outline*. Warsaw: National Research Institute. 1935.
Peterson, Arnold. *Stalin's Corruption of Marxism: A Study in Machiavellian Duplicity*. New York, 1940.
Pigido, F. *Visim mil'ioniv: 1933—i rik na Nkraini* [Eight Millions: The Ukraine in 1933]. Winnipeg, 1951.
[A description of the terrible famine in the Ukraine in 1932–1933.]
Pilsudska, Alexandra. *Pilsudski: A Biography by His Wife*. New York, 1941.
Pipes, Richard. *The Formation of the Soviet Union: Communism and Nationalism, 1917–1923*. Cambridge, Mass., 1954.
The Politics of Aristotle. Translated with notes by Ernest Barker. Oxford, 1950.
Polonskii, M. L., and Rostovtsev, M. I. *Belorusskaia SSR* [The Belorussian SSR]. Moscow, 1964.
Ponomarev, B. N., ed. *Politicheskii slovar'* [Political Dictionary]. 2d ed. Moscow, 1958.
Rahulia, Vasil'. *Uspaminy* [Memories of the Past]. New York, 1957.
Rauch, Georg von. *A History of Soviet Russia*. New York, 1958.
———. *Russland: Staatliche Einheit und Nationale Vielfalt* [Russia: State Unity and National Diversity]. Munich, 1953.
Rose, William John. *Poland, Old and New*. London, 1948.
Seduro, Vladimir I. "Belorussian Culture and Totalitarianism." *Proceedings of the Conference of the Institute for the Study of the History and Culture of the USSR*. New York, 20–22 March 1953.
Shapiro, Leonard, ed. *Soviet Treaty Series: A Collection of Bilateral Treaties, Agreements and Conventions, Etc., Concluded between the Soviet Union and Foreign Powers, 1917–1939*. 2 vols. Washington, D. C., 1950–1955.
Shcharbakou, V. K. *Kastrychnitskaia Revaliutsyia na Belarusi i belapol'skaia akupatsyia* [The October Revolution in Belorussia and the Polish Occupation]. Minsk, 1930.
Shkliar, M. E. *Kommunisticheskaia Partiia (bol'shevikov) Belorussii v period perekhoda na mirnuiu rabotu po vosstanovleniiu narodnogo khoziaistva, 1921–1925 gg*. [The Communist Party (Bolsheviks) of Belorussia in the Period of Transition to a Time of Peaceful Reconstruction of the National Economy, 1921–1925]. Minsk, 1950.
Shotwell, James T., and Laserson, Max M. *The Curzon Line: The Polish-Soviet Dispute*. New York, [1940s].
Solovei, Dmytro. *The Golgotha of the Ukraine: Eye-Witness Accounts of the Famine in Ukraine Instigated and Fostered by the Kremlin in an Attempt to Quell Ukrainian Resistance to Soviet Russian National*

and Social Enslavement of the Ukrainian People. New York: Ukrainian Congress Committee of America, 1953.

Souvarine, Boris. *Stalin: A Critical Survey of Bolshevism.* New York, 1939.

Stalin, Iosif Vissarionovich. *Marksizm i natsional'no-kolonial'nyi vopros* [Marxism and the National-Colonial Problem]. Moscow, 1937.

———. *Sochineniia* [Works]. 1st ed. 13 vols. Moscow, 1946–1952. [Bibliographical references are included at the end of each volume.]

———. *Voprosy Leninizma* [Problems of Leninism]. 11th ed. Moscow, 1947.

Stiapura, Z. "Shto zroblena u haline useahul'naha navuchan'nia u BSSR za 1926–1927 navuchal'ny hod?" [What Was Done in the Field of Education in the Belorussian SSR in the 1926–1927 Academic Year?]. *As'veta,* nos. 5–6 (1927).

Strokovskii, V. *Promyshlennost' BSSR* [The Industry of the Belorussian SSR]. Moscow, 1931.

Stukalich, Iurka. "Kvitneiuts' na ikh mahile viarhini" [Dahlias Are Blooming on Their Grave]. *Bats'kaushchyna,* no. 18 (1 May 1955).

Sullivant, Robert S. *Soviet Politics in the Ukraine, 1917–1957.* New York, 1962.

Temperley, Harold William Vazeille, ed. *A History of the Peace Conference of Paris.* 6 vols. London, 1920–1924.

Tokaev, Grigori A. *Betrayal of an Ideal.* Bloomington, Ind., 1955.

———. *Comrade X.* London, 1956.

Trainin, I. *Natsional'noe i sotsial'noe osvobozhdenie zapadnoi Ukrainy i zapadnoi Belorussii* [National and Social Liberation of West Ukraine and West Belorussia]. Moscow, 1939.

Trotsky, Leon. *Stalin: An Appraisal of the Man and His Influence.* London, 1947.

Tsvikevich, A. "Berlinskaia Kanferentsyia" [Berlin Conference]. *Polymia,* no. 4 (1926).

———. *Kratkii ocherk vozniknoveniia Belorusskoi Narodnoi Respubliki* [A Brief Account of the Origins of the Belorussian National Republic]. Kiev, 1918.

Vakar, Nicholas P. *Belorussia: The Making of a Nation.* Cambridge, Mass., 1956.

Vernadsky, George. *A History of Russia.* New York, 1944.

Vikhrev, Semen Romanovich. *Suverinetet Belorusskoi SSR v sostave Soiuza SSR* [The Sovereignty of the Belorussian SSR within the USSR]. Minsk, 1958.

Vishniak, M. V. *Dva puti, Fevral' i Oktiabr'* [Two Roads, February and October]. Paris, 1931.

Volacic, Mikola. "The Curzon Line and Territorial Changes in Eastern Europe." *Belorussian Review,* no. 2 (1956).

———. "The Population of Western Belorussia and Its Resettlement in Poland and the USSR." *Belorussian Review,* no. 3 (1956).

Volkov, I. "Na Belorussii" [In Belorussia]. *Sotsialisticheskii vestnik*, no. 7 (30 July 1948).
Vyshinskii, Andrei. *Sudebnye rechi* [The Trial Speeches]. Moscow, 1948.
Walles, Sam. *People of Europe*. New York, 1948.
Wandycz, Piotr S. *Soviet-Polish Relations, 1917-1921*. Cambridge, Mass., 1969.
Wheeler-Bennett, John W. *The Treaty of Brest-Litovsk and Germany's Eastern Policy*. Oxford, 1940.
Zaprudnik, Jan. "The Communist Party of Belorussia: An Outline of Its History." *Belorussian Review*, no. 7 (1957).
Ziuz'kou, A. *Kryvavy shliakh Belaruskai natsdemokratyi* [The Bloody Path of Belorussian National-Democracy]. Minsk, 1931.

ENCYCLOPEDIAS AND HANDBOOKS

Belorusskaia Sovetskaia Sotsialisticheskaia Respublika v tsifrakh: k desiatiletiiu sushchestvovaniia BSSR, 1919-1929 [The Belorussian Soviet Socialist Republic in Figures: On the Tenth Anniversary of the Belorussian SSR, 1919-1929). Minsk, 1929.
Bol'shaia sovetskaia entsiklopediia [Great Soviet Encyclopedia]. 1st ed. 65 vols. Moscow, 1929-1948.
Bol'shaia sovetskaia entsiklopediia. 2d ed. 51 vols. Moscow, 1950-1958.
Polen: Osteuropa-Handbuch [Poland: An East-European Handbook]. Edited by Werner Markert. Cologne, 1959.
Russia, Poland, Lithuania and White Russia: Handbook Prepared under the Direction of the Historical Section of the Foreign Office. Handbook no. 44. London, 1920.

PERIODICALS AND SERIALS

Ahliad dzeinastsi Savetu Narodnykh Kamisarau i Ekanamichnae Narady BSSR: zbornyia matar'ialy [A Survey of the Activities of the Council of People's Commissars and the Economic Council of the Belorussian SSR: Collected Materials]. Minsk, 1925-.
As'veta [Education]. Minsk, 1924-1929.
 [A periodical of the People's Commissariat of Education and the Union of Workers in Education. After December 1929 it appeared under the title *Kamunistychnae vykhavan'ne* (Communist Upbringing).]
Belaruski zbornik [Belorussian Collection]. Munich: Institute for the Study of the USSR, 1955-.
Belorussian Review. Munich: Institute for the Study of the USSR, 1955-.
Belorusskaia kul'tura [Belorussian Culture]. Minsk, 1928-.
Bol'shevik. Moscow, April 1924-November 1952.
 [Official organ of the Central Committee of the All-Union Communist

Party (Bolsheviks). After November 1952, this journal appeared under the title, *Kommunist*.]

Istoricheskii arkhiv [Historical Archives]. Moscow, 1956–.
[Bimonthly publication of the Institute of History of the Academy of Sciences of the USSR.]

Istoricheskii zhurnal [Historical Journal]. Moscow, February 1931–July 1945.
[Superseded in July 1945 by *Voprosy istorii* (Problems of History).]

Izvestiia Akademii Nauk BSSR [News of the Academy of Sciences of the Belorussian SSR]. Minsk, 1940–.

Kamunistychnae vykhavan'ne [Communist Upbringing]. Minsk, January 1930–.
[Official organ of the Commissariat of Education and the Union of Workers in Education. See also *As'veta*, above.]

Kommunist [Communist]. Moscow, 1952–.
[Official organ of the Central Committee of the Communist Party of the Soviet Union. See also *Bol'shevik*, above.]

Nauchnye izvestiia Smolenskogo Gosudarstvennogo Universiteta [Scientific Information of the Smolensk State University]. 7 vols. Smolensk, 1923–1930.

Partiinaia zhizn' [Party Life]. Moscow, 1946–1954.
[Journal of the Central Committee of the Communist Party of the Soviet Union.]

Polymia [Flame]. Minsk, 1924–.
[A Belorussian periodical of literature, politics, economics, and history.]

Satsyialistychnae budaunitstva [Socialist Construction]. Minsk, 1925–.
[Official organ of the State Planning Committee of the Belorussian SSR.]

Sotsialisticheskii vestnik [Socialist Messenger]. New York and Paris, 1920–.
[A central organ of the Russian Social-Democratic Working Party founded by L. Martov.]

Voprosy istorii [Problems of History]. Moscow, July 1945–.
[Official organ of the Institute of History of the Academy of Sciences of the USSR.]

NEWSPAPERS

Bats'kaushchyna [The Fatherland]. Munich, 1946–.
[The weekly Whiteruthenian (Belorussian) newspaper, organ of Belorussian national liberation thought.]

Belarus [Belorussian]. New York, 1949–.
[A Belorussian newspaper published by the Belorussian-American Association, Inc.]

Belaruskae slova [Belorussian Word]. Backnang, Germany, 1948–.
Izvestiia [News]. Moscow, 1917–.
   [Official daily newspaper of the Soviets of the Workers' and Peasants' Deputies of the USSR.]
Pravda [Truth]. Moscow, 1912–.
   [Official daily newspaper of the Central Committee of the Communist Party of the Soviet Union.]
Rabochii [Worker]. Minsk, 1922(?)–1937.
   [Official daily newspaper of the Central Committee of the Communist Party (Bolsheviks) of Belorussia and the Central Soviet of the Trade Unions of Belorussia. From the very beginning it was published irregularly. In September 1937, it was superseded by *Sovetskaia Belorussiia* (see below).]
Sovetskaia Belorussiia [Soviet Belorussia]. Minsk, 1937–.
   [Official daily newspaper of the Central Committee of the Communist Party (Bolsheviks) of Belorussia.]
Zvezda [Star]. Minsk, July 1917–1927.
   [Official daily newspaper of the Central Bureau of the Communist Party (Bolsheviks) of Belorussia, published in Russian. In 1927 it became the official newspaper of the government of the Belorussian SSR; since then it has been published in the Belorussian language under the title *Zviazda* (Star).]

INDEX

Academy of Sciences of the USSR, 72–73
Adamovich, Iazep, 29, 48, 50, 94
Agriculture, 6–7, 10; Belorussian State Academy of, 75, 89; collectives, 74; Commissariat of, 74; improvement of conditions, 75–76; Stolypin's reforms, 9. *See also* Collective Farms; Collectivization; Land
Akinshyts, Fabian, 161
Aliakhnovich, Frantsishak, 83, 161
All-Belorussian Congress of Soviets: First (1919), 29, 30, 49; Second (1920), 74; Third (1921), 48–50
All-Belorussian National Congress: First (1917), 24, 25; Second (1944), 163–64, 169
All-European Economic Conference (Genoa, 1922), 50
All-Russian Central Executive Committee, 29–30
All-Russian Congress of Soviets: Second (1917), 23; Tenth (1922), 55
All-Union Central Executive Committee (V.Ts.I.K.), 56, 57, 65, 66, 117
All-Union Communist Party (Bolsheviks), 60; Central Committee, 95, 96, 98–99, 100, 113, 116, 125, 155; Central Control Commission, 113
All-Union Congress of Soviet Writers: First (1934), 120
All-Union Congress of the Soviets: First (1922), 56–57
Antanovich, Apanas, 160
Antipov, Nikolai Kirillovich, 113, 114, 116
Antonov, 62
Astrouski, Radaslau, 18, 109, 159, 162
As'veta (Education), 110

Augustov districts, 177
Aukhimovich, N. E., 155, 176

Balitski, Anton, 86, 94, 111
BCD (Belorussian Christian Democratic Party), 130
Belaruskaia hazeta (Belorussian Gazette), 161
Belaruskaia Nazalezhnitskaia Partyia (Party of Belorussian Independence), 161
Belaruskaia Tsentral'naia Rada. See Belorussian Central Council
Belaruski Narodny Front (Belorussian People's Front), 161
Belorussia: boundaries of, 1, 2, 66, 177–80; Communist control of, 13–16, 19, 20–21, 23, 47–50, 125–26, 144, 148, 169–70; Communist purges of, 110–15, 123–25, 144–45, 170–73; cultural development, 80–92; deportations to USSR, 145; early revolutionary movement in, 8–10; economic conditions, 62; ethnic origins, 36, 80; formation of parties, 6, 27–28; German occupation, 142–64; history of, 1–11; laws, 2–3; Marxism in, before Revolution, 7; national movement, 6–7, 158–59, 161, 187, 191; national movement destroyed, 108–10, 114–16, 173–74; and negotiations at Brest-Litovsk, 25–26; under NEP, 62–64, 76, 189; origin of name, 1; partition of, 31–38; Polish occupation, 35, 38–40, 42–45, 76; and Russian Provisional Government, 187; results of World War II, 166–68; and Russian-Polish treaty of 1921, 45–46; struggle with Poland, 31–34; treatment by Russia, 4; underground movement (World War

Belorussia *(continued)*:
  II), 155–56; in World War I, 11, 13–14; in World War II, 142–64. *See also* Belorussian National Republic; Belorussian Soviet Socialist Republic; West Belorussia
Belorussian Academy of Sciences, 89, 165, 175
Belorussian Association of Proletarian Writers, 91
Belorussian Autocephalous Orthodox Church, 159
Belorussian Autonomous Union, 17n
Belorussian Central Council, 22, 162, 163
Belorussian Central Executive Committee (B. Ts. I. K.), 49, 66, 68, 72, 84, 86
Belorussian Christian Democratic Party (BCD), 130
Belorussian Communist Party (Bolsheviks), 15, 28, 55, 70, 96, 113, 173; Central Committee, 60–61, 84, 112, 113, 116, 119, 123, 172; purges, 108; ruled by Moscow, 60
Belorussian Hramada. *See* Hramada
Belorussian Institute of Agriculture and Forestry, 75
Belorussian language, 2, 3, 4, 10, 80–81, 84–85, 90–91, 112; in Poland, 133–35; reforms, 175
Belorussian Military Rada, 21n
Belorussian Military Region, 86
Belorussian National Committee, 17
Belorussian National Museum, 134
Belorussian National Republic (BNR): conversion of exiled leaders, 82–83; formation of, 24
Belorussian Peasants' and Workers' Association, 130
Belorussian People's Front, 161
Belorussian Peoples' University, 27
Belorussian Revolutionary Hramada. *See* Hramada
Belorussian Soviet Socialist Republic (BSSR), 46, 49, 64, 65, 66; Communists secure governance, 49; constitution of 1927, 71–72; elections to soviets, 66–70; and formation of USSR, 55, 189; granted independence, 188; membership in U.N., 180–85; national composition of, 67; population (1926), 67; reestablished, 47; since Stalin's death, 176, 191; sovereignty of, 29–30
Belorussian State University, 88, 89
Belorussian Teachers' Association, 134
Belorussification, 84–85
Bel'ski, I. A., 155
Bereza Kartuska, concentration camp at, 137
Beshankovichy district, 100
Biadulia, Zmitrok, 39
Bialystok region, 35, 177
Bierut, Boleslaw, 179
BNR. *See* Belorussian National Republic
BNS. *See* Samapomach
Bodunova, Paluta, 18
Bol'shevik (journal), 175
Bolsheviks, 12; activity in Belorussia, 13–17, 19–23; agrarian policy, 15; 1917 coup d'état in Minsk, 20; Decree on Land, 23; mishandle Belorussian question, 26; national policy, 19. *See also* All-Union Communist Party; Belorussian Communist Party; Russian Communist Party
Bonder, V. I., 155
Borman, Martin, 152, 159, 160
Brest: union of Catholic and Orthodox Church at (1596), 3
BSSR. *See* Belorussian Soviet Socialist Republic
B. Ts. R. *See* Belorussian Central Council
Bug River, 42
Bukharin, Nikolai, 59, 93, 94, 95, 108, 124, 188
Burbis, Ales', 21
Busel, S., 145
Butenev, Count, 132

Catherine II, 4
Central Committee. *See* All-Union Communist Party; Belorussian Communist Party; Russian Communist Party
Central Executive Committee. *See* All-Union Central Executive Committee; Belorussian Central Executive Committee
Charles XII: invasion of Belorussia, 146

Index

Charnushevich, Zmitrok, 29
Charviakou, Aleksandr, 29, 48, 49, 50, 123
Chechen-Ingush Autonomous Soviet Republic, 167
Cheka (Security Police), 62, 64. *See also* GPU; NKVD
Chicherin, Grigori Vasilievich, 40
Christian Democratic Union, 17n
Christian Democrats, 161
Churches. *See* Religion
Churchill, Winston, 179, 180, 182, 183
Clergy, persecution of, 99
Collective farms, 74, 144, 190. *See also* Agriculture; Collectivization; Land
Collectivization: creates black market, 104; cruelty in, 98; extent and success of, 98–99, 102–06; famine caused by, 103–05; Lenin opposed to force, 96; progress of, 95–103; results of, 190; revolts by peasants, 100; Stalin's duplicity in, 99–100; three regions of, 95–96; in West Belorussia, 143–44
Commissariat: of Agriculture, 75; of Education, 114; of Nationalities, 19; of Workers' and Peasants' Inspection, 54
Committee to Save the Revolution and the Fatherland, 19, 20
Communist Party of Belorussia. *See* Belorussian Communist Party
Communist Party of Russia. *See* Russian Communist Party
Communist Party of the USSR. *See* All-Union Communist Party
Communist Party of West Belorussia (KPZB), 137, 144, 145
Communist University (Minsk), 89
Communist Youth (Komsomol), 155
Concentration camps, 168
Conference of the All-Union Communist Party: Sixteenth (1929), 108
Conference of the Central Committee of the Russian Communist Party: Fourth, 82
Congress of Belorussian Peasants: First, 14
Congress of Soviets of the USSR: Eighth (1936), 120
Congress of the All-Union Communist Party: Twelfth (1923), 58–59; Fifteenth (1927), 96, 97; Sixteenth, 113; Seventeenth (1934), 116; Eighteenth (1939), 125
Congress of the Belorussian Communist Party: First (1918), 28, 60; Sixteenth (1937), 125
Congress of the Belorussian Political Parties: Second, 18
Congress of the Communist Party of the Soviet Union (Twentieth, 1956), 175–76. *See also* Congress of the All-Union Communist Party
Congress of the Representatives of the Soldiers' Committees of the Western Front: Second, 20
Congress of the Russian Communist Party: Tenth, 63; Twelfth, 113
Constitution of the USSR: 1924, 83, 180–81; 1936, 120, 180
Council of People's Commissars of the Western Region and the Front (Sovnarkom), 20, 22, 39, 49, 86, 94, 125
Curzon, George Nathaniel, Lord, 44–45
Curzon Line, 141, 177, 179

Declaration of the Rights of the Peoples of Russia (1917), 19
Dmowski, Roman, 32, 42
Dounar-Zapolski, Mitrafan, 86
Dowbor-Musnicki, General, 23
Duma. *See* Russia
Dvarchanin, Ihnat, 115, 136, 137
Dylo, Iazep, 18
Dzerzhinski, Feliks Edmundovich, 45, 58

Education, 7, 10; development of schools, 86–90; elementary schools organized, 170; growth of schools for adults, 87; lack of teachers and texts, 115; national composition of schools, 90; under Nazis, 159–60; professional, 88; prohibition of textbooks, 110; purges, 110–15; social origins of students, 91; university, 88–89; in West Belorussia, 134–35. *See also* Illiteracy
Elections, 121
Ermachenko, Ivan, 159, 160, 161
Estonians, 67

Farming. *See* Agriculture; Collective farms; Collectivization; Land
February Revolution of 1917, 10, 12, 13, 14, 187
Feudalism, in Poland, 136
Foch, Marshal Ferdinand, 35
Food, scarcity of, 103–05
Frunze, Mikhail V., 14, 15, 16, 57

Gaisin, General, 142
Georgia, Republic of, 54, 55
Germans, 67
Germany: atrocities against Belorussians, 149, 152–57, 167–68; attacks Poland (1939), 139; conquers Belorussia, 147; devastation of Belorussia, 165–66; division of Belorussia, 150–51; extermination of Jews, 153–54; 1918 defeat, 25; Nonaggression Pact with USSR, 139; negotiations at Brest-Litovsk, 25–26; occupation of Belorussia, 76, 146–64, 191; occupation of Minsk, 23–25, 27; partisan warfare against, 154–56; and partition of Poland, 141; in Poland, 127; in West Belorussia, 129. *See also* Hitler; Nazis
Gogenloe, Princess, 7
Gomel region, 65, 66
Gorki Institute of Agriculture, 75
Gottberg, General, 157, 162
GPU (State Political Administration): attacks Natsdems, 109; complimented by Stalin, 113; requires interior passports, 117. *See also* Cheka; NKVD
Grabski, Wladyslaw, 43–44
Great Russians, 67; chauvinism, 112–13, 171
Grodno, 29, 35, 36
Guderian, Heinz, 154–55
Gusarov, Nikolai, 172
Gypsies, 67

Hadleuski, Father, 161
Haladzed, Mikola, 78, 123
Halavach, Platon, 18
Haller, General Josef, 37–38
Hanenko, I. P., 155
Harkavy, Vasil', 100
Harriman, W. Averell, 179
Hauryliuk, Iazep, 115, 137
Herzen, Aleksandr, 50

Higher Pedagogical Institute (Minsk), 114
Himmler, Heinrich, 149, 154, 165
Hitler, Adolph, 143; Hitlerism applied to Belorussia, 153-54; *Mein Kampf*, 146, 149; viewed as savior, 147. *See also* Nazis
Hoffman, General Max, 26
Homan (Talk), 6
Horetski, M., 83
Howard, Roy: interviews Stalin, 121
Hramada: of Belorussia, 6, 9, 10, 17, 17n, 18, 21, 115; Congress of 1917, 17; of West Belorussia, 137

Ihnatouski, Usevalad, 27, 39, 50, 86, 110, 111
Illiteracy, 7, 86, 87
Industry: destruction of, 165; heavy, 167; increase in, 76–77; output, 77–79; in West Belorussia, 133
Institute of Belorussian Culture (Inbelkult), 80, 90
Institute of Linguistics, 175
Interior passports, 117
Ivan IV, 81
Ivanouski, Vatslau, 162

Jadwiga, Queen, 3
Jagiello, Grand Duke of Lithuania. *See* Ladislaus II
Jews, 67, 68, 89–90; in Belorussia, 36; in Poland, 127; under Nazis in occupied Belorussia, 153; in West Belorussia, 129

Kalinin, Mikhail, 66
Kalinouski, Kostus' (or Constantine), 5
Kamenev, Lev, 26, 58n, 93
Kamenskaia, N. V., 28
Karaneuski, I., 39
Karski, Efim, 27, 86
Kazlouski, Uladyslau, 161
Keitel, Wilhelm, 152–53, 156
Khrushchev, Nikita, 175–76, 191
Kiev: invasion of (1240), 1, 2; Pilsudski takes, 43
Kievan Russia, 1–2
Kiselev, V. K., 125
Kleshchev, A., 173
Knorin, Vilhelm, 16, 19, 20, 50, 84–85
Koch, Erich, 152
Kolas, Iakub, 9–10, 39, 91

Index

Komsomol, 155
Kon, 45
Kornilov, General Lavr Georgievich, 16
Kostsevich, Makar, 145
Koval'chuk (Comrade), 112
Kozlov, B. N., 173
Kozlov, V. I., 155
KPZB. *See* Communist Party of West Belorussia
Kraevaia Aborona (Country's Defense), 163
Kronstadt, 62
Krutalevich, Aleksandr, 86
Krynitski, 96
Kube, Wilhelm, 151, 152n, 157, 159, 162
Kulaks, 75, 94, 97–98, 103. *See also* Peasants
Kupala, Ianka, 9–10, 39, 91; quoted, 92
Kurchevich-Seuruk, 18

Ladislaus II, 3
Lagun, I., 29
Land: codes, 73; distributed to peasants, 64, 73–74, 97n; ownership of, 75; reform in Poland, 131–32; reform in West Belorussia, 135–36. *See also* Agriculture; Collective farms
Lander, Karl, 19, 20
Language. *See* Belorussian language; Old Slavonic language; Poland, language
Lastouski, Vatslau, 38, 43, 83, 109, 111
Latvia, 67
Lawyers, deficiency of, 71
League of Nations, 40
Lenin, Vladimir [Nikolai], 40; agrarian policy, 15; and dictatorship of Communist Party, 189; and New Economic Policy, 62–63, 93; on self-determination, 12; "Report Delivered to the Tenth Congress of the Central Committee of the RKP(b)," 96; "Report on the Political Activities of the Central Committee," 63; role in formation of USSR, 55–59; "To the Rural Poor," 111, 117; and unity of Soviet republics, 51; view of collectivism, 96; 105–06; wanted devotion to cause, 107; *What Is to Be Done*, 107; writings, 7–8
Lenin State Library, 165
Liosik, Iazep, 18, 27, 86, 110
Litbel, 30
Literature, 90–92
Lithuania: 30, 67, 81; Grand Duchy of, 2–5; in West Belorussia, 129; peasant uprising in, 5; and Poland, 3–4, 32; proposed for U.N., 182; slice of BSSR transferred to, 143
Lithuanian Communist Party, 48
Lloyd George, David, 40, 42–44
Lodysev, S. I., 125
Ludwig, Emil, 102
Lutskevich, Anton, 36, 109, 145
Lychev, I. A., 113

Makeev, General, 142
Maladniak, 91
Malenkov, Georgi, 173
Marchlewski, 45
Marxism: in Belorussia, 7–11
Masul'ski, General, 155
Mazurau, Kiryl, 176
Mensheviks, 16, 19, 108; in Georgia, 54
Meshkov, Comrade, 112
Miasnikov [Miasnikian], Aleksandr, 15–16, 19, 29
Miatla, Piatrok, 136
Mickiewicz, Adam, 42
Mikhailov, M. A., 14
Mikolajczyk, Stanislaw, 179
Military Revolutionary Committee (Revkom), 19, 21, 48; authority terminated, 49
Minsk: Bolshevik coup d'état in (1917), 20; City Council, 23; Communist University at, 89; congresses in, 48–50; Duma, 23; destruction of war, 165; Germans capture (1941), 147; German occupation of, 23–25, 27; Higher Pedagogical Institute at, 114; land ownership in, 7; Marxist party in, 7; meetings in, 18, 48; military school opened, 85; Polish occupation of, 38; population, 11; populist club in, 6; revolutionary activities in, 8; Soviet of Workers' and Soldiers' Deputies, 23

Minskaia hazeta (Minsk Gazette), 14
Mogilev: province of, 10, 11, 14, 29; region, 159; medical institute opened, 160
Molotov, Viacheslav, 143, 180, 182
Molotov-Ribbentrop Line, 141
Mongolia, 1, 2, 81
Moscow: doctrine of primacy of, 171–72; Sixteenth Congress in (1930), 108; Conference (1944), 179

Napoleon, 146
Nasedkin, A. A., 125
Nasha dolia (periodical), 9
Nasha niva (newspaper), 9, 10
Natalevich, Mikola, 142, 173
National Communists, 69
National Democrats (Natsdems) (Belorussian), 69; attacked by press and security police, 108–09
National Democrats, Polish. See under Poland
Nationalism. See Belorussia, national movement
Nationalities: in formation of USSR, 47, 53, 56–60
Natsdems. See National Democrats
Natsional'no-Trudovoi Soiuz (N.T.S.), 158
Nazis: barbarity of, 152–53; theory of master race applied to USSR, 152; welcomed by Belorussians, 146–47. See also Germany
Nekrashevich, Stsiapan, 110
New Economic Policy (NEP): concessions to peasants, 63–64; element of democracy under, 64; introduced by Lenin, 62–63, 93; Party members support, 108; reconciles Communist Party and local nationalism, 82. See also under Belorussia
Nicholas I, 4
Nicholas II, 8
Nikolai Nikolaevich, Grand Duke, 31
NKVD (People's Commissariat of Internal Affairs), 122, 124; behind German lines, 156–57; retreats before Germans, 148; slaughter and deportation by, 145; in West Belorussia, 144–45; after World War II, 167. See also Cheka; GPU
Novaia Vileika: medical institute in, 160
October Revolution of 1917, 13, 18, 20, 22, 25, 91, 92
Old Slavonic language, 2
Orgburo, 54
Ostarbeiters, 154, 168

Panteleimon, Metropolitan, 159
Paskevich-Erivanski, Prince, 165
Patek, Stanislaw, 40
Patolichev, Nikolai, 173, 176
Pazniak, Ianka, 145
Peasants: deportation of, 103; exploited by Stalin, 190; under German occupation, 25; increase of income, 76; land distribution to, 64, 73, 97n; movement organized (1905), 8; NEP introduced to placate, 63; not free to move, 117–18; oppression of, 6–7; organized by Communists, 14–15, 23; percentages of poor and middle class, 75; Polish treatment of, 136; position in Belorussia, 4, 5, 6, 10, 11; revolt of (1863), 5; uprisings (1920–1921), 62; in West Belorussia, 132–33. See also Kulaks
People's Commissariat of Education, 110
People's Commissariat of Internal Affairs. See NKVD
People's Commissariat of Nationalities, 54
Petrograd, 17
Picheta, Uladimir, 111
Pilsudski, Jozef, 32–35, 40, 131, 136; defeats Bolsheviks, 38; invades Ukraine, 43
Poets, 90–92
Poland, 67, 89–90; annexes part of Belorussia and Ukraine, 127; attacked by Communist press, 108–09; in Belorussia under Nazis, 158–59; boundary negotiations, 177–80; colonization of West Belorussia, 132; constitution of 1935, 131; desire to rule, 40–42; dispute with Soviet Russia over Belorussia, 25; elections, 130; exchange of population with

Belorussia, 168; feudalism in, 136; fights Red Army, 42–43, 177; Germans attack, 139; heterogeneity of population, 4; independence of, 32; land reform, 131–32; language, 2, 38; and Lithuania, 3–4, 32; minorities in politics, 130–31; 1917 campaign in Belorussia, 23; occupation of Belorussia, 76; occupation of Minsk, 38; partitioned, 4, 140–41, 177; parties in, 6, 42, 132; peasant uprising, 5; National Democrats, 42; political terror, 136–37; Polonization of Lithuania, 3; Sejm, 35, 115; struggle with Bolsheviks, 30–46; West Belorussia under, 127–38; after World War I, 127
Polish Peasant Party, 132
Polish Socialist Party, 6
Politburo, 54, 55, 61, 95, 125, 172
Polotski, Symon, 81
Polymia (literary association), 91
Poniatowski, Stanislaus Augustus, King, 136
Ponomarenko, Panteleimon, 155, 172n
Populist movement (1870s), 6
Potocki, Count, 7
Potsdam Conference, 180
Private enterprise, 76–78
Prochniak, 45
Provisional Government. *See* Russian Provisional Government
Provisional Polish Revolutionary Committee, 45
Provisional Workers' and Peasants' Revolutionary Government (of BSSR), 28
Pryshchepau, Zmitrok, 74, 94
Purges, 107–08, 110–15, 123–25, 144–45, 170–73

Rabochii (Worker), 119
Rada, 18, 21n, 23, 27, 38
Rada Muzhou Daveru (Council of Men of Confidence), 162
Rahulia, Vasil', 135
Rak-Mikhailouski, Symon, 115, 136
Rakovsky, Christian, 57
Red Army, 67, 125; invades Poland, 139; verge of collapse, 147–48
Red Cross, 160

Red Navy, 62
Reform of 1861, 4, 5, 6
Religion: churches closed, 99; during Nazi occupation, 159; inherited from Kievan Russia, 1; for minorities in Poland, 135; Orthodox Church, 3; Roman Catholic Church, 3. *See also* Brest
Responsible Workers of the National Republics and Regions, 82
Revkom. *See* Military Revolutionary Committee
Revolutionary Military Council (Revvoensovet), 85–86
Revolution of 1905, 9
RKP(b). *See* Russian Communist Party (Bolsheviks)
Rogozinskii, N., 20
Roosevelt, Franklin D., 180, 182, 183
Rosenberg, Alfred, 150, 158
RSDRP. *See* Russian Social Democratic Labor Party
RSFSR. *See* Russian Soviet Federated Socialist Republic
Rurik, founder of first Russian state (c. 862), 1
Russia: Dumas, 8–9, 10; defeat by Japan (1905), 8; descended from eastern Slavic tribes, 1; dispute with Poland over Belorussia, 25; treatment of Belorussians, 4; treatment of minority groups, 12. *See also* Great Russians, Kievan Russia; Union of Soviet Socialist Republics
Russian Communist Party (Bolsheviks): activity after partition, 47–49; Central Committee, 54, 55; concept of, 59; Northwestern Regional Committee, 28; Politburo and Orgburo, 54; renamed, 60; rules all soviets through their parties, 60. *See also* All-Union Communist Party
Russian Council of Labor and Defense, 64
Russian Provisional Government, 31, 187
Russian Social Democratic Labor Party (RSDRP), 7, 8, 12; monolithic, 107; purges of, 107–08
Russian Socialist Revolutionary Party, 18

Russian Soviet Federated Socialist Republic (RSFSR), 27, 46, 64, 65, 102; Central Executive Committee, 29; constitution, 52; dominance over USSR, 56–61; power of, 51–52
Russification, 175
Rykov, Aleksei, 93, 94, 108, 188

Sabaleuski, Iury, 136
St. Vladimir, 1
Saiuz Belaruskai Moladzi (Union of Belorussian Youth), 162
Sakharova, Praskoviia Fedorovna, 113
Samapomach (BNS), 160–61, 162
Samoila, U., 145
Schools. See Education
Sejm: elections to (1922), 130; and land reform, 131–32
Serfs. See Peasants
Shantyr, Fabian, 18
Sharanhovich, Vasil', 123–24
Siberia, concentration camps in, 168
Skaryna, Frantsishka, 81
Slavs, 1, 2
Slutsk district, 153; uprising in, 45
Smolensk: Belorussian SSR formed in, 29; congress at (1918), 60; region, 10, 65, 66, 159
Smolich, Arkadz, 18
Social Democrats. See Russian Social Democratic Labor Party
Social Revolutionary Party, 48
Sovetskaiia Belorussiia (newspaper), 126
Soviet of Peasants' Deupties, 14
Soviet of the People's Commissars of the Western Region and the Front, 21
Soviet of Workers' and Soldiers' Deputies, 14
Soviets of Workers', Soldiers', and Peasants' Deputies of the Western Region and the Front, 20
Soviet republics: questions of unity and independence, 51–56
Soviets: elections to, 66–70; blamed for failure of collectivization, 100–101
Sovkhozes (state farms), 64
Sovnarkom: All-Union, 72, 98; Belorussian, 64, 72, 74
Spasin, General, 142
Stalin, Iosif, 22, 27; attacks Belorussian Natsdems, 108; becomes tyrant and dictator, 114, 190; and collectivization, 99–100; conducts Great Purge, 122; and constitution, 120; continues rule by terror, 167; cult of personality, 174; "Dizzy from Success," 98–99; eliminates civil rights, 111–12; eliminates opposition, 93–95; explanation of Lenin's agrarian policy, 15; exploits workers, 190; flattery of required, 118–20; guilt of, 105–06; Howard interviews, 121; lies about peasant conditions, 105; as linguist, 174–75; on local nationalism, 82; Ludwig interviews, 102; "The National Question and Leninism," 112; on "national question," 47, 53–54; "Political Report of the Central Committee to the 15th Congress of the All-Union Communist Party," 76; purges in Belorussia, 110–14; "Report to the Seventeenth Party Congress on the Work of the Central Committee of the VKP(b)," 105; results of death, 175–76; role in formation of USSR, 53–59; on Russian minorities, 13; selects candidates for BSSR, 28; view of Curzon Line, 179; view of NEP, 93–94; "Work in the Village," 102
State Veterinary Institute (Vitebsk), 89
Stettinius, Edward R., 184
Stolypin, Peter, 9
Supreme Allied Council, 40, 43
Supreme Soviet, 125; elections for, 121; Fifth Extraordinary Session, 142, 143; tenth session, 181, 182
SVB ("Union for the Liberation of Belorussia"), 109
Sverdlov, Iakov, 14, 29, 49

Talash, Vasil', 39
Tambov Province, 62
Tarashkevich, Branislau, 136, 137
Tartars, 67; of Crimea, 167
Tehran Conference, 178, 179
Teutonic Knights, 2, 3
Treaties: Brest-Litovsk, 23, 24, 25, 62–63; of Minority Nationalities,

Index

131; of Rapallo (1922), 50; of Riga (1921), 127, 128, 177; of Versailles (1919), 128
Trepka, Anton, 145
Trotsky, Leon, 25–26, 40, 124
Truman, Harry S, 184
Ts. I. K. *See* All-Union Central Executive Committee; Belorussian Central Executive Committee
Tsvikevich, Aleksandr, 83, 110, 111, 137
Tukhachevskii, Mikhail, 123
Tumash, Vitaut, 159

Uborevich, Ieronim, 123
Ukraine, 26, 31, 55, 67; admitted to U.N., 184; constitution of, 71; descended from eastern Slavic tribes, 1; division of Kievan Russia, 2; language, 2; and Poland, 127–29; proposed for U.N., 182; treatment by Russia, 4; trial of alleged conspirators, 109; western boundary, 177
Ulasau, Aleksandr, 145
U.N. *See* United Nations
"Union for the Liberation of Belorussia" (SVB), 109
"Union for the Liberation of the Ukraine," 109
Union of Belorussian Teachers, 134
Union of Krevo (1386), 3
Union of Lublin (1569), 3
Union of Soviet Socialist Republics (USSR): agreement with Poland (1941), 177–78; Constitutions, 56, 71, 83; Council of People's Commissars, 117; formation of, 47–61; Nonaggression Pact with Germany, 139; partition of Poland, 141; rights of Soviet republics, 51–56, 185; Sovnarkom, 72, 98; State Planning Committee, 78; West Belorussia included in, 142. *See also entries for* All-Union
Union of the Farmer Defenders of the Eastern Borderlands, 132 n
United Nations: BSSR an original member of, 177, 180–85; Lithuanian membership proposed, 182; Ukraine admitted to, 184
Unszlicht, 45
Uprava (Municipal Council), 159

Uralova, E. I., 125
USSR. *See* Union of Soviet Socialist Republics

Valoshyn, Pavel, 136
Varashenia, I. D., 155
VKP(b). *See* All-Union Communist Party (Bolsheviks)
Vilna, 36; becomes part of Lithuania, 143; University of, 134
Vitebsk: province of, 10, 29, 65, 66, 100; jail burned, 148; destruction of, 165
Vladimir I (St. Vladimir), 1
Voroshilov, Klimenti, 121
Voznesenskii, Nikolai A., 173
V. Ts. I. K. *See* All-Union Central Executive Committee
Vydra, 111

West Belorussia: censuses of 1921 and 1931, 129; disillusionment, 137–38; education, 134–35; ethnographic composition, 129; Hramada dissolved, 137; industry, 133; land reform, 132–33, 135–36; minorities in Poland, 127–29; minorities in politics, 130–31; Polish policy of colonization, 132; religion, 135; reunited with BSSR, 142; treatment of peasants, 136
Western Military Region, 86
White Russia. *See* Belorussia
White Ruthenia. *See* Belorussia
Wilson, Woodrow, 25, 32
Witos, Vincent, 132
Workers: exploited by Stalin, 190; fired for unexcused absence, 118
World War I, 10–11, 13–14, 31
Wrangel, General Pëtr Nikolaevich, 43
Writers, 90–92

Yagoda, Genrikh, 122
Yalta Conference, 179, 182, 184
Yezhov, Nikolai, 122

Zhdanov, Andrei, 172, 173
Zhylka, V., 83
Zhylunovich, Zmitrok, 18, 28, 29, 60, 82, 91
Zinoviev, Grigory, 93
Zvezda (Star, newspaper), 16

This book has been set in
Hermann Zapf's Palatino
with G. G. Lange's uncial
type, Solemnis, used
for display.

Composition & printing
by Heritage Printers, Inc.

Binding by The C. J. Krehbiel Co.

Design by Jonathan Greene

www.ingramcontent.com/pod-product-compliance
Lightning Source LLC
Chambersburg PA
CBHW021839220426
43663CB00005B/325